William Stanley Braithwaite
Photograph by Carl Van Vechten, 1947,
courtesy of Saul Mauriber

THE
WILLIAM
STANLEY
BRAITHWAITE
READER

edited by
PHILIP BUTCHER

Ann Arbor
THE UNIVERSITY OF MICHIGAN PRESS

To My Father

Acknowledgments

Many individuals have given generous assistance to my work on this book, and I regret that it is not feasible to name them all. I am greatly indebted to Mr. William S. Braithwaite, Jr., who gave his full cooperation at every stage of the project, and to Mr. Edward J. Starr, whose extensive collection of Braithwaite documents and memorabilia, now at Morgan State College, has been, like Mr. Starr himself, a major resource. Many librarians have aided me, but I am especially obliged to Mr. Walter Fisher, Mrs. Virginia Richardson, Mrs. H. Florine Williams, and other members of the staff of the Morgan State College Library, and to Miss Ruth Ann Stewart of the Schomburg Collection of the New York Public Library. I am grateful to the American Philosophical Society and the Morgan State College Committee on Faculty Research for grants which made the preparation of this volume possible. I thank also my friend and colleague Harold B. Chinn, who first aroused my interest in research on William Stanley Braithwaite.

For permission to reprint copyrighted materials written by William Stanley Braithwaite, grateful acknowledgment is made to the following individuals and publishers:

Black World
   "Negro America's First Magazine." Reprinted by permission of *Black World* from *Negro Digest*. Copyright © December, 1947, by *Negro Digest*.
   "I Saw Frederick Douglass." Reprinted by permission of *Black World* from *Negro Digest*. Copyright © January, 1948, by *Negro Digest*.

The William Stanley Braithwaite Reader

The Boston *Globe*
"A Grave Wrong to the Negro." Reprinted from The Boston *Globe*, ca. 1906.

Coward, McCann and Geoghegan, Inc.
"Where Did You Get This?" Chapter xxi reprinted from *The Bewitched Parsonage: The Story of the Brontës*, 1950.

Crisis Publishing Company, Inc.
"Some Contemporary Poets of the Negro Race." Reprinted from *The Crisis*, April, 1919.

Dodd, Mead, & Company
"The Year in Poetry." Reprinted from *Bookman*, March, 1917.

Clarence E. Farrar, Marshall Jones Company
"Introduction," *The Heart of a Woman*, by Georgia Douglas Johnson. Published by Cornhill Publishing Company, 1918.

National Urban League, Inc.
"The Novels of Jessie Fauset." Reprinted from *Opportunity*, January, 1934.
Review of *On These I Stand*, by Countee Cullen. Reprinted from *Opportunity*, Summer, 1947.

The New Pittsburgh Courier Publishing Company
"The First Negro Novelist." Reprinted from the *Pittsburgh Courier*, May 30, 1953.

The New Republic
"Imagism: Another View." Reprinted from *The New Republic*, June 12, 1915.

Phylon
Selections from "The House Under Arcturus" (An incomplete serial autobiography). Reprinted from *Phylon*, 1941–42.
"Poems of Mood and Substance." A Review of *Powerful Long Ladder*, by Owen Dodson. Reprinted from *Phylon*, vii, 1946.
Review of *A History of American Poetry, 1900–1940*, by Horace Gregory and Marya Zaturenska. Reprinted from *Phylon*, viii, 1947.
"A Tribute to W.E.Burghardt Du Bois." Reprinted from *Phylon*, x, 1949.
"The Passing of Alain Leroy Locke." Reprinted from *Phylon*, xv, 1954.
"Alain Locke's Relationship to the Negro in American Literature." Reprinted from *Phylon*, xviii, 1957.

Acknowledgments

Letters and other manuscripts, printed here with the permission of Mr. William S. Braithwaite, Jr., have been made available for publication through the courtesy of the following institutions:

Columbia University Library: Letter to Edmund C. Stedman.

Fisk University Library: Letter to Charles W. Chesnutt.

Harvard College Library: Letters to Amy Lowell and Carl Sandburg.

Morgan State College Library: "My Journal—An Autobiographical Record" and letters to William Dean Howells, James D. Corrothers, Thomas Wentworth Higginson, J. Max Barber, Ray Stannard Baker, Emma K. Braithwaite, Claude McKay, Mary Church Terrell, George E. Haynes, W. E. B. Du Bois, Alain Locke (April 13, 1925), Nella Larsen, Benjamin Brawley, and Florence Read.

Northwestern University Library, Special Collections Department, Evanston, Ill.: Letters to Lew Sarett.

Syracuse University Library: "Mrs. Washburn," "Memories of the Boston *Transcript*," "To Marianne Moore, For Her Birthday," "Countee Cullen," "Amy Lowell," and letters to L. C. Page & Co., Miss Robinson, Richard A. Carroll, Olive Lindsay Wakefield, Walter de la Mare, Marianne Moore, Benjamin W. Huebsch, George F. Brown, Burton J. Kline, J. Donald Adams, Mary Altizer Roberts, Margaret Widdemer, Robert Frost, Joseph Auslander, James B. Meriwether, and the *Christian Science Monitor*.

Tulane University Library: Letter to George W. Cable.

University of Virginia Library: Letters to the New York *World*, Temple Scott, Maxwell Perkins, Chard Powers Smith, William Lyon Phelps, Alain Locke (June 28, 1926), Willard H. Wright, E. Merrill Root, Lawrence Lee, and Howard G. Schmitt.

The William Stanley Braithwaite Reader

Grateful acknowledgment is made to Mr. Saul Mauriber, photographic executor of Carl Van Vechten, and the James Weldon Johnson Collection, Collection of American Literature, Yale University, for permission to use the photograph of William Stanley Braithwaite taken by Carl Van Vechten.

It is fitting that I close with an expression of appreciation for the unfaltering interest and invaluable insights provided by my wife, Ruth.

PHILIP BUTCHER

Baltimore, Maryland

Contents

Contents

Introduction

Writing in praise of William Stanley Braithwaite, awarded the 1918 Spingarn Medal as "the American citizen of African descent who made last year the highest achievement in any field of elevated human endeavor," W. E. B. Du Bois called him "the most prominent critic of poetry in America." So influential was Braithwaite at the time that a celebrated rival, Harriet Monroe, dubbed him "Sir Oracle" and "the Boston dictator." Poets as notable as Robert Frost and Amy Lowell courted his favor, as did Claude McKay and Countee Cullen. William Dean Howells, who spoke with the highest authority, once said Braithwaite was "the most intelligent historian of contemporary poetry I know." Yet this poet, critic, editor, anthologist, and publisher, whose books fill a whole shelf, has been ignored or slighted in most textbooks and histories of American literature as a whole, and even in the current flood of anthologies and studies of "the black experience" he has received less recognition than his labors and accomplishments merit. This volume of selections from his works is designed to rescue the achievement of William Stanley Braithwaite from undeserved neglect.

Braithwaite's long life — he died at eighty-three — began in Boston on December 6, 1878. His father, whose line of descent included on one hand a Barbadian shoe merchant of African ancestry and on the other the daughter of a French nobleman, was born in British Guiana, where his family had attained distinction in public affairs. He had come to America after interrupting medical studies in England, and in Boston met and married a beautiful young woman whose mother had been a slave in North Carolina. Braithwaite's father died in 1886, leaving his widow and children without assets. The boy stopped school at twelve to help support the family. Being poor was more an inconvenience than a stigma and his boyhood differed little from the typical American pattern for that time and place. He sold papers behind City Hall, played hockey on the Common, and worked at a variety of jobs before he became a typesetter for a Cambridge publisher and surreptitiously acquired a personal library composed of the galley proofs that were produced each day in the print shop. At fifteen, when he had read Keats and Burns and Wordsworth, he was overcome by a passion for poetry that never after relinquished its hold on him.

Soon he was writing poetry and some of his verses found their way into print in periodicals. Persevering in his literary ambitions despite many discouragements, he contrived to publish a thin book of verse, *Lyrics of Life and Love,* in 1904 and issued another, *The House of Falling Leaves,* four years later. His career as editor and anthologist began in 1906 with *The Book of Elizabethan Verse,* which was followed a few years later by volumes of Georgian and Restoration verse. It must be noted that his preoccupation with poetry and his interest in the English Renaissance did not prevent him from contributing to the Boston *Globe,* sometime in 1906, the attack on racist caricatures in American culture which is the first selection in this book. And before he edited the collection of Elizabethan poetry he did his best to find a publisher for quite a different project, *The Anthology of Negro Authors: Prose and Verse,* that he never succeeded in getting into print. Like every author who must live by his pen, Braithwaite was at the mercy of the publishing world and the reading public. His literary career did not

2

begin in a period hospitable to black writers unwilling to use the approved formulas, dialect pathos, and minstrel comedy.

On February 14, 1906, Braithwaite began to contribute to the Boston *Evening Transcript,* a newspaper that enjoyed at that time a status not unlike that of today's *New York Times.* The reviews and essays he published in its pages were a major source of income for him for twenty years, though he was never a salaried staff member. They constitute the bulk of his critical writing and the principal basis for his authority in the world of letters. Through them, he labored to enlarge the audience for verse, encourage and assist fledgling poets, and win for talent and genius appropriate recognition. He became a significant force in revitalizing poetry in America.

One outgrowth of his work with the *Transcript* was his publication of a slender *Anthology of Magazine Verse for 1913.* For the next sixteen years he issued his annual selection of the best poetry printed in the nation's periodicals. Braithwaite exhibited a wide range of taste, conscientious objectivity, and a fine capacity for identifying poetry that would endure. His personal predilection for the Pre-Raphaelites and late romantics did not affect his appreciation for other kinds of poetry. (His own verse, much overshadowed in importance by his other writing, has a richer variety than is supposed; though he wrote often in the manner of Ernest Dowson, his model was sometimes Edwin Arlington Robinson, Marianne Moore, or even Dylan Thomas.) Conservative critical pronouncements in the *Transcript* and elsewhere did nothing to enhance his influence once conservative tenets ceased to be the rule in American poetry. And the very pursuits that brought him prestige doomed him to a diminishing stature. No one engaged in writing appreciative newspaper essays on poets for a livelihood could help but be unduly generous in the long run, and no annual selection of the "best" verse, largely dependent for survival

3

on the commercial support of the poets themselves, could hold to rigid standards of excellence and a careful discrimination.

Yet poets regarded an invitation to reprint their lines in "Braithwaite" as tantamount to an award of merit; scholars still find the bibliographies and other editorial paraphernalia of these volumes valuable to their studies; and bibliophiles treasure the books because they first acclaimed poems that are now accepted as minor classics. Especially demonstrative of Braithwaite's discernment is the 1915 anthology which included E. A. Robinson's "Flammonde," Amy Lowell's "Patterns," Wallace Stevens's "Peter Quince at the Clavier," and Robert Frost's "Birches," "The Road Not Taken," and "The Death of the Hired Man." That volume also offered a poem by James Weldon Johnson, and black poets were represented in the later annuals in increasing numbers. As Margaret Haley Carpenter has said, no other annual collections of poetry "commanded the literary excitement, the prestige, or the popularity accorded these volumes." Both Braithwaite's position and disposition encouraged a wide acquaintance among aspiring and established poets; the Index of Names for correspondence in the William Stanley Braithwaite Papers at Harvard University runs to more than thirteen typed pages, single-spaced and double column. His reputation as discoverer and mentor of new talent is thoroughly deserved.

Though poetry was the field of his acknowledged competence, he felt at home in the whole world of letters and also in public affairs. Many of the books of prose and verse that he planned to write (and sometimes actually announced as in print) never appeared, mainly for lack of a publisher's willingness to risk an advance. The range of his ventures is attested by the books he produced in 1919: an anthology of modern British verse, a history of World War I for juveniles, and a collection of poems written at his invitation to celebrate America's victory in that conflict. One of the contributors was Fenton Johnson, who wrote of return-

4

ing black soldiers "proud to give the world / The Freedom that we never knew nor shared."

Braithwaite's career altered its course somewhat in 1922, when he became president of B. J. Brimmer Publishing Company. The name was a composite. The first initial stood for Braithwaite himself, and Brimmer was the name of a grammar school at which he spent happy years as a boy. The "J." must have stood for his partner and the company treasurer, Winifred Virginia Jackson. The Brimmer spring list for 1924, announced in a full-column ad in *The New Republic,* included Miss Jackson's book of poems about New England life, for which Braithwaite wrote one of his many introductions. Among the other titles was a novel about the "Race Problem" by Joshua Henry Jones, and *Confusion,* the first novel by Harvard sophomore James Gould Cozzens, a Braithwaite discovery. The loss of a major book, an anthology of prose and verse readings used by a famous Harvard professor on his platform appearances, helped bring about the demise of the firm in the following year. Braithwaite never really got over the Brimmer failure, a severe blow both to his hopes and his precarious finances. It did serious damage, too, to his long-standing supposition that race was not an insurmountable barrier to full acceptance in the business world in Boston or the academic community in Cambridge.

How he managed to support a wife and rear seven children in relative comfort remains a mystery. His financial circumstances became desperate when the Depression struck. He had no regular employment or assured income until he accepted a professorship at Atlanta University, where he spent ten years guiding black students in the study of English and American literature and pioneered by introducing his graduate classes to writing not previously regarded as worthy of serious study. Some of the master's essays written under his direction would be classified today under Black Studies, though American Literature is just as appropriate a designation.

On his retirement from Atlanta in 1945 Braithwaite returned to the North, but now his residence was an apartment in Harlem. *Selected Poems* appeared in 1948 and *The Bewitched Parsonage,* a book on the Brontës, was published a year later. Several projects in which he had a compelling interest, among them a biography of his friend Alain Locke and a collection of critical essays to be titled *The Contemporary Negro Novelist,* were abortive. Because of his failing eyesight, Margaret Haley Carpenter, a Virginia poet and critic, bore the brunt of the work on their *Anthology of Magazine Verse for 1958.* He died on June 9, 1962.

No more than this summary of Braithwaite's life is needed here, for several of the readings in this volume are autobiographical and many of the selections document details of his history and illuminate his character. One way to give Braithwaite his due is to let him speak for himself.

Volumes of his poems may be had in reprint editions, and several of his lyrics are available in anthologies, so none of his previously published verse is presented in this book. Of the critical essays here, only two or three have been reprinted since their original appearance. First publication of these and other essays is specified in the headnotes. Where no reference is made to original publication they are printed here for the first time, except that a portion of Braithwaite's recollection of E. A. Robinson appeared in *New Letters,* Fall, 1971, and some other passages from this oral history, *The Reminiscences of William S. Braithwaite,* are presented in my "W. S. Braithwaite's Southern Exposure: Rescue and Revelation," *Southern Literary Journal,* Spring, 1971, and "William Stanley Braithwaite and the College Language Association," *CLA Journal,* December, 1971. The former article also quotes from a few of the letters published here, a mere fragment of the voluminous correspondence preserved at Morgan State College, Syracuse University, the University of Virginia, and other libraries.

It has seemed desirable to restrict editorial intrusions and keep scholarly paraphernalia at a minimum. Braithwaite's writing, so much of it done for periodicals, is sprin-

Introduction

kled with more than the usual quota of slips and errors. On occasion I have silently supplied a missing element or made a correction required for clarification; ellipses mark editorial deletions. For the selections offering Braithwaite's memories of the Boston *Transcript*, E. A. Robinson, and Amy Lowell I have supplied titles. Though I have aimed for consistency within individual pieces, I have not tried to achieve uniformity in Braithwaite's use of "Race" and "race," "Negro" and "negro," etc., since the variations are instructive reflections of the practices of different periodicals. The correspondence has presented special problems, since some of the letters are drafts in a handwriting that is nearly indecipherable and others are carbon copies replete with errors attributable to failing eyesight or imperfect typing. The absence of an index will inconvenience some readers, but a comprehensive list of names and topics would have stretched to unmanageable proportions and a restricted one would be of dubious value. It is hoped that a judicious use of the Contents will serve instead.

William Stanley Braithwaite's stature is sure to grow as scholars give attention to the records of his life and work, and one purpose of this book is to inspire and facilitate their labors. Another is to make available to the general reader representative writing by an admirable man whose career in American letters is without parallel.

Criticism
(ca. 1906 – 1957)

Braithwaite's opinions about literature and the race problem, the two matters in which he had an abiding interest, found early expression in various forms in newspapers and journals. A month after William Monroe Trotter founded the belligerent Boston *Guardian*, "an organ to voice intelligently the needs and aspirations of the colored American," he wrote, on December 14, 1901, to thank young William Stanley Braithwaite for a newsletter which he had contributed, and for his help in promoting the paper in Newport, R. I. The item below, preserved in an undated clipping, was published in the Boston *Globe*, evidently about 1906.

A Grave Wrong to the Negro

The world has moved from words to pictures since the 18th century to criticise by satire public events and men and racial characteristics. In this evidence of modern progress, economizing time and the means to the end, few will, indeed, be found to say that in all but one direction of the evolution of satire into caricature has there not been a real advance in the new over the old method. But the paradox is incontrovertible that the rise, growth and perfection of modern democracy has been the soil out of which has grown the expression of a more brutal antagonism waged in the interest of racial prejudice.

We deem as the largest legacy of our democracy freedom of speech and press; we builded these edifices on our belief in the brotherhood of man; but we have used the privileges born of our belief against our cherished convictions by applauding and encouraging the agency of a false institution to keep separate man from his brother, by endowing him with particular ridicules and vices, exaggerating them into "national" and "racial" characteristics which very promptly earn abhorrence and contempt for physical and mental defects that do but exist as the common inheritance of all mankind.

In this respect the case of the American negro is in a far worse plight than that of any other people, since his calumniators attempt to reserve him as the ultimate plaything for all sorts and conditions of men to scorn and laugh at, leaving him deprived of those personal altars of self-pride and manliness which are allowed to other men by right divine. The caricaturists have emphasized in him lust, avarice, falsehood — in fact, the whole decalogue of crimes and vices which arose like a ghost from the ashes of Eden's asbestos-purity when burned by the fire of God's wrath — by using as a contrast of degradation to other men the divine inheritance of his complexion and features.

The American — whatever the name may denote in the way of a distinct national type — has come to look upon with ridicule all other national and racial types that are purely such, because they do not happen to be what he terms ideally American, and yet it is from these heterogeneous nationalities and races the nation expects to secure the material to mold that type of the individual which it prophesies is to be the world's superior manhood and womanhood. But this assimilation that is sought for the growth of nationalism is retarded by the applause public opinion gives to, and the non-suppression of, the blatant, anathematizing caricatures of racial and national characteristics. They also impede the progress of a race by forcing upon it a pessimism, dampening and dulling, born of the influence of a self-portrait whose composition is made of weird and ugly lines, which in its unfaithfulness ostensibly strives to hide and distort the true model.

Criticism

There was never in real life a prototype of the negro of the execrable "coon song," the vaudeville stage, the musical comedy, or the pages of the comic weeklies; yet this exotic individual has been so long and so persistently exploited that the world believes in these "fundamentals" of his character and has become callous to the difference between the "chicken-stealing preacher" and a bishop of the [African Methodist Episcopal] church. . . . Now, it were better if this country were a nation of chicken-stealers than one of money-thieves, soul-murderers and home-destroyers who are bank and insurance presidents, for a surfeit of chicken meat can only at worst beget indigestion, much more easily cured than the decay of bad morals and ethics whose decomposition no power but the resurrection day or revolution can restore to the salvation of clean social and civil life.

Yet the chicken-stealer because he is a negro is caricatured into a vice, while the bank and insurance presidents, because they are Americans of the Mayflower or Jamestown colony descent, are idealized into portraits of oil, softened into masterpieces of pity and forgiveness out of sympathy for a universal human weakness. One does not complain of clean, wholesome humor at the expense of individual or race; but the caricatures of these defects should be relative and not positive. Since, however, our American caricaturists are vulgarists instead of satirists for the most part, without the artistic sense of subtlety in uncovering motives, they are no better than the offenders and insulters of national and racial pride — which consequently reveal their false pretensions to be above the weaknesses of human nature.

———————

Braithwaite's career as a critic began with a contribution to the Boston *Transcript*, February 14, 1906. Most of his reviews and articles in that newspaper and other journals treated poetry. Some (like his piece on *The Quest of the Silver Fleece*, a novel by W. E. B. Du Bois, in *Crisis* for December, 1911) appraised fiction and other prose works. His stature as a critic, however, rests on his knowledge and judgment not of prose but of poetry. That his competence extended to English verse as well as American is established by this selection from his long essay in the *Forum* for December, 1913.

The Lyrical Poetry of the New Laureate

o   o   o

Twenty-one years ago the death of Tennyson was flashed over the wires of the world. Two great English laureates had honored the post within half a century. Tennyson's death still left England rich in poets of lofty attainments. William Morris, Coventry Patmore, Swinburne, and Meredith, the older singers, would, had the choice fallen to any one of them, have continued to shed glory on a post that had been raised in public esteem by the two preceding incumbents. Henley and Watson and Kipling were the younger men who added an embarrassment of riches from which to select Tennyson's successor. The Marquess of Salisbury, coming into office after Lord Rosebery's futile year of erratic administration and power, waited three years before doing otherwise than what was expected of him. The reading of the *Autobiography* of Alfred Austin gives, I think, a very good reason why Salisbury appointed the journalist-poet to the vacant laureateship. I do not hold so mean an opinion of Alfred Austin's verse as has been quite frankly expressed in almost every critical quarter. Many of his earlier nature-lyrics are exquisite: and he told a verse-narrative, if not with arresting poetic power, delicately. But he was for all that a political journalist; an ardent worshipper of the person and policies of Disraeli; and Disraeli's pupil (can we ever erase the memory of these two figures from the Budget of '67 and the Berlin Congress!) rewarded him with the laureateship, to the disappointment of the English-speaking world.

1 4

For the seventeen years that Alfred Austin held the laureateship, he never emerged from the eclipse that the genius
of his predecessor cast upon his rising fame. The memory of
Tennyson was, to the public, like a shadow his name could
not escape. In the meantime many new figures rose in the
poetic heavens. Henley passed: Watson and Davidson had
large powers; Kipling was a driving and irresistible force,
whose song had the blood of the Empire in its substance;
Stephen Phillips was weaving dramatic spectacles in the
fabric of verse; Francis Thompson and William Butler Yeats
were building magnificent palaces of lyric art: the entrance
to one through ecclesiastical mysticism and Catholic faith,
and to the other, through a symbolism both natural and
spiritual; and preceding the late laureate's death, the attain-
ment of popular recognition by still younger men like John
Masefield and Alfred Noyes gave them a public claim to be
considered in succession. In 1910 all of this company of English poets who were living — it had grown two less by the
deaths of Thompson and Davidson — would have acknowledged one absolute master — Swinburne: and they were of
no divided opinion as to who should succeed him when he
passed away — Meredith. Death claimed both within a
month. By priority of age and achievement, the honor of the
foremost place among English poets, in my opinion, be-
longed to a poet whose art had never solicited any honor;
whose exclusiveness and retirement had made him known
but to a small circle of readers and critics; and who had
scarcely uttered a line but for his own joy in making something lovely out of the "flying vapors of the world," — to a
poet by the name of Robert Bridges. . . .

Of Mr. Bridges' style there is little or nothing that is
strikingly original. He has carried on, with the practice of
certain principles of variations of stress in the lyric, the best
tradition of English poetry. As Arthur Symons says, his
"finest lyrics might have found their place among the lyrics
in an Elizabethan song-book. And yet they are not archaic,
a going back, as of one who really, in thought, lives in an-

other age, to which his temper of mind is more akin." These variations of stress are nothing more than metrical experiments in which he has proved himself a skilled and successful craftsman in subduing balance, measure and harmony of rhythm. He allows no chance for violence of any kind; he produces a sort of conscious rapture, a felicitous flow, within defined bounds, of music, to which one must attune the ear to catch the delicate inweaving of harmonies. Perhaps no lyric poetry in English is more consciously artistic in verse-structure, none that more apparently seems to exist for the sake of art; and yet we find constant surprises, a quiet thrilling of the emotions, and delight in them, when once the full flavor and meaning of his language is scrutinized. It is in his rare and choice treatment of words that Mr. Bridges' style has its perfection. He finds an original association hidden in their opposites, and by bringing them together in most unusual circumstances awakens and unites qualities that produce the most subtle significance. He chooses them deliberately for their beauty, but they are no less valuable for their singing quality, and in no instance do they ever fail to make clear the precise meaning for which he has enlisted their services in rendering thought or feeling. In no lyric does his style in its purity and subtlety show to a higher degree than in *I Have Loved Flowers That Fade*, perhaps the best-known of his songs.

> *"I have loved flowers that fade,*
> *Within whose magic tents*
> *Rich hues have marriage made*
> *With sweet unmemored scents.*
> *A honeymoon delight, —*
> *A joy of love at sight,*
> *That ages in an hour: —*
> *My song be like a flower!*
>
> *I have loved airs that die*
> *Before their charm is writ*

Along a liquid sky
Trembling to welcome it:
Notes, that with pulse of fire
Proclaim the spirit's desire,
Then die, and are nowhere: —
My song be like an air!

Die, song, die like a breath,
And wither as a bloom:
Fear not a flowery death,
Dread not an airy tomb!
Fly with delight, fly hence!
'Twas thy love's tender sense
To feast; now on thy bier
Beauty shall shed a tear."

The specific quality of Mr. Bridges' work as art can hardly be better shown than in this example, wherein all his special effects are woven into one pattern. Here is magic of a kind that is evoked out of elements that one does not find lying about close to one's experience. And yet it is not made of any ethereal substance. If we can work our own emotions into clear enough definitions to understand our desires, we shall find embedded within them potent sentiments to which this remote magic gives utterance.

Mr. Bridges has been charged with a lack of human sentiment. It is true he speaks no large language of humanity. There are no outcries of passion, no deep thoughtfulness that would tend to render some solution to the evil and hard circumstances that beset deed or will in human experience; there are no intensities illuminating either ethical or moral ideals; he cannot take an attitude that is even conjecturally humane. All his songs are narrowly personal; but the belief in his own experience has a kind of relative exactitude to what must occur in life as men live it under different influences and environments. Sheltering himself in some happy retreat from the troubled affairs of the world he

would still desire, as he declares in the XXXVIIIth sonnet in
The Growth of Love, to have life —

> *"I would have life — thou saidst — all as this day,*
> *Simple enjoyment calm in its excess,*
> *With not a grief to cloud, and not a ray*
> *Of passion overhot my peace to oppress;*
> *With no ambition to reproach delay,*
> *Nor rapture to disturb its happiness."*

But it is a life rather of essence than of substance, of
brooding and meditation rather than of decision and action,
and into which there comes a realization no less of dejection
and sorrow, of the pains and joys of love, of poignant grief,
of vain aspiration. It was as if these various human states of
being had by others been mostly used in their unripe development; in that way they made art rough, violent, wild, full
of sharp and bitter memories; — at fruition, no passion, no
bitterness, no disappointment that had not been transfig-
ured into beauty which was the residue of all experience.
It is this feeling at the base of that austere self-control, that
continual ecstatic suspension of mood, which centres in the
utterance which we must accept as the key to all Mr.
Bridges' work:

> *"I love all beauteous things,*
> *I seek and adore them;*
> *God hath no better praise,*
> *And man in his hasty days*
> *Is honored for them.*
>
> *I too will something make*
> *And joy in the making;*
> *Although to-morrow it seem*
> *Like the empty words of a dream*
> *Remembered on waking."*

○   ○   ○

Braithwaite's praise was a factor in the rise of Robert Frost's literary reputation and the popularity of his poetry. The article below appeared in the Boston *Transcript,* May 8, 1915. Frost cultivated Braithwaite, as he did other poets and critics whose approval he wanted. See Lawrance Thompson, *Robert Frost: The Years of Triumph,* 1915–1938 (1970) on the Frost-Braithwaite relationship.

Robert Frost, New American Poet

The success which has immediately come to the poetry of Robert Frost is unique. It has no exact parallel in the experience of the art in this country during the present generation. It makes us consider for a moment the forces and circumstances which bring recognition, and the various degrees of recognition, to work of undoubted achievement, and in the achievement of a special quality and unpracticed method. One must not consider this recognition entirely on the basis of popularity; it must have a degree of popularity among the limited circle of readers who are always ready to appreciate poetry, but which forms itself into groups, each having sympathy and an active enthusiasm for a particular poetic expression.

All kinds of poetry do not attract people who may care for poetry itself as an art. One may find this a point of difference in the appreciation and enjoyment that the lover of music, the lover of painting, the lover of sculpture, the lover of drama, finds in the arts of music, painting, sculpture and drama. I do not mean that the lover of these four arts just mentioned will accept all that is given them in those creative forms. What I do mean is that however critical the initiate may be of the details in the rendition of laws and forms, however antagonistic they find themselves to the impressions and meanings which are conveyed in no uncertain terms, they are immediately in the atmosphere of the art and enjoy that as a sort of primary interest which at least puts them into an emotional response with the piece in spite of the fact that sympathy and understanding may revolt against it.

A profound lover of poetry will fail, or often find it very difficult, to enjoy the atmosphere of the art in the special kind of poetry for which his sympathy is not absolute and his understanding enlightening though not comprehensive. This point of difference, then, makes it very hard for a poet to win readers outside the group who immediately grasp his intention and the peculiar beauty of embodiment which conveys that intention. The more originally that intention is presented, the slower is the poet to extend the influence of his work. Poetry of unusual substance and expression which commands an immediate attention beyond a group acceptance is certain to have behind it a history of great critical importance. It is rooted deeply in the traditions of the art. What it is, though a part of the very texture and tone of the work itself, is not clearly defined as a separate quality, and until the public is given the key to the secret by which the fundamental moods of the poet are shaped into expression, the work cannot be appreciatively understood and enjoyed.

No American poet of today has come into so sudden a recognition as Robert Frost. I do not take into account such reputations as Mr. Markham's and some others whose burst into popularity may be suggested in comparison. The reason I think is obvious. Nor do I consider Mr. Masters, whose "Spoon River Anthology" is commanding attention everywhere at present. Mr. Masters's alliance is more with prose than poetry. In the case of the others it was the fortuitous circumstance of nearly everything else except the subtle manifestation of an original and fresh artistic impulse which made them suddenly known to all classes of readers, the larger number of which cared little or nothing for the progress of poetry as an art. Mr. Frost must be considered not only from the point of view of his material, but from the point of view of his art. In both of these points of view he strikes fresh and original ground; in neither does he present exactly new methods or new substance.

In 1913 appeared Mr. Frost's first book, "A Boy's Will," a slender little volume of lyrical verse; the following year "North of Boston" was issued. Originally brought out in England, both volumes have just been issued in this country. The poet is just forty years old, and this fact is significant in a consideration of the poet's art. It shows an apprenticeship of the most rigorous sort. Unlike most poets, he did not rush into print without first knowing exactly what he wanted to do and how to do it. It will be noted that the American poets who accomplish impressive and beautiful work are the poets who have mastered the medium through which they speak. It has been said time and time again that the American poets do not know the technique of their art, as the English and Continental poets do. For the rank and file this criticism is true. Often this criticism is meant to apply to the lack of new forms among our poets or to the failure to obtain the best and most subtle rhythmical effects from the metres commonly used. The marvel among foreign poets is that often the least endowed substantially are enabled by the extraordinary technical proficiency they command to accomplish such beautiful artistic results.

To appreciate Mr. Frost's poetry perfectly one has got to regard carefully the two backgrounds from which it is projected; fully under the influence of his art these two backgrounds merge into one, though each has its special distinction. There is the background of his material, the environment and character which belong to a special community; and there is the background of art in which the fidelity of speech is artistically brought into literature. This latter is a practice that brings up large and important questions of language and meaning in relation to life on the one hand and to literature on the other. Mr. Frost has been through the longest period of experimentation in mastering the technique of his art of any other American poet. What he finally

2 1

arrived at in poetic expression he finds as the highest accomplishment in the greatest English poets, and asserts that the American poets who have shown unquestionable genius, especially a man like Edwin Arlington Robinson, have in a large measure the same quality of speech which is at once both artistic and the literal tone of human talk. But no poet in either England or America, except this newly arrived New England poet, has consciously developed and practised this essential and vital quality of poetry which he characterizes as sound-posturing.

The poet was in his twentieth year when he realized that the speech of books and the speech of life were far more fundamentally different than was supposed. His models up to this period, as with all youthful poets and writers, had been literary models. But he found quite by accident that real artistic speech was only to be copied from life. On his New Hampshire farm he discovered this in the character of a man with whom he used to drive along the country roads. Having discovered this speech he set about copying it in poetry, getting the principles down by rigorous observation and reproduction through the long years which intervened to the publication of his books. He also discovered that where English poetry was greatest it was by virtue of this same method in the poet, and as I shall show in his talk with me, he illustrated it in Shakespeare, Shelley, Wordsworth and Emerson. That these poets did not formulate the principles by which they obtained these subtle artistic effects, but accomplished it wholly unconscious of its exact importance, he also suggested; but with a deliberate recognition of it as a poetic value in the poets to come he sees an entirely new development in the art of verse.

The invitation which brought Mr. Frost to Boston to read the Phi Beta Kappa poem on Wednesday at Tufts College gave me the opportunity to get from the poet his views on the principles of sound-posturing in verse and some reflections on contemporary poets and poetry in England and America. Before returning home, it will be interesting to note, the publication of Mr. Frost's books in England awakened a critical sympathy and acceptance among English writers of his ideas. His work won over, by its sheer poetic achievement, critics and poets, who had not realized before the possibilities of reproducing the exact tone of meaning in human speech in literary form. Where the poet's work is not fully appreciated in this country is where this principle is not understood. The substance of New England farm life of which his poetry is made has attracted immense interest, but in some quarters the appreciation of this substance is a little modified because the reader has only partially grasped the significance of the form. So it was this I wished the poet to explain in my very first question.

"First," he said, "let me find a name for this principle which will convey to the mind what I mean by this effect which I try to put into my poetry. And secondly, do not let your readers be deceived that this is anything new. Before I give you the details in proof of its importance, in fact of its essential place in the writing of the highest poetry, let me quote these lines from Emerson's 'Monadnoc,' where, in almost a particular manner, he sets forth unmistakably what I mean:

> *Now in sordid weeds they sleep,*
> *In dullness now their secret keep;*
> *Yet, will you learn our ancient speech,*
> *These, the masters who can teach.*
> *Four-score or a hundred words*
> *All their vocal muse affords;*
> *But they turn them in a fashion*
> *Past clerks' or statesmen's art or passion.*
> *I can spare the college bell,*
> *And the learned lecture well;*
> *Spare the clergy and libraries,*
> *Institutes and dictionaries,*
> *For that hearty English root*
> *Thrives here, unvalued, underfoot.*

Rude poets of the tavern hearth,
Squandering your unquoted mirth,
Which keeps the ground and never soars,
While Dick retorts and Reuben roars;
Scoff of yeoman strong and stark,
Goes like bullet to its mark;
While the solid curse and jeer
Never balk the waiting year.

"Understand these lines perfectly and you will understand what I mean when I call this principle 'sound-posturing,' or more literally, getting the sound of sense. What we
do get in life and miss so often in literature is the sentence
sounds that underlie the words. Words in themselves do not
convey meaning, and to provide this, which may seem entirely unreasonable to any one who does not understand the
psychology of sound, let us take the example of two people
who are talking on the other side of a closed door, whose
voices can be heard but whose words cannot be distinguished. Even though the words do not carry, the sound of
them does, and the listener can catch the meaning of the
conversation. This is because every meaning has a particular
sound-posture, or to put it in another way, the sense of
every meaning has a particular sound which each individual
is instinctively familiar with, and without at all being conscious of the exact words that are being used is able to understand the thought, idea or emotion that is being conveyed. What I am most interested in emphasizing in the
application of this belief to art, is the sentence of sound, because to me a sentence is not interesting merely in conveying a meaning of words; it must do something more; it must
convey a meaning by sound."

"But," I queried, "do you not come into conflict with
metrical sounds to which the laws of poetry conform in creating rhythm?"

"No," the poet replied, "because you must understand
this sound of which I speak has principally to do with tone.

It is what Mr. Bridges, the poet-laureate, characterized as
speech-rhythm. Metre has to do with beat, and sound-posture has a definite relation as an alternate tone between the
beats. The two are one in creation, but separate in analysis.
If we go back far enough we will discover that the sound of
sense existed before words, that something in the voice or
vocal gesture made primitive man convey a meaning to his
fellow before the race developed a more elaborate and concrete symbol of communication in language. I have even
read that our American Indians possessed besides a pic-
ture-language, a means of communication, though it was not
said how far it was developed, by the sound of sense. And
what is this but calling up with the imagination, and recog-
nizing, the images of sound? When Wordsworth said, 'Write
with your eye on the object,' or in another sense, it was important to visualize, he really meant something more. That
something carries out what I mean by writing with your ear
to the voice.

"This is what Wordsworth did himself in all his best poetry, proving that there can be no creative imagination unless there is a summoning up of experience, fresh from life,
which has not hitherto been evoked. The power, however,
to do this does not last very long in the life of a poet. After
ten years Wordsworth had very nearly exhausted his, giving
us only flashes of it now and then. As language only really
exists in the mouths of men, here again Wordsworth was
right in trying to reproduce in his poetry not only the
words — and in their limited range, too, actually used in
common speech — but their sound.

"To carry this idea a little further, it does not seem possible to me that a man can read on the printed page what
he has never heard. Nobody today knows how to read
Homer and Virgil perfectly, because the people who spoke
Homer's Greek and Virgil's Latin are as dead as the sound
of their language. On the other hand, to further emphasize
the impossibility of words rather than sound conveying the
sense of meaning, take the matter of translation. Really to

understand and catch all that is embodied in a foreign masterpiece it must be read in the original, because while the words may be brought over, the tone cannot be.

"In the matter of poetry," the poet continued, "there is a subtle differentiation between sound and the sound of sense which ought to be perfectly understood before I can make clear my position. For a second let me turn aside and say that the beginning of literary form is in some turn given to the sentence in folk speech. Art is the amplification and sophistication of the proverbial turns of speech. All folk speech is musical. In primitive conditions man has not at his aid reactions by which he can quickly and easily convey his ideas and emotions. Consequently he has to think more deeply to call up the image for the communication of his meaning. It was the actuality he sought; and thinking more deeply, not in the speculative sense of science or scholarship, he carried out Carlyle's assertion that if you 'think deep enough you think musically.' Poetry has seized on this sound of speech and carried it to artificial and meaningless lengths. We have it exemplified in Sidney Lanier's musical notation of verse, where all the tones of the human voice in natural speech are entirely eliminated, leaving the sound of sense without root in experience."

Braithwaite's defense of Imagism, for which he had really only limited admiration, may be explained in part by his differences with Conrad Aiken, reared in the South, and Ezra Pound, whose bigotry was expressed in a derogatory reference to Braithwaite's racial identity in a letter to the *Transcript*. This article was in *New Republic*, June 12, 1915.

Imagism: Another View

It was an ingenious attempt on the part of Mr. Aiken in his recent article to define the place of imagism in contemporary poetry. It is a comparatively easy task to differentiate a "new" movement in art, but a difficult process to place it in the constantly shifting ground of artistic progress. We cannot make a thing by wishing it so; even our dislike of a thing is no assurance that we have broken through more than the surface-meaning; and this fact is often betrayed by uttering irrelevancies and confusing relations. Now to call *vers libre* a fad is to go wide of the mark; very wide of the mark, when it is realized that there are no classic metres in English poetry, and that because of this the French consider that English poets have always written in *vers libre*. Imagism has made a logical reappearance in English poetry for centuries; certain modern poets have given it a name, because it is the habit of the time to find a name for truths. I doubt if many of us would question the critical authority of Remy de Gourmont. In him, as in all French criticism, is the essential quality of balanced judgment. Of the movement to which Amy Lowell, John Gould Fletcher and Richard Aldington belong, he has written: "The Imagists are evidently descended from the French Symbolists. One sees that at once in their horror of the *cliché*, the horror of rhetoric and of the grandiose, of the oratorical style, that easy style with which the imitators of Victor Hugo have disgusted us forever. As positive precepts, they wish precision of language, clearness of vision, concentration of thought, and they like to combine these in a dominant image. Mr. Harold Munro, who has given an excellent outline of Imagism in the last number of *The Egoist*, finds the greater part of these principles in the best English poets and theorists of poetry, from Dryden to Matthew Arnold, but recent poets have neglected them too much. It is in this way that new literary schools are formed; they are always a reaction against the carelessness of the leading school and the worship which it necessarily has for *clichés* started during its ascendancy. In poetry, even more than in any other art, constant renewal is necessary, and when we see a school endeavoring to do this, above all by invoking eternal, although disregarded, principles, we can only augur well for its future."

That these aims are acknowledged by the imagist poets this preface proves; and better than acknowledged, they are constantly practiced. A reliance on Mr. Pound's statement is likely to involve one who heeds it in contradictions. In the first place Mr. Pound approaches every artistic theory through a series of negations; in the second place, a versifier so derivative as Mr. Pound negatives himself from, as he has amply proven in his prose ramblings, the influence of one theory and school by another. Imagism is, in every sense, made up of positive forces.

After all, a name is only a convenient handle by which we carry the identification of things. You cannot isolate a force or degree or quality of feeling, because the shape and material of language is custom-made rather than ready-made. All poetry comes out of feeling; the degree to which feeling is personalized in images determines not the logic of form but the measure of emotion and imagination which gets into the substance. It is on this basis that the poetry of Amy Lowell, John Gould Fletcher, Mr. Flint and Mr. Aldington must be judged. They believe that what they feel, experiencing life and observing nature, concerning the mystery and wonder of things, can be better reproduced for communication if certain artificial, misleading, and useless impedimenta of language are eliminated. This is not to say that there must not be any decoration, any more than to say that in abandoning, for the purpose, the rhythm of metres, rhythm cannot find any other laws of control. A fallacy long accepted by the conventional-minded is the fallacy that the genius of the poet is revealed by what he can do under the restrictions of form. All really great poets have broken the traditional regularities of forms handed on to them by their predecessors; they found their genius could not achieve within the restrictions, and instead of adding to the mediocrity of the art, imposed technical obligations upon themselves which only the most rigorous and persistent labors could accomplish. This, it seems to me, is what the imagists are doing. It is what Chaucer, Shakespeare, Coleridge,

Blake, Poe and Henley have done. And it is precisely the imagistic principle in the work of these poets I have just named which gives them a preëminent position in the art of English poetry. Whether the poetry of this modern imagist group is great poetry is a matter with which we ought to have but little concern at present; that it is good poetry can easily be proved. To prove it is all a matter of being able to demonstrate the difference between what is verse and what is poetry in their primary significances.

All art is artifice, Arthur Symons once declared, and the scope of poetry is neither enlarged nor restricted by the range of subjects with which it deals. It depends entirely upon the force of symbols in words, reproducing upon the mind an impression corresponding in exactitude to the gradations of a state of being in objects or experience, and thereby presenting a reality. This is what Poe accomplished, whose telescopic imagination observed but a small space of the starry emotions of humanity. So if the imagists in their poems show a vibratory sensitiveness to natural realities, and actually bring to us sensations of heat and light, of windy beaches, meadows, city streets, and leaves, it must be the result of an active imagination stimulated by the only force upon which it is dependent and interrelated — the emotional. But to say that the imagists are only concerned in their poetry with natural objects is to disregard the human relations that are woven in the essential spirit of this external world.

Writing in *vers libre* does not consitute the whole purpose of the imagist poets. In fact, they have employed both regular rhythms and rhyme in their work. Whether employing the medium of *vers libre* or metre, they have shown, especially in a certain intensifying quality of mood, the first note of pure romanticism in English poetry of the last decade. The final test of poetry is not that it stirs one — for to be stirred is only a transitory experience, and this the merest jingle has often effected — but that it haunts one. It is not the feeling of contemplative anxiety aroused by the philosophic or moral imagination that gives to poetry its highest value, but the agitated wonder awakened in the spirit of the reader by the sudden evocation of magic. This is the haunting quality in poetry, a thing that has no web of reasoning, and whose elements are so unaccountably mixed that no man has yet learned its secret.

Now I contend that this is what the contemporary imagists are striving for. They do not always get it, but they get it, this subtle quality of magic, in a measure beyond the reach of all but a few poets of to-day. From the poems of Amy Lowell, of John Gould Fletcher, of H. D., of Richard Aldington, of D. H. Lawrence, if one had the space to go into detail here, quotations could be brought into evidence to prove the case. I approached the work of the imagists with considerable doubt, but soon found myself surrendering to an influence that was different from any other in the poetry of the day. It was often deeper than the theme of the poem — it was a force, an element, which created beauty on a strange new pattern.

———————

This appraisal of Amy Lowell's *Men, Women and Ghosts* appeared in the Boston *Transcript*, October 12, 1916, when she and Braithwaite were collaborating on *The Poetry Review*. He wrote this epigram about forty years later:

Amy Lowell

Poly-this and poly-that and poly-sized;
A flair for drama, and for breaking rules;
Herself a genius by herself emprized —
And those that dared to differ — simply fools!

Amy Lowell Again Assails Tradition

When I began the reading of "Men, Women and Ghosts," like the undercurrent of a tune this observation of a modern critic kept beating in my mind, and I must satisfy its insistence by quoting it here: "The principle of destruction is the principle of life. It is your business, if you are bringing a new force into the world, to begin by killing, or at least wounding, a tradition, even if the tradition once had all the virtues." This same critic again remarks: "True originality will but disconcert the student of poetry who has come to love certain formulas, the formulas of his masters, which seem to him, as every form of truth must seem to 'young ignorance and old custom,' a form immortal in itself." Miss Lowell has been wounding tradition ever since the publication of "Sword Blades and Poppy Seeds," two years ago; and "young ignorance and old custom" have been disconcerted in championing the old formulas. It has been, this spectacle of passionate protection against originality, very largely on the surface, a voluntary confession that form is immortal only when barricaded with imitations. But the point is missed by every student of poetry who shows himself disconcerted by new formulas that a "limitation, which in the artist is often strength, shutting him in more securely on his own path, in the critic is mere weakness of sight, an unpardonable blindness. In no two ages of the world has eternal beauty manifested itself under the same form."

I open myself to the charge of inconsistency when I agree that the "poetry that is at once recognized by its resemblance to other poetry must always be second-rate work," but I have not been inconsistent because what I have recognized is that a degree of intensity and a mode of spiritual intuition is often comparable in poets far apart in total achievement. Judged by the above statement the poems in this volume are not second-rate work because they have no resemblance to any other poetry. One may look around and examine all the other poetry in English that has lately, with new formulas, departed from traditional modes of expression, and find nothing exactly like the art in Miss Lowell's "Men, Women and Ghosts." There are her confreres in "Imagism," but even among them there is no such advance, which has taken the principle of form out of a narrow practice and set it constructively upon the fundamental base of rhythmic laws. "It has long been a favorite idea of mine," she states in the preface to this new volume, that "the rhythms of vers libre have not been sufficiently plumbed, that there is in them a power of variation which has never yet been brought to the light of experiment." The "power of variation" that has been attempted in the present collection offers results that carry the art of "Men, Women and Ghosts" beyond experimentation. "This is a book of stories," the poet declares in her preface. "For that reason I have excluded all purely lyrical poems. But the word 'stories' has been stretched to its fullest application. It includes both narrative poems, properly so called; tales divided into scenes, and a few pieces of less obvious story-telling import in which one might say that the dramatis personae are air, clouds, trees, houses, streets, and such things." These stories, however, are not only told in the "fluctuating rhythm of vers libre," in which the movement of poetry is associated with the movement of music, but in the ordered pattern of Chaucerian stanzas and strict metrical forms, sometimes the two forms blending as in the narrative of "The Cremona Violin," and also in polyphonic prose, a form of Miss Lowell's own invention in which the typographical arrangement of the words gives elaborate and effective aid to the dramatic substance, having recurrent pulses and rhyme.

There are five groups of poems in the volume, and the caption of each is an ornament in itself. "Figurines in Old Saxe" contains the incomparable "Patterns" which opens the book; "Pickthorn Manor," a long narrative in metre and rhyme of the eighteenth century in which love hallucinations result tragically; "The Cremona Violin," another long narrative, of eighteenth century Germany; "The Cross-Roads," a ghostly tale of New England; "A Roxbury Garden," a delightful chronicle of two girls and their games; and "1777," in which our own Revolutionary atmosphere and Venetian pictures depend for their dramatization upon natural objects. Next comes "Bronze Tablets," four poems of the Napoleonic era, containing "The Fruit Shop," "Malmaison," "The Hammers," and "Two Travellers in the Place Vendôme," veritable achievements of historical narratives with something of an epical significance condensed in their human characterization in which the figure of Napoleon is woven with the destinies of his career. "War Pictures" contains the well-known "The Bombardment," but a more remarkable accomplishment is "The Allies," which I believe stands with Masefield's "August, 1914," at the head of all poems inspired by the war. "The Overgrown Pasture" is a series of poems in Yankee dialect, and finally "Clocks Tick a Century," with a supplementary section of "Towns in Color," in which the attempt is to give the "color, and light, and shade of certain places and hours, stressing the purely pictorial effect."

The very bewilderment of riches in this volume makes quotation a difficult thing. Miss Lowell's subjects are so varied and their aspects so manifold, that to illustrate her poems by quotation is to have been eluded by a general sense of her substance and treatment. However, I want to hazard a few lines from "The Hammers," a poem in which, from the building of a ship to the building of a coffin, hammering is finely symbolic of the tragic ending of Napoleon's life and career. These for instance:

> Tap! Tap! Tap!
> Marble likeness of an Emperor,
> Dead man, who burst your heart against a world too
> narrow,
> The hammers drum you to your last throne
> Which always you shall hold alone.

And in "Malmaison," a tremendous inscription of Josephine's fate, this picture of that desolate and abandoned woman is fine: "Night. The Empress sits alone, and the clock ticks, one after one. The clock nicks off the edges of her life. She is chipped like an old bit of china; she is frayed like a garment of last year's wearing. She is soft, crinkled, like a fading rose."

The substance of that impressive poem "The Allies," may be gathered from these extracts: "This is the war of wars, and the cause? Has this writhing worm of men a cause? . . . In the shoulder of the worm is a teacher. . . . A dust speck in the worm's belly is a poet. . . . The eye of the serpent is an owner of mills. . . . Bankers, butchers, shopkeepers, painters, farmers — men, sway and sweat. They will fight for the earth, for the increase of the slow, sure roots of peace, for the release of hidden forces. They jibe at the eagle and his screeching sound. . . . Each man pulls his belt a little tighter, and shifts his gun to make it lighter. Each man thinks of a woman, and slaps out a curse at the eagle. The sword jumps in the hot sky, and the worm crawls on to battle, stubbornly. This is the war of wars, from eye to tail the serpent has one cause: Peace!"

Clearly and definitely the verse-stories in "Men, Women and Ghosts" place Miss Lowell among the contemporary poets who have arrived. Now that her art, an art built upon the elements of revolt against tradition, has amply and fully functioned to a degree where it can no longer be assailed for either inadequacy or willfullness, her substance alone offers a matter for controversy. But after all, substance is the point of vital discussion in all poets. She wisely, taking a last stand on the question of form, remarks, "For the substance of the poems — why, the poems are here." Yes, they are here with an astonishing measure of emotional and visionary power. They are seldom to be discerned by any test of subjective sentiment; she knows experience as something spun like fine sunshine thrown over life from which she evokes an objective pattern more universal than particular. It is a reading of life, dramatic, vivid, effective, in which delicate and tender moods are as expressive as those vigorous strokes in which qualities of romantic terror and naturalism abound. The energy alone which could produce a collection of poems such as "Men, Women and

Ghosts" is remarkable, but when that energy is touched
with that power of insight and emotion which endows the
results with beauty, then the poet is of that creative fellowship with the divine, which is shared by no other of the sons
of man.

Published in March, 1917, this is the first part of a long essay
that appeared in *Bookman.* In the second part, in the June issue, Braithwaite treated in detail a multitude of individual works
and poets. In *The Poetic Year for 1916: A Critical Anthology,*
he reprinted reviews and a series of articles, "The Lutanists of
Midsummer," written for the *Transcript.*

The Year in Poetry

All the glamour about our present renaissance of poetry carries with it a palpable danger: the danger of disintegrating
criticism. My belief is that the year 1916 may be the pivot
upon which the art of poetry in America will advance or re-
cede. Poets are born — but fine poetry is encouraged by
public patronage and appreciation. Neither patronage nor
appreciation is to be had from the public, if criticism poi-
sons the art at its root. The tradition of criticism is nearly always the attempt to do this: Francis Jeffrey stands as the
typical example of the destructive critic, who gave us no insight into his personal knowledge of life, and now nobody
reads him except out of curiosity; Charles Lamb is a typical
example of the creative critic, who seeks in his author a contact with life: he is not erudite but human, he measures
rather than judges, and so we never cease to delight in his
wisdom. With these examples, the right aims of criticism
ought to appear quite positive. Contrary to popular belief
— and the theory of literary individuals — criticism is not a
judgment of literary styles and materials, but an interpreta-

tion of life through the creative use of language and expression. Not the form, but the substance is the main thing. Life is supplemented by expression. Facts are never visualized except through spiritual recognition. Form — conventional or free — with literary or colloquial diction, is nothing but a chaos of words unless the theme or subject which it gives being to has glowed to the "Let there be light" of the imaginative emotion.

The year 1916 witnessed the development of the present growth in American poetry to the point where a critical reaction will be fatal to its further progress. This renascence, now firmly accepted by everybody as a definite movement in American life and literature, was fully a decade coming to maturity. It grew upon the fostering appreciation of the few who created a hearing for the art; that hearing established an audience, and the audience quickened the creative impulse of the poets. The Renaissance became a fact. The corollary to all this has been the evidence during the past year of an impulse to criticism which has taken hold of the poets themselves.

The last decade, while poetry was developing, criticism as a function of appraisal did not exist. There was, of course, a body of critical writing in America, but when it concerned itself with poetry, it dealt mainly with the past. This critical writing, which could praise Keats and Shelley, Poe and Emerson, would have hesitated to commend comparable poetic virtues in Hovey and Moody, even if a self-reliant study of contemporaneous values had been bold enough to hazard opinions. What Arthur Symons was doing in England nobody dared to do in America. Joel E. Spingarn gave comforting assurance ten years ago, in promulgating the ideal of creative criticism, that America need not lack an accomplishment in disengaging contemporary literary values. It was Europe and not America that recognized Dr. Spingarn's humane scholarship. America chose to go barren of interpretive writing, dealing with contemporary literature.

Criticism

Now, as I have said, there is an incipient critical utterance, mainly the work of a few, and led by poets who have until very recently been out of touch with the current of American art, and it gives warning of being destructive. It is for the good of the art of poetry that it intends to be destructive — so it claims. It is dogmatic, as all such criticism is. It denies taste to those who differ in opinion from itself, forgetting the proverb *de gustibus non est disputandum*. It clings to the tradition that artistic standards must be imported, and in applying those standards compares American poetry to its disadvantage with English and European poetry, forgetting that in all essentials of life, experience, and culture America is fundamentally and superficially different from Europe; and it has never yet in all the examples I have read of this criticism understood the vital matter of substance and spiritual qualities, or given one-tenth of the attention to ideas and emotion that it has to questions of style and form, and to the discussion of rules and tradition.

The influence of this kind of criticism can do more harm to American poetry at present than any other influence whatever. The harm it does is by misrepresenting the art. If the public heeds such criticism, audiences will diminish, and the consequent discouragement of the poets themselves will produce a decline in creativeness. It must be realised that no poet to-day works and starves in obscurity till chance or influence brings a patron to reward him with fame and a competence, as was true in the past; fame and fortune for the modern poet are the gifts of public recognition and appreciation, and if these do not come before youth advances to that vague borderland where it is lost, the modern poet gives the best of himself to other things. That poets have made money during the past few years is no proof that poetry to-day is less an art than a profession, but under the dispensation of modern democracy it *does* prove that poetry must make good business to flourish as an art.

37

I will not admit that there is any such thing as a *new* poetry; there are *new* aspects and meanings to life, and poetry, eternal as the primary instincts of man, finds new symbols, images, and personalisations to express and interpret them; and so with the old formulæ of poetic forms and diction, old formulæ of criticism become inadequate by which to judge the new embodiments of poetic art. The fundamentals of criticism may be in Aristotle as the fundamentals of poetry are in the folk chants of antiquity and the communal chant of primitive peoples in the world to-day; but Professor Saintsbury has shown that centuries of practice have made the function of criticism a subtle evaluation of life in dealing with the direct evidence of creative literature; so poetry has advanced from the oral communal chant to a highly developed organism in which formal diction and forms of fixed patterns are more or less standardised. Art is the evidence of spiritual forces in man's nature working through experience, reflective and active, and criticism is a luminous annotation of this evidence, defining through interpretation the degree of intensity in which the evidence presents the artist's attempt to realise truth and beauty.

Criticism has always lagged behind creation; which is natural, since it must first have a body of evidence upon which to work. When it does catch up it begins to pound with the guns of orthodoxy; it brings precedent and tradition as tests, and not finding the progressive era of new art adhering to the fundamentals of a past period, it fails to understand the impulse and aims of the new conceptions and embodiments. The first urge of incomprehension in art is to attack the thing that cannot be explained in the common terms of the particular artistic medium, and so this criticism at once begins a destructive career. In orthodox criticism there is more energy than reason, more blind logic than evocative enthusiasm. In this you have again the contrast of Jeffrey and Lamb. The same intellectual temper which applies orthodox criticism to contemporary work will change its method when applied to the art of a past era and will come forward with a creative exposition of literature.

Contemporary painting, music, architecture and the drama have been fortunate in having trained creative critics in America, but poetry has lacked such interpreters. I do not mean to say there has not been an occasional essay here and there which practised this method. And yet poetry is the one art through which America has nationally influenced European culture — there will immediately come to the reader's mind the influence of Poe and Whitman in England, France, Italy and Germany — is the one art which during the past decade has brought the American spirit into the international comity of Western culture, though receiving the least critical attention of the interpretive kind. The future of American poetry depends seriously upon the present and future quality of criticism. I have the greatest faith that the quality of that criticism will be creative. A significant editorial recently printed in the *Boston Evening Transcript* on "Our Consumption of Art," suggests the hopeful tendency of American criticism in general, and it cannot be so general without concerning itself with the art of poetry in particular. "Ever and ever," it said, "the course of the advance in criticism is away from the exposition merely of the forms and of the technique of the arts and on to the exposition of the emotions and ideas — to the spirit of the artists who determined and created these forms. . . . As this type of criticism increases in America, we shall be nearing the day when its value will tell in America's power to create art, for this critical insight informs its audience what are really the qualities of soul, of mind and of character which sufficed to the production of great art."

In the nineteenth century American poetry was differentiated by locality, though it was only in New England that a group rose to the dignity and influence of a "school." The tradition of the New England group was English, its artistic culture was a provincial branch of British art. The culture of the northeastern seaboard about used up the nineteenth century in completing the exhausted reign of British ideals over the art in America. In Walt Whitman was the declaration of poetic independence, but it was not until 1900 that his thoroughly American principles were confederated into the spiritual constitution of native poetry. The two most conspicuous figures in American poetry at the end of the last century were Hovey and Moody; Moody reacted to European influences, in style and conception he adhered to the traditions of British culture; Hovey carried on the spiritual and emotional revolt of Whitman, and while refusing to go as far as the latter in the matter of form, yet practised an elasticity in the use of fundamental rhythms which gave him all the prestige of an innovator. He was the first link in the chain of continuity which America was creating in the art of poetry.

To-day American poetry is differentiated by aims, principles, and forms. Physical boundaries, in determining the character of expression, are obliterated. There are, of course, centralised forces, but they are forces of individual power, rather than propinquity of ideals. There are *tendencies* and *schools;* and they are struggling against each other for predominance. This is a state of affairs that has never happened before in the history of American poetry. And it proves two things that are of the utmost importance: first, that the condition of American poetry is persuasively healthy, and secondly, that a continuity is defining itself underneath the shifts and changes of expression — showing a rooted poetic impulse in the American people that is going to grow and develop into larger achievements of which the present accomplishments are only the significant and convincing indications.

The present accomplishment, if we take the year 1916, has variety in the individual and unity in the group. It is not with any arbitrary intention that I have arranged the volumes supplying the text for this article into three groups. Two groups are American, and are opposed in the matter of form, though in the instance of a few poets we find them utilising two methods of expression, and sometimes producing a hybrid form of rhythm. Some of the work of Conrad Aiken and John Gould Fletcher is of this character, and in each case the practice is a purely literary device rather than a natural and colloquial rendering of spoken sounds. Amy Lowell employs this form, too, and it is an effort to produce scale values in colour and sound, a combination of exact pictorial and emotional effects. Robert Frost may also be said to produce this form; but if you study his blank verse closely, and particularly the idioms of his lyrics, it will be seen that it is not a literary innovation that he achieves but the unconscious tone of colloquial speech in which the *sense* of sound moulds the rhythmic outlines. But this middle ground — on which stand some others that are important though not as notable in actual results as those I have mentioned — is flanked with work that is tenaciously conservative and traditional on the one hand, and work that is radical and revolutionary on the other. Within both these limits of expression — the formal and free — there is a range of inventiveness that might furnish a thesis for the erudite, *but should be of concern to the true lover of poetry only where, in either case, the invention fails to communicate adequately and appealingly the substance dealt with.* So much for the matter of form. It becomes a fallacy when you conceive it to be anything else than a kind of function performing through symbols the revelations and evocations *enjoyed* by the individual. After all it is only a medium, and as such must obey laws, but these laws, generally well defined in the abstract, change aesthetically in their manifestations, and the most convincing artist is he who can penetrate the veil of secrecy that surrounds them and force their elements into service.

The third group of volumes is made up of the English poets. I separate them from either of the American groups to contrast both form and interest. As to form they are all working in the main current of English poetry. Certain distinctions they possess, a subtle verbal ease, not common to the conservative American group. This gives them a quality of magic that is delightful — a quality that is mellow, atmospheric, retrospective. This is offset in the work of the Americans by magical glamour, by a fiercer tussle with the issues of life, a vibrant sense of the destinies that envelop the mind and soul of man, and a stronger personal reaction to normal experience. It is a difference of culture, not spirit, that contrasts this English group of conformists with the Americans, but the advantage is certainly not all on the side of culture. It may produce a ripeness of art that has charm and distinction, but it loses a freshness, a buoyancy, a flexible adaption of mood and sympathy toward the fermentations of new life. The anarchistic principle must violate culture to propagate a new and vivid content in poetry. Abercrombie, considered by many the greatest of all living English poets today, Masefield and Gibson, have done this. Behind them for the most part is a welter of clean workmanship, illumined here and there with a special quality of one kind or another, which can set no fair claim to be as good as or better than our contemporary poets of America.

The spirit of the American conformists is a greater element of poetic strength than the culture of the English conformists. Beauty it regards as desirable, but truth is essential. And it is very largely this motive which has made so intense a response on the part of the American mind to the new art forms. That other group of American poets who practise free verse or *vers libre* has emancipated emotion for the full exercise of the intellect. Here the situation is similar to the situation among the English poets of to-day. The anarchistic principle has not only violated form but made substance yield a new significance. It is to art what the liberal influence has been in latter-day English politics. The particular merit of this group, mostly carried by two or three strong figures, is an intellectual advance over their contemporaries in both England and America. However are regarded the forms in which they write, they have revived a note of romanticism in American poetry, and given to its expression a stimulus that will impart a tone to invention of whatever pattern, and make it worthy of the intense substance whch is the fibre and texture of our national existence. The thing criticism should remember when it considers American poetry to-day is, that it must be studied as *American poetry.* It is already a little too old to be regarded as an experiment, and it is yet too young to render a judgment as to its ephemeral or permanent character. But it is worthy of the highest appreciation and the most sympathetic interpretation, because it has seized upon and embodied aspects of character and life hitherto unrealised in rhythmic expression, and registered them upon the spirit of the nation.

Braithwaite regarded James Weldon Johnson as an intimate friend. They exchanged an extensive correspondence and shared many interests. Braithwaite's review of Johnson's autobiography, *Along This Way,* in *Opportunity* for December, 1933, especially praises his long service as an official of the National Association for the Advancement of Colored People. The following review, of *Fifty Years and Other Poems,* appeared in the Boston *Transcript* on December 12, 1917.

The Poems of James Weldon Johnson

One should not in the least be interested in the fact of Mr. Johnson being a colored man, who has written these poems, if he did not compel such considerations by taking, on occasions the most significant and interesting, a racial attitude. The expression in this key is a sentiment, though of the profoundest, and should be distinguished in art, not as a cause and characteristic, but as impulse and inspiration in the human scale. Brander Matthews, in his introduction to these poems, discusses the two currents of tradition of the colored man in American art, which merge in Mr. Johnson. The mistake Professor Matthews makes in this account is the common mistake of not differentiating between the negro and the man of color. No matter what may be the social economic classification of the whole, there is a difference in the stock. Of the mass Professor Matthews can say that "They are not as we are; they stand apart, more or less; they have their own distinct characteristics;" but of the individual it cannot be said because the facts present no difference in nature, intellect, or spirit. This is wholly the difference in verse for instance, between Paul Laurence Dunbar and Mr. Johnson.

"In the following pages," writes Professor Matthews, "Mr. James Weldon Johnson conforms to both of these traditions. He gathers together a group of lyrics, delicate in workmanship, fragrant with sentiment, and phrased in pure and unexceptional English. Then he has another group of dialect verses, racy of the soil, pungent in flavor, swinging in rhythm and adroit in rhyme. But where he shows himself a pioneer is in the half-dozen larger and bolder poems, of a loftier strain, in which he has been nobly successful in expressing amply the higher aspirations of his own people. It is in uttering this cry for recognition, for sympathy, for understanding, and, above all, for justice, that Mr. Johnson is most original and most powerful. In the superb and soaring stanzas of 'Fifty Years' (published exactly half a century after the signing of the Emancipation Proclamation) he has given us one of the noblest commemorative poems yet written by any American — a poem sonorous in its diction, vigorous in its workmanship, elevated in its imagination and sincere in its emotion. In it speaks the voice of a race, and the race is fortunate in its spokesman. In it a fine theme has been finely treated. In it we are made to see something of the soul of the people who are our fellow-citizens now and forever — even if we do not always so regard them. In it we are glad to acclaim a poem which any living poet might be proud to call his own."

The titular poem of this collection is worthy of all the

praise Professor Matthews bestows upon it. Personally there are other poems in this volume I like better, and in which I think Mr. Johnson's qualities as a poet are more instinctive. In the "O Black and Unknown Bards," the tribute he pays to the folk-singers of the negro spirituals, there is a deeper imaginative mood, a graver possessive memory of racial glory. I quote the second and third stanzas:

Heart of what slave poured out such melody
As "Steal Away to Jesus?" On its strains,
His spirit must have nightly floated free,
Though still about his hands he felt his chains.
Who heard great "Jordan roll?" Whose starward eye
Saw chariot "swing low?" And who was he
That breathed that comforting, melodic sigh,
"Nobody knows de trouble I see"?

What merely living clod, what captive thing,
Could up toward God through all its darkness grope,
And find within its deadened heart to sing
These songs of sorrow, love and faith, and hope?
How did it catch that subtle undertone,
That note in music heard not with the ears?
How sound the elusive reed so seldom blown,
Which stirs the soul or melts the heart to tears.

I would like to quote here the sonnet on "Mother Night," which depends upon nothing but the poetic mood of abstraction for its theme, and the accomplishment of which confirms the important universality supporting Mr. Johnson's gifts as a poet:

Eternities before the first-born day,
Or ere the first sun fledged his wings of flame,
Calm Night, the everlasting and the same,
A brooding mother over chaos lay.
And whirling suns shall blaze and then decay,
Shall run their fiery courses and then claim

The haven of darkness whence they came;
Back to Nirvanic peace shall grope their way.
So when my feeble sun of life burns out,
And sounded is the hour for my long sleep,
I shall, full weary of the feverish light,
Welcome the darkness without fear or doubt,
And heavy-lidded, I shall softly creep
Into the quiet bosom of the Night.

As Professor Matthews claims, it may be through those "half dozen larger and bolder poems," where "he shows himself a pioneer" — in such poems as the "Fifty Years," "Brothers," "The White Witch," "Fragment," "The Color Sergeant," and the sonnet, "To Horace Brumstead," that Mr. Johnson may claim the attention of many who want some tangible evidence with the purposeful web of racial life and aspiration; significant as these pieces are in conception and workmanship, they are not from an artistic point of view the best gifts from the poet's store. Mr. Johnson is a man of wide and deep experience. In the consular service of the Government, he was for a number of years in South America, and of Spanish life and literature he is a sympathetic interpreter. The fruits in this volume are showered in the group of light and delicate lyrics and songs "Down by the Carib Sea," and of some epigramatic translations from the Spanish with a sonnet or two from Placido. The Carib Sea Trees have all the quality of the luxuriant tropics; the passionate in consequence to energy and reality, all the fine efflorescence of a nature indulging in its own sensations.

And in the other verses that strike a universal note there is more often both felicity of conception and expression. Particular reference should be made to Mr. Johnson's poem "The Young Warrior," which, set to music of Mr. Harry T. Burleigh, has been sung throughout Italy as a martial song inspiriting the Italian soldier on his way to the front. The pieces in negro dialect are characteristic of work of this kind, and Mr. Johnson's possess the usual intensity of pathos and the usual humorous abandon. One notes particularly, however, in the dialect verses in this volume, the absence of coarseness, of crudity, in the humor which has more or less pervaded the racial writers of dialect since Dunbar. Mr. Johnson, if he has done nothing else to enhance the value of this kind of speech in verse, has given it a quality of refinement.

If we care to regard "Fifty Years and Other Poems" racially there can be no doubt but what it is the most significant accomplishment in verse since the publication of Dunbar's poems, that Mr. Johnson is the most important poet of the race. But the implication of his volume is deeper. He has intellectual qualities that Dunbar did not possess. He is also free of the sensuality which so immeasurably helped the earlier poet to his wide recognition. He stands more squarely upon his own achievement as a man and poet, and his contribution to the verse of today, if less glamorous and less applauded, is more practical and more commendable in its natural development. His career already distinguished in diplomacy and journalism, as a publicist, novelist and translator (he translated the libretto of "Goyescas" produced at the Metropolitan Opera House three winters ago, and has done besides Spanish dramas and verse), with this volume he gives assurance of a career in poetry to outshine his other accomplishments.

Braithwaite wrote a number of prefaces and endorsements for books of verse. Most were gratuitous offerings of praise for the poetry of friends, work he genuinely admired. Some were evidently part of the package of services he was sometimes commissioned to perform as editorial guide and agent. This introduction, to *The Heart of a Woman* (1918) by Georgia Douglas Johnson, is a representative piece. W. E. B. Du Bois wrote the foreword for her second book, *Bronze, A Book of Verse*, which Braithwaite's publishing firm issued in 1922.

Introduction, The Heart of a Woman

The poems in this book are intensely feminine and for me this means more than anything else that they are deeply human. We are yet scarcely aware, in spite of our boasted twentieth-century progress, of what lies deeply hidden, of mystery and passion, of domestic love and joy and sorrow, of romantic visions and practical ambitions, in the heart of a woman. The emancipation of woman is yet to be wholly accomplished; though woman has stamped her image on every age of the world's history, and in the heart of almost every man since time began, it is only a little over half a century since she has either spoke or acted with a sense of freedom. During this time she has made little more than a start to catch up with man in the wonderful things he has to his credit; and yet all that man has to his credit would scarcely have been achieved except for the devotion and love and inspiring comradeship of woman.

Here, then, is lifted the veil, in these poignant songs and lyrics. To look upon what is revealed is to give one a sense of infinite sympathy; to make one kneel in spirit to the marvelous patience, the wonderful endurance, the persistent faith, which are hidden in this nature.

> *The heart of a woman falls back with the night,*
> *And enters some alien cage in its plight,*
> *And tries to forget it has dreamed of the stars*
> *While it breaks, breaks, breaks on the sheltering bars.*

sings the poet. And

> *The songs of the singer*
> *Are tones that repeat*
> *The cry of the heart*
> *Till it ceases to beat.*

This verse just quoted is from "The Dreams of the Dreamer," and with the previous quotation tells us that this woman's

48

heart is keyed in the plaintive, knows the sorrowful agents of life and experience which knock and enter at the door of dreams. But women have made the saddest songs of the world, Sappho no less than Elizabeth Barrett Browning, Ruth the Moabite poetess gleaning in the fields of Boaz no less than Amy Levy, the Jewess who broke her heart against the London pavements; and no less does sadness echo its tender and appealing sigh in these songs and lyrics of Georgia Douglas Johnson. But sadness is a kind of felicity with woman, paradoxical as it may seem; and it is so because through this inexplicable felicity *they* touch, intuitionally caress, reality.

So here engaging life at its most reserved sources, whether the form or substance through which it articulates be nature, or the seasons, touch of hands or lips, love, desire, or any of the emotional abstractions which sweep like fire or wind or cooling water through the blood, Mrs. Johnson creates just that reality of woman's heart and experience with astonishing raptures. It is a kind of privilege to know so much about the secrets of woman's nature, a privilege all the more to be cherished when given, as in these poems, with such exquisite utterance, with such a lyric sensibility.

————

Poems by half a dozen of the writers treated in this article in *Crisis* in April, 1919, had been included in Braithwaite's annual anthologies of magazine verse. Fenton Johnson, whose *Champion Magazine*, "a monthly account of Negro achievement," won compliments from Braithwaite, is represented also in his *Victory! Celebrated by Thirty-Eight American Poets* (1918).

Some Contemporary Poets of the Negro Race

The present revival of poetry in America could scarcely advance without carrying in its wake the impulse and practice of a poetic consciousness in the Negro race.

While we have no traditions in the art, we have a rich and precious tradition in the substance of poetry: vision, intense emotionalism, spiritual and mystical affinities, with both abstract and concrete experience, and a subtle natural sense of rhythmic values. All these are essential folk-qualities, primal virtues in the expression of impassioned experience, whether festive or ceremonial, in all the indigenous folk-literatures of the world. But when a race advances from primitive life and customs, or when the divisions of a particular race become sharply differentiated by learning and culture, and intercourse with other peoples with modes of culture more perfect in certain respects affects them, there is produced a standard of form in written and oral speech that becomes a characteristic of class co-racial consciousness. This standard becomes the medium of literary expression in which taste is the vital essence, and is opposed by the "vulgar tongue" of the "people" in which the vigorous and imaginative folk-ballads are recited, the communal chants of traditional custom and ritual dramatized, and national songs sung.

The survival of the vulgar tongue in modern times, where the influence of formal and conventional civilization has penetrated among primitive communities, is in dialect, the attempt of the invaded, enslaved, and suppressed peoples to imitate phonetically the speech of the dominant class or race. Dialect is, thus, not the corruption of the folk or tribal language, of the Frankish invaders of Gaul, of the Anglo-Saxon conquest of ancient Britain, of the absorption of the African savages — who may be likened in every tribal respect to the Franks, Angles and Saxons — by America, but of the language of the Latins, the Britons, and the English.

Dialect may be employed as the *langue d'oc* of Frédéric Mistral's Provençal poems, as a preserved tongue, the only adequate medium of rendering the psychology of character, and of describing the background of the people whose lives and experience are kept within the environment where the dialect survives as the universal speech; or it may be employed as a special mark of emphasis upon the peculiar characteristic and temperamental traits of a people whose action and experiences are given in contact and relationship with a dominant language, and are set in a literary fabric of which they are but one strand of many in the weaving.

I have gone to some length in the foregoing because the matter is of vital importance to those who regard the future of the Negro in American literature. It holds, too, I think, the explanation of that gap which exists between the mysterious and anonymous period of the "Sorrow Songs" — vivid, intense poetry of a suffering, but eternally confident folk — and the advent of Paul Laurence Dunbar. The Negro poet, as such, can be said to have inherited no poetic traditions which would make him a bi-national artist: that is to say, he had no precursors sufficient in numbers and of decided genius, the substance of whose song was racial, while the expression was national—the glorious and perfect instrument of English poetic art, which we know as the common possession of Chaucer, Shakespeare, Milton, Wordsworth, Keats, Shelley, Swinburne, Browning, Longfellow, Poe and Lowell.

This gap I postulate as a silent transition to a new order of imaginative and emotional racial utterance. Remember that here was a race of many tribes, members of which amounting to hundreds of thousands were stolen from their native homes, from their immemorial customs and traditions, which in many instances have been proven to be the traits of a highly organized primitive culture and social code, and forcibly held in a captivity that suppressed every virtue but work and every ideal but obedience. The struggle through two centuries under this unchristian suppression was toward the acquisition of a new language which in all its unfamiliar and tortuous meanings had to be learned through the auditory sense, as the invaluable aids of reading and writing were denied; and it is little wonder that the earliest and latest folk utterance of these people was the collective yearning of sorrow, impassioned and symbolic, addressed to the one benign spirit their masters taught them from whom to seek love and mercy in a mystical hereafter as a compensation for their miserable existence on earth. It was the poetry of an ancient race passing through the throes of an enforced re-birth into the epoch of an alien and dominating civilization.

When it sought voice in Paul Laurence Dunbar, it did so with old memories and impulses; it was the finale, in a rather conscious manner, of centuries of spiritual isolation, of a detached brooding and yearning for self-realization in the universal human scale, and in a childish gayety in eating the fruits of a freedom so suddenly possessed and difficult to realize. Dunbar was the end of a régime, and not the beginning of a tradition, as most careless critics, both white and colored, seem to think. But his niche is secure because he made the effort to express himself, and clothe his material artistically; though he never ventured into the abstract intricacies and wrung from the elements of rhythmic principles the subtle and most haunting forms of expression. His work reflected chiefly the life of the Negro during the era of Reconstruction and just a little beyond, when the race was emerging from the illusion of freedom to the hard and bitter reality of how much ground still remained to be dishearteningly but persistently fought for before a moral and spiritual liberty, as well as a complete political freedom and social fraternity, was attained. When Mr. Howells said that Dunbar was the first poet of his race to express and interpret the life of his people lyrically, he told only a half-truth; what survives and attracts us in the poetry of Dunbar is the life of the Negro in the limited experience of a transitional period, the rather helpless and still subservient era of testing freedom and adjusting in the mass a new condition of relationship to the social, economic, civil and spiritual fabric of American civilization. Behind all this was an awakening impulse, a burning and brooding aspiration, creeping like a smothered fire through the consciousness of the race, which broke occasionally in Dunbar as through the crevices of his spirit — notably the sonnet "Robert Gould Shaw," the "Ode to Ethiopia," and a few other poems—but which he did not have the deep and indignant and impassioned vision, or the subtle and enchanting art to sustain.

Such a poet we did have in substance, though he chose to express himself in the rhythms of impassioned prose rather than the more restricted and formal rhythm of verse. But the fact is as solid as the earth itself, that Dr. Du Bois in "The Souls of Black Folk" began a poetic tradition. This book has more profoundly affected the spiritual nature of the race than any other ever written in this country; and has more clearly revealed to the nation at large the true idealism and high aspiration of the American Negro; and the intellectual mind of the country accepted it as the humanistic doctrine by which on terms of equal economic, political and social endeavor the Negro was to work out his destiny as an American citizen — sharing pound for pound the weight of responsibility, enjoying the same indivisible measure of privilege in the American democracy.

It is only through the intense, passionate, spiritual idealism of such substance as makes "The Souls of Black Folk" such a quivering rhapsody of wrongs endured and hopes to be fulfilled that the poets of the race with compelling artistry can lift the Negro into the only full and complete nationalism he knows — that of the American democracy. "There is no difference between men;" declared G. Lowes Dickinson, the English Platonist, "wealth, position, race or nationality, make no difference between men: it is only the growth of the soul." And the poets of a race give expression and reality to the soul of a people through whose eternal laws no unnatural impediments of injustices or wrongs can keep from ascendency to the highest fulfillment and the fullest participation in ideal and eternal privileges of life.

I am not one who believes that a Negro writer of verse — or of fiction, for that matter — must think, feel, or write racially to be a great artist; nor can he be distinctively labeled by the material he uses. This is a fallacy too often expressed by critics to confirm the desired hypothesis that the Negro is humanly different in the scale of mankind, that even after some centuries of civilizing process in America he is still nearer in his most cultivated class to the instincts of his ancestral forebears than any other of the conglomerate races who compose the citizenry of the Republic. In every race and nation there are primitives who retain the impulses of barbarism, more evident and prevalent among peoples of the Teutonic stock than among those of the Latin stock. But the Negro has absorbed in his advanced class, just as in the advanced class of any other people, the culture of the best civilizations in the world today, and in his imaginative and artistic expression he is universal. What I said about embodying racial aspirations and material does not alter this fact. All great artists are interracial and international in rendering in the medium of any particular art the fundamental passions and the primary instincts of humanity.

The promise of this I seem to detect in the spiritual voice of the Negro becoming articulate in the poets who are beginning to emerge from the background of the people. They are springing up around us everywhere, and it is the profound duty of the race to encourage and support them. There is power and beauty in this pristine utterance — wood notes wild that have scarcely yet been heard beyond the forest of their own dreams. But if we will cherish these with a responsive audience, one day, and not very long hence, we shall have a great chorus of these singers to glorify our souls and the soul of America.

These notes do not include all the poets who have published books within recent years; they are intended rather to indicate tendencies, which I regard as more important for the moment, and illustrated by the examples of representative work printed during the past year. Thus, such writers as the late James D. Corruthers, Edward Smyth Jones, George Reginald Margetson, and others, do not fall within the scope of this paper. Nor do these writers quite reach the artistic development of those I deal with, neither does Mr. Fenton Johnson, a young man already the author of three volumes, and whose recent work shows a rapid and steady progress. This question of equipment, of a thorough grounding in the technical elements of the science of versification, is the greatest handicap to the progress of many contemporary writers of verse. It is the hard and laborious task of mastering the subtle and fluctuating rhythms of verse that the average individual tries to escape which produces such a mass of mediocre work, often choking and wasting the substance of a passionate and imaginative poetic spirit. It is difficult to impress upon such individuals that they must serve a jealous and consecrated apprenticeship to this divine mistress, and that ambition is but a humble offering upon the altar of her sacred mystical religion.

There are, however, three books recently published, which show not only a distinctive poetic quality, but also an artistic adequacy of expression and which promise the fulfillment of the Negro in poetry I have so confidently predicted for the future. Besides these books, I have in the past year come across single poems in the magazines by unknown writers confirming more specifically the rapid development of the higher poetic qualities that are manifesting themselves in the Negro. These latter I will deal with first, because they represent what I hope most to see accomplished; because they are the proofs of my contention that poets of the race may deal with a rich and original vein of racial material and give it the highest forms of creative literary expression, which neither differentiates the author from the artist in general nor tolerates for a moment the false psychology of that gratuitous, separate standard by which white critics are prone to judge the works of Negro authors.

The most significant accomplishments among these recent poems are two sonnets signed by "Eli Edwards" which appeared in *The Seven Arts* for last October. "Eli Edwards," I understand, is the pseudonym of Claude McKay, who lives in New York City, choosing to conceal his identity as a poet

from the associates among whom he works for his daily
bread. His story as it is, which I had from Mr. Oppenheim,
who accepted his poems when editor of *The Seven Arts,* is
full of alluring interest, and may one day be vividly featured
as a topic of historic literary importance. For he may well
be the keystone of the new movement in racial poetic
achievement. Let me quote one of the sonnets:

The Harlem Dancer

Applauding youths laughed with young prostitutes
   And watched her perfect, half-clothed body sway;
Her voice was like the sound of blended flutes
   Blown by black players upon a picnic day.
She sang and danced on gracefully and calm,
   The light gauze hanging loose about her form;
To me she seemed a proudly-swaying palm
   Grown lovelier for passing through a storm.
Upon her swarthy neck black, shiny curls
   Profusely fell; and, tossing coins in praise,
The wine-flushed, bold-eyed boys, and even the girls,
   Devoured her with their eager, passionate gaze;
But, looking at her falsely-smiling face
   I knew her self was not in that strange place.

Here, indeed, is the genuine gift — a vision that evokes
from the confusing details of experience and brings into the
picture the image in all its completeness of outline and its
gradation of color, and rendered with that precise surety of
form possessed by the resourceful artist. The power in this
poet is, I think, his ability to reproduce a hectic scene of
reality with all the solid accessories, as in "The Harlem
Dancer," and yet make it float as it were upon a background
of illusion through which comes piercing the glowing sense
of a spiritual mystery. Note the exalted close of Mr. Edwards's riotous picture of the dancer when

    . . . . *looking at her falsely-smiling face,*
   I knew her self was not in that strange place—

he translates the significance of the intoxicated figure with its sensuous contagion into something ultimate behind the "falsely-smiling face," where "her self" — be it the innocent memory of childhood, perhaps of some pursuing dream of a brief happiness in love, or a far-away country home which her corybantic earnings secure in peace and comfort for the aged days of her parents — is inviolably wrapped in the innocence and beauty of her dreams. This sonnet differs in both visionary and artistic power from anything so far produced by the poets of the race. The visual quality here possessed is extraordinary; not only does Mr. Edwards evoke his images with a clear and decisive imagination, but he throws at the same time upon the object the rich and warm colors of his emotional sympathies.

Another poem of last year is by a young man, Roscoe C. Jamison. His "Negro Soldiers," first published in *The Crisis* for September, 1917, is undeniably the finest contribution in verse to the Negro's participation in the war. In such a brief compass the poet has focused the heart-burning predicament of a many-millioned people, and yet unfalteringly he points the inevitable self-sacrificing way, fervently believing that it will not be in vain. And underneath it all is a current of exaltation in that allusion to the crucified Christ which makes these people the victors in the anguish of their treatment. Though it was first printed in this magazine, and many times reprinted since, I shall quote it here, because it cannot be too often read and cherished:

> *These truly are the Brave,*
> *These men who cast aside*
> *Old memories, to walk the blood-stained pave*
> *Of Sacrifice, joining the solemn tide*
> *That moves away, to suffer and to die*
> *For Freedom — when their own is yet denied!*
> *O Pride! O Prejudice! When they pass by,*
> *Hail them, the Brave, for you now crucified!*
> *These truly are the Free,*
> *These souls that grandly rise*

Above base dreams of vengeance for their wrongs,
Who march to war with visions in their eyes
Of Peace through Brotherhood, lifting glad songs
Aforetime, while they front the firing-line.
Stand and behold! They take the field today,
Shedding their blood like Him now held divine,
That those who mock might find a better way!

Need a race despair which possesses a voice of flame and dew like that — a voice, too, that has in it the solacing and uplifting strains of confident tomorrows?

This young man had a future of immense possibilities. Unfortunately he has died since this appreciation was written.

In Georgia Douglas Johnson we have the foremost woman poet of the race, a writer whose lyrics have some of that flame-like intensity and delicate music which makes Christina Rossetti the foremost woman poet of England. But I do not mean, and I do not wish it to be understood, that I limit her horizons when I characterize her as the foremost woman poet of the race. She expands beyond into the universal, and as the title of her volume, "The Heart of a Woman," indicates, she renders and interprets the mysterious and inexplicable secrets of femininity. The key that unlocks her dreams, her unique sensibility, to revealing those shadowy and passionate depths which lie in a woman's heart, seems to mould itself out of the abstraction of this mood in "Contemplation":

We stand mute!
No words can paint such fragile imagery,
Those prismic gossamers that roll
Beyond the sky-line of the soul;
We stand mute!

The soul of this sex, playing for so many centuries the rôle of Lady Shalott, has at last refused to take the world reflected through a mirror; she will look with her own eyes through the window of experience down upon the many-towered Camelot; the shattered mirror has brought her face to face with reality. That is why, perhaps, that women — before they gained the defiant courage of the new art with the Freudian psychology of erotic motorism — made most of the frail, pensive songs of the world. Whether in religion or love, or in the descriptive rendering of nature, they always extracted the substance to which clung the mist of tears. Not always the tears of despair, but tears of joy and exultation as well. This exquisite quality gives a charming atmosphere to Mrs. Johnson's lyrics.

There is in Mrs. Johnson the pure poetic temperament, burning, quivering, thrilling, through the subjective lyric emotion into delicately textured and colored speech. Through these lyrics the whole scale of a woman's heart is sounded, and as if a little tired with so much giving, and so much like a woman, too, when she has lavished her soul upon life, she folds in the end her little dreams up in her heart:

> *I'm folding up my little dreams*
> *Within my heart to-night,*
> *And praying I may soon forget*
> *The torture of their sight.*
>
> *For Time's deft fingers scroll my brow*
> *With fell relentless art —*
> *I'm folding up my little dreams*
> *To-night, within my heart!*

In Mr. Waverley Turner Carmichael's "The Heart of a Folk" we have a spontaneous singer who has written the raciest and most indigenous dialect verse since Dunbar. His gift is natural and unforced; humor and pathos blending with instinctive utterance throughout his work. His volume contains a number of pieces that can come under no other

classification than that of the "Spirituals" of the ante-bellum
Negro; he has accomplished the rare thing of reproducing
both the haunting rhythm and the fervid imagery of the
"Sorrow Songs," to a degree I did not think possible today.
They are not exactly the same, but they come so close to the
original impulse and expression that they might easily deceive one unacquainted with the inexplicable modulations
of the genuine product. Here is a sample:

> *Keep me, Jesus, keep me;*
> *Keep me 'neath Thy Mighty Wing,*
> *Keep me, Jesus, keep me;*
> *Help me praise Thy Holy Name,*
> *Keep me, Jesus, keep me.*
> *O my Lamb, come my Lamb,*
> *O my good Lamb,*
> *Save me, Jesus, save me.*

Here is a poet who might restore something of that peculiar artlessness of praise and longing of the ante-bellum
Negro and thus preserve a lingering echo of that tradition —
if he returns from the furnace of war whither he has gone to
help make safe his country for the democracy that wrung
such bitter anguish out of his forebears.

Looked at in every way the foremost poet of the race
today is Mr. James Weldon Johnson, whose "Fifty Years and
Other Poems" has recently been published. Certainly Mr.
Johnson has proven himself more versatile than his brother-
poets, and he has been able to define certain characteristics
in his verse more broadly based upon experience. He is also
more ably equipped to bend his material to the specific purpose in hand, so that there is no indefinite vagueness in his
work. He has rather a full-bodied instead of a subtle music,
and his emotions, enraptured as they are, never wander in-
coherently out of control. He brings, too, a wealth of ideas
into his poems, and presents them with that finality which
sometimes makes you gasp at their audacity, and at others

submit to the chastisements of truth. As Professor Brander Matthews remarks in his Introduction to Mr. Johnson's poems, he shows himself a "pioneer in the half-dozen larger and bolder poems, of a loftier strain, in which he has been nobly successful in expressing the higher aspirations of his own people. It is in uttering this cry for recognition, for sympathy, for understanding, and above all for justice, that Mr. Johnson is most original and most powerful. In the superb and soaring stanzas of 'Fifty Years' (published exactly half a century after the signing of the Emancipation Proclamation) he has given us one of the noblest commemorative poems yet written by any American — a poem sonorous in its diction, vigorous in its workmanship, elevated in its imagination and sincere in its emotion. In it speaks the voice of his race; and the race is fortunate in its spokesman. In it a fine theme has been finely treated. In it we are made to see something of the soul of the people who are our fellow-citizens now and forever — even if we do not always so regard them. In it we are glad to acclaim a poem which any living poet might be proud to call his own."

Mr. Johnson's poems are so much better known, most of them having originally appeared in the leading magazines of the country, than those of the other poets treated in this paper, that I shall not lengthen the already overlengthened space allowed me. And I wish, too, I might comment on Mr. Benjamin Brawley's fine ballad, "The Seven Sleepers of Ephesus," and the verses of Jessie Fauset, which I have noticed in the magazines from time to time as having a certain wistful note of their own. Both these poets, I trust, will soon give us a collection of their poems, and thus give me the pleasure of writing about them.

When *Spring in New Hampshire and Other Poems* was published in London, Claude McKay promptly sent a copy to

Braithwaite, with whom he had been in correspondence for several years. Braithwaite's review, below, appeared in the *Transcript* on May 25, 1921.

Spring in New Hampshire

This little book of poems was published in London and is the work of a young negro who has had a varied and adventurous career. Mr. McKay is at present an associate editor of Max Eastman's magazine, "The Liberator." The title of the collection is reminiscent of the poet's attendance at Dartmouth College five or six years ago. In the brief preface, written by I. A. Richards, we are told that "The writer of these verses was born in the Clarendon Hills of Jamaica (British West Indies) in 1889. In 1911 he published a small volume in the negro dialect, and later left for the United States, where he worked in various occupations and took courses in agriculture and English at the Kansas State College. In the spring of this year (1920) he visited England to arrange for the publication of his poems.

"Claude McKay is a pure-blooded negro, and though we have recently been made aware of some of the more remarkable achievements of African art typified by the sculpture from Benin, and in music by the 'Spirituals,' this is the first instance of success in poetry with which we in Europe at any rate have been brought in contact. The reasons for this late development are not far to seek, and the difficulties presented by modern literary English as an acquired medium would be sufficient to account for the lacuna; but the poems here selected may, in the opinion of not a few who have seen them in periodical form, claim a place beside the best work that the present generation is producing in this country."

The English reception of Mr. McKay's poems ought, according to custom, to be of great advantage to the progress of his career in this country, where he is living and

pursuing his literary work; but there is no immediate promise of an American edition of his book, the New York publisher failing, as was announced, to issue the book simulta-
neously with Grant Richards.

There are no dialect poems in this book but there is an
intense racial feeling, a passionate mood of censure for the
wrongs and oppressions imposed upon the poet's race, and
in this a deep sense of individual suffering. The subjective
note that Mr. McKay gets into his verses is very different
from any similar note that is to be found in the verses of the
native negro poets. It must be remembered in this respect
that Mr. McKay is a foreigner whose formative years were
entirely influenced by traditions and associations wholly different from the American negro, and in his art it has in certain very cogent aspects enabled him to regard his themes
with the detached attitude of the artist. That has not in any
sense smothered or made inarticulate the poignancy of moods
or experiences that are very unhappy and very real. He
can feel all the bitterness and all the shame, the unjust
and oppressive conditions which his color subjects him to
and being endowed with the sensitiveness of the artist, suf-
fers infinitely, but the very quality of this artistic sensibility
enables him to vision images and experiences with a detached temperament. This is successfully illustrated in one
of the most striking of contemporary sonnets, "The Harlem
Dancer":

Applauding youths laughed with young prostitutes
And watched her perfect, half-clothed body sway;
Her voice was like the sound of blended flutes
Blown by black players upon a picnic day.
She sang and danced on gracefully and calm,
The light gauze hanging loose about her form;
To me she seemed a proudly swaying palm
Grown lovelier for passing through a storm.
Upon her swarthy neck black, shiny curls
Profusely fell; and, tossing coins in praise,

The wine-flushed, bold-eyed boys, and even the girls,
Devoured her with eager, passionate gaze;
But, looking at her falsely smiling face,
I knew her self was not in that strange place.

The atmosphere, background and figure here painted
with something of the feverish and exotic passion that Mo-
reau got into his canvases, has long waited for a poet of Mr.
McKay's sympathy and imagination to describe, and the
fact that he has done it proves that he alone has had the
power to do it. Again in the stanza called "Alfonso, Dressing
to Wait at Table, Sings," he has touched with his vivid poetic insight a certain common aspect of negro life into art:

Alfonso is a handsome bronze-hued lad
*   Of subtly changing and surprising parts;*
His moods are storms that frighten and make glad,
*   His eyes were made to capture women's hearts.*

Down in the glory-hole Alfonso sings
*   An olden song of wine and clinking glasses*
And riotous rakes; magnificently flings
*   Gay kisses to imaginary lasses.*

Alfonso's voice of mellow music thrills
*   Our swaying forms and steals our hearts with joy;*
And, when he soars, his fine falsetto trills
*   Are rarest notes of gold without alloy.*

But O! Alfonso, wherefore do you sing
*   Dream-songs of carefree men and ancient places?*
Soon shall we be beset by clamouring
*   Of hungry and importunate palefaces.*

The temperament in this quite perfect piece of mellow
irony is the temperament of the artist with an exposed and
quivering nerve.

Again and again one is reminded in the verses of a
storm-tost dreamer, wandering about an unsympathetic

world and among unfriendly men. This stanza from "The
Spanish Needle" —

> *Shadowed by the spreading mango,*
> *Nodding o'er the rippling stream,*
> *Tell me, dear plant of my childhood,*
> *Do you of the exile dream?*

With a wistfulness that is very appealing the poet recalls his
childhood in the poem called "The Tropics in New York" —

> *Bananas ripe and green and ginger-root,*
> *Cocoa in pods and alligator pears,*
> *And tangerines and mangoes and grapefruit*
> *Fit for the highest prize at parish fairs*
>
> *Set in the window, bringing memories*
> *Of fruit trees laden by low-singing rills,*
> *And dewy dawns and mystical blue skies*
> *In benediction over new-like hills.*
>
> *Mine eyes grew dim and I could no more gaze;*
> *A wave of longing through my body swept,*
> *And, hungry for the old, familiar ways,*
> *I turned aside and bowed my head and wept.*

There is very solid accomplishment in this book of Mr.
McKay's, and evidence of power that ought to go far and
away from that direction where a common critical fallacy
has placed all negro poets dealing with racial themes in the
roots of Dunbar. There is a very different temper of both vision and expression in Mr. McKay and in Dunbar, and I
think in certain respects of far greater importance.

———

An educator trained at Harvard, Leslie Pinckney Hill published
The Wings of Oppression, which Braithwaite reviewed in the

Transcript for December 10, 1921, and a blank-verse drama, *Toussaint L'Ouverture — A Dramatic History* (1928).

A Poet of His Race

There is the full racial allegiance in Mr. Hill's muse and when it is paid he seems somehow to breathe a deeper poetic air. The imagination is an impartial bestower of gifts, and when those gifts are used for any special racial purpose it is always better for art rather than for polemics. Mr. Hill divides his collection into five groups, which consist of "Poems of My People," "Poems of the Times," "Poems of Appreciation," "Songs" and "Poems of the Spirit." These are all prefaced with some five stanzas called "The Wings of Oppression," after which the book is named. "A serious, dignified and artistic expression of the Negro race — ideals of which the world wrongfully believe this race to be quite incapable," we are told is presented in these poems. In the opening poem are martialed all the moods which express the position of a race burdened with prejudice and scorn and struggling against these to find an honorable and worthy place in the community. But in the lines called "My Race" Mr. Hill sings

> *My life were lost, if I should keep*
> *A hope-forlorn and gloomy face,*
> *And brood upon my ills, and weep*
> *And mourn the travail of my race.*

These lines may suggest to us why only fourteen poems out of the sixty-nine the book contains are devoted to "My People." These deal with the meaning of the World War to the American Negro, with a tribute to Tuskegee on freedom, on the Jim Crow, on lynching, on "To a Caged Canary in a Negro Restaurant," on "Self Determination," as the philosophy of the American negro and "The Black Man's Bit" in the war. In the other groups Mr. Hill deals with a variety

Criticism

of subjects which make the ordinary poetic appeal. They are neither better nor worse than the average poetic attempts of a cultivated mind without the vivid poetic temperament. Indeed there is a great deal of conventionality in the poetic impulse which is lured to express itself in "Lines Written in the Alps Above Chamounix." We quote the first of the two sonnets named "A Call to Poets," as representative of Mr. Hill's work.

> Rise up from dalliance with little things,
> O poets of all lands. Your golden age
> Is now, and all the world your heritage.
> The nations perish till ye sweep the strings
> With re-creative music. He that sings
> With power now to calm the peoples' rage
> Will bind the future to his tutelage,
> And give the heavy-laden present wings.
> Where is your lost dominion? Once ye framed
> A heaven of beauty pillared firm in peace,
> And ye were called the shepherds of the soul.
> By what default was that high priesthood shamed?
> How did the magic of your music cease
> To win the human heart, and keep it whole?

Even in his conventional habit of poetic thought and expression Mr. Hill's verse is disciplined, a virtue not always common among writers who bring no fresh quality of substance.

Alain Locke's *The New Negro* (1925), a manifesto and a monument, featured this essay by Braithwaite, a revision of an earlier piece of similar title he had published in September, 1924, in *Crisis*. It is a pioneering and remarkably perceptive critique, offering judgments that are generally as sound now as when they were first pronounced.

The Negro in American Literature

True to his origin on this continent, the Negro was projected into literature by an over-mastering and exploiting hand. In the generations that he has been so voluminously written and talked about he has been accorded as little artistic justice as social justice. Ante-bellum literature imposed the distortions of moralistic controversy and made the Negro a wax-figure of the market place: post-bellum literature retaliated with the condescending reactions of sentiment and caricature, and made the Negro a *genre* stereotype. Sustained, serious or deep study of Negro life and character has thus been entirely below the horizons of our national art. Only gradually through the dull purgatory of the Age of Discussion, has Negro life eventually issued forth to an Age of Expression.

Perhaps I ought to qualify this last statement that the Negro was *in* American literature generations before he was part of it as a creator. From his very beginning in this country the Negro has been, without the formal recognition of literature and art, creative. During more than two centuries of an enslaved peasantry, the race has been giving evidence, in song and story lore, of an artistic temperament and psychology precious for itself as well as for its potential use and promise in the sophisticated forms of cultural expression. Expressing itself with poignancy and a symbolic imagery unsurpassed, indeed, often unmatched, by any folk-group, the race in servitude was at the same time the finest national expression of emotion and imagination and the most precious mass of raw material for literature America was producing. Quoting these stanzas of James Weldon Johnson's *O Black and Unknown Bards,* I want you to catch the real point of its assertion of the Negro's way into domain of art:

O black and unknown bards of long ago,
 How came your lips to touch the sacred fire?
How, in your darkness, did you come to know
 The power and beauty of the minstrel's lyre?
Who first from midst his bonds lifted his eyes?
 Who first from out the still watch, lone and long,
Feeling the ancient faith of prophets rise
 Within his dark-kept soul, burst into song?

There is a wide, wide wonder in it all,
 That from degraded rest and servile toil
The fiery spirit of the seer should call
 These simple children of the sun and soil.
O black slave singers, gone, forgot, unfamed,
 You — you, alone, of all the long, long line
Of those who've sung untaught, unknown, unnamed,
 Have stretched out upward, seeking the divine.

How misdirected was the American imagination, how blinded by the dust of controversy and the pall of social hatred and oppression, not to have found it irresistibly urgent to make literary use of the imagination and emotion it possessed in such abundance.

   * * *

Controversy and moral appeal gave us *Uncle Tom's Cabin,* — the first conspicuous example of the Negro as a subject for literary treatment. Published in 1852, it dominated in mood and attitude the American literature of a whole generation; until the body of Reconstruction literature with its quite different attitude came into vogue. Here was sentimentalized sympathy for a down-trodden race, but one in which was projected a character, in Uncle Tom himself, which has been unequalled in its hold upon the popular imagination to this day. But the moral gain and historical effect of Uncle Tom have been an artistic loss and setback. The treatment of Negro life and character, overlaid with these forceful stereotypes, could not develop into artistically satisfactory portraiture.

Just as in the anti-slavery period it had been impaled upon the dilemmas of controversy, Negro life with the Reconstruction became involved in the paradoxes of social prejudice. Between the Civil War and the end of the century the subject of the Negro in literature is one that will some day inspire the literary historian with a magnificent theme. It will be magnificent not because there is any sharp emergence of character or incidents, but because of the immense paradox of racial life which came up thunderingly against the principles and doctrines of democracy, and put them to the severest test that they had known. It was a period when, in literature, Negro life was a shuttlecock between the two extremes of humor and pathos. The Negro was free, and was not free. The writers who dealt with him for the most part refused to see more than skin-deep, — the grin, the grimaces and the picturesque externalities. Occasionally there was some penetration into the heart and flesh of Negro characters, but to see more than the humble happy peasant would have been to flout the fixed ideas and conventions of an entire generation. For more than artistic reasons, indeed against them, these writers refused to see the tragedy of the Negro and capitalized his comedy. The social conscience had as much need for this comic mask as the Negro. However, if any of the writers of the period had possessed gifts of genius of the first caliber, they would have penetrated this deceptive exterior of Negro life, sounded the depths of tragedy in it, and produced a masterpiece.

American literature still feels the hold of this tradition and its indulgent sentimentalities. Irwin Russell was the first to discover the happy, care-free, humorous Negro. He became a fad. It must be sharply called to attention that the tradition of the ante-bellum Negro is a post-bellum product, stranger in truth than in fiction. Contemporary realism in American fiction has not only recorded his passing, but has thrown serious doubts upon his ever having been a very

genuine and representative view of Negro life and character. At best this school of Reconstruction fiction represents
the romanticized high-lights of a régime that as a whole was
a dark, tragic canvas. At most, it presents a Negro true to
type for less than two generations. Thomas Nelson Page,
kindly perhaps, but with a distant view and a purely local
imagination did little more than paint the conditions and at-
titudes of the period contemporary with his own manhood,
the restitution of the over-lordship of the defeated slave
owners in the Eighties. George W. Cable did little more
than idealize the aristocratic tradition of the Old South with
the Negro as a literary foil. The effects, though not the motives of their work, have been sinister. The "Uncle" and the
"Mammy" traditions, unobjectionable as they are in the setting of their day and generation, and in the atmosphere of
sentimental humor, can never stand as the great fiction of
their theme and subject: the great period novel of the South
has yet to be written. Moreover, these type pictures have
degenerated into reactionary social fetishes, and from that
descended into libelous artistic caricature of the Negro;
which has hampered art quite as much as it has embar-
rassed the Negro.

Of all of the American writers of this period, Joel Chandler Harris has made the most permanent contribution in
dealing with the Negro. There is in his work both a deepen-
ing of interest and technique. Here at least we have something approaching true portraiture. But much as we admire
this lovable personality, we are forced to say that in the
Uncle Remus stories the race was its own artist, lacking
only in its illiteracy the power to record its speech. In the
perspective of time and fair judgment the credit will be divided, and Joel Chandler Harris regarded as a sort of provi-
dentially provided amanuensis for preserving the folk tales
and legends of a race. The three writers I have mentioned
do not by any means exhaust the list of writers who put the
Negro into literature during the last half of the nineteenth
century. Mr. Howells added a shadowy note to his social rec-

ord of American life with *An Imperative Duty* and pro-
phesied the Fiction of the "Color Line." But his moral
scruples — the persistent artistic vice in all his novels —
prevented him from consummating a just union between
his heroine with a touch of Negro blood and his hero. It is
useless to consider any others, because there were none who
succeeded in creating either a great story or a great character out of Negro life. Two writers of importance I am re-
serving for discussion in the group of Negro writers I shall
consider presently. One ought perhaps to say in justice to
the writers I have mentioned that their non-success was
more largely due to the limitations of their social view than
of their technical resources. As white Americans of their
day, it was incompatible with their conception of the ine-
qualities between the races to glorify the Negro into the serious and leading position of hero or heroine in fiction. Only
one man that I recall, had the moral and artistic courage to
do this, and he was Stephen Crane in a short story called
The Monster. But Stephen Crane was a genius, and therefore could not besmirch the integrity of an artist.

With Thomas Dixon, of *The Leopard's Spots,* we reach
a distinct stage in the treatment of the Negro in fiction. The
portraiture here descends from caricature to libel. A little
later with the vogue of the "darkey-story," and its devotees
from Kemble and McAllister to Octavus Roy Cohen, sentimental comedy in the portrayal of the Negro similarly degenerated to blatant but diverting farce. Before the rise of a
new attitude, these represented the bottom reaction, both in
artistic and social attitude. Reconstruction fiction was passing out in a flood of propagandist melodrama and ridicule.
One hesitates to lift this material up to the plane of literature even for the purposes of comparison. But the gradual
climb of the new literature of the Negro must be traced and
measured from these two nadir points. Following *The Leopard's Spots,* it was only occasionally during the next twenty
years that the Negro was sincerely treated in fiction by
white authors. There were two or three tentative efforts to

dramatize him. Sheldon's *The Nigger* was the one notable early effort. And in fiction Paul Kester's *His Own Country* is, from a purely literary point of view, its outstanding performance. This type of novel failed, however, to awaken any general interest. This failure was due to the illogical treatment of the human situations presented. However indifferent and negative it may seem, there is the latent desire in most readers to have honesty of purpose and a full vision in the artist: and especially in fiction, a situation handled with gloves can never be effectively handled.

The first hint that the American artist was looking at this subject with full vision was in Torrence's *Granny Maumee*. It was drama, conceived and executed for performance on the stage, and therefore had a restricted appeal. But even here the artist was concerned with the primitive instincts of the Race, and, though faithful and honest in his portrayal, the note was still low in the scale of racial life. It was only a short time, however, before a distinctly new development took place in the treatment of Negro life by white authors. This new class of work honestly strove to endow the Negro life with purely aesthetic vision and values, but with one or two exceptions, still stuck to the peasant level of race experience, and gave, unwittingly, greater currency to the popular notion of the Negro as an inferior, superstitious, half-ignorant and servile class of folk. Where they did in a few isolated instances recognize an ambitious impulse, it was generally defeated in the course of the story.

Perhaps this is inevitable with an alien approach, however well-intentioned. The folk lore attitude discovers only the lowly and the naïve: the sociological attitude finds the problem first and the human beings after, if at all. But American art in a reawakened seriousness, and using the technique of the new realism, is gradually penetrating Negro life to the core. George Madden Martin, with her pretentious foreword to a group of short stories, *The Children in the Mist*, — and this is an extraordinary volume in many ways — quite seriously tried, as a Southern woman, to elevate the Negro to a higher plane of fictional treatment and interest. In succession, followed Mary White Ovington's *The Shadow*, in which Miss Ovington daringly created the kinship of brother and sister between a black boy and white girl, had it brought to disaster by prejudice, out of which the white girl rose to a sacrifice no white girl in a novel had hitherto accepted and endured; then Shands' *White and Black*, as honest a piece of fiction with the Negro as a subject as was ever produced by a Southern pen — and in this story, also, the hero, Robinson, making an equally glorious sacrifice for truth and justice, as Miss Ovington's heroine; Clement Wood's *Nigger*, with defects of treatment, but admirable in purpose, wasted though, I think, in the effort to prove its thesis on wholly illogical material; and lastly, T. S. Stribling's *Birthright*, more significant than any of these other books, in fact, the most significant novel on the Negro written by a white American, and this in spite of its totally false conception of the character of Peter Siner.

Mr. Stribling's book broke ground for a white author in giving us a Negro hero and heroine. There is an obvious attempt to see objectively. But the formula of the Nineties, — atavistic race-heredity, still survives and protrudes through the flesh and blood of the characters. Using Peter as a symbol of the man tragically linked by blood to one world and by training and thought to another, Stribling portrays a tragic struggle against the pull of lowly origins and sordid environment. We do not deny this element of tragedy in Negro life — and Mr. Stribling, it must also be remembered, presents, too, a severe indictment in his painting of the Southern conditions which brought about the disintegration of his hero's dreams and ideals. But the preoccupation, almost obsession of otherwise strong and artistic work like O'Neill's *Emperor Jones, All God's Chillun Got Wings*, and Culbertson's *Goat Alley* with this same theme and doubtful formula of hereditary cultural reversion suggests that, in spite of all good intentions, the true presental of the real tragedy of Negro life is a task still left for Negro writers to perform. This is especially true for those phases of culturally representative race life that as yet have scarcely at all found treatment by white American authors. In corroborating this, let me quote a passage from a recent number of the *Independent*, on the Negro novelist which reads:

"During the past few years stories about Negroes have been extremely popular. A magazine without a Negro story is hardly living up to its opportunities. But almost every one of these stories is written in a tone of condescension. The artists have caught the contagion from the writers, and the illustrations are ninety-nine times out of a hundred purely slapstick stuff. Stories and pictures make a Roman holiday for the millions who are convinced that the most important fact about the Negro is that his skin is black. Many of these writers live in the South or are from the South. Presumably they are well acquainted with the Negro, but it is a remarkable fact that they almost never tell us anything vital about him, about the real human being in the black man's skin. Their most frequent method is to laugh at the colored man and woman, to catalogue their idiosyncrasies, their departure from the norm, that is, from the ways of the whites. There seems to be no suspicion in the minds of the writers that there may be a fascinating thought life in the minds of the Negroes, whether of the cultivated or of the most ignorant type. Always the Negro is interpreted in the terms of the white man. White-man psychology is applied and it is no wonder that the result often shows the Negro in a ludicrous light."

I shall have to run back over the years to where I began to survey the achievement of Negro authorship. The Negro as a creator in American literature is of comparatively recent importance. All that was accomplished between Phillis Wheatley and Paul Laurence Dunbar, considered by critical standards, is negligible, and of historical interest only. Historically it is a great tribute to the race to have produced in Phillis Wheatley not only the slave poetess in eighteenth century Colonial America, but to know she was as good, if not a better, poetess than Anne Bradstreet whom literary historians give the honor of being the first person of her sex to win fame as a poet in America.

Negro authorship may, for clearer statement, be classified into three main activities: Poetry, Fiction, and the Essay, with an occasional excursion into other branches. In the drama, until very recently, practically nothing worth while has been achieved, with the exception of Angelina Grimké's *Rachel*, notable for its sombre craftsmanship. Biography has given us a notable life story, told by himself, of Booker T. Washington. Frederick Douglass's story of his life is eloquent as a human document, but not in the graces of narration and psychologic portraiture, which has definitely put this form of literature in the domain of the fine arts. Indeed, we may well believe that the efforts of controversy, of the huge amount of discursive and polemical articles dealing chiefly with the race problem, that have been necessary in breaking and clearing the impeded pathway of racial progress, have absorbed and in a way dissipated the literary energy of many able Negro writers.

Let us survey briefly the advance of the Negro in poetry. Behind Dunbar, there is nothing that can stand the critical test. We shall always have a sentimental and historical interest in those forlorn and pathetic figures who cried in the wilderness of their ignorance and oppression. With Dunbar we have our first authentic lyric utterance, an utterance more authentic, I should say, for its faithful rendition of Negro life and character than for any rare or subtle artistry of expression. When Mr. Howells, in his famous introduction to the *Lyrics of Lowly Life*, remarked that Dunbar was the first black man to express the life of his people lyrically, he summed up Dunbar's achievement and transported him to a place beside the peasant poet of Scotland, not for his art, but precisely because he made a people articulate in verse.

The two chief qualities in Dunbar's work are, however, pathos and humor, and in these he expresses that dilemma of soul that characterized the race between the Civil War and the end of the nineteenth century. The poetry of Dunbar is true to the life of the Negro and expresses characteristically what he felt and knew to be the temper and condition of his people. But its moods reflect chiefly those of the era of Reconstruction and just a little beyond, — the limited experience of a transitional period, the rather helpless and subservient era of testing freedom and reaching out through the difficulties of life to the emotional compensations of laughter and tears. It is the poetry of the happy peasant and the plaintive minstrel. Occasionally, as in the sonnet to *Robert Gould Shaw* and the *Ode to Ethiopia* there broke through Dunbar, as through the crevices of his spirit, a burning and brooding aspiration, an awakening and virile consciousness of race. But for the most part, his dreams were anchored to the minor whimsies; his deepest poetic inspiration was sentiment. He expressed a folk temperament, but not a race soul. Dunbar was the end of a régime, and not the beginning of a tradition, as so many careless critics, both white and colored, seem to think.

After Dunbar many versifiers appeared, — all largely dominated by his successful dialect work. I cannot parade them here for tag or comment, except to say that few have equalled Dunbar in this vein of expression, and none have deepened it as an expression of Negro life. Dunbar himself had clear notions of its limitations; — to a friend in a letter from London, March 15, 1897, he says: "I see now very clearly that Mr. Howells has done me irrevocable harm in the dictum he laid down regarding my dialect verse." Not until James W. Johnson published his *Fiftieth Anniversary Ode* on the emancipation in 1913, did a poet of the race disengage himself from the background of mediocrity into which the imitation of Dunbar snared Negro poetry. Mr. Johnson's work is based upon a broader contemplation of life, life that is not wholly confined within any racial experience, but through the racial he made articulate that universality of the emotions felt by all mankind. His verse possesses a vigor which definitely breaks away from the brooding minor undercurrents of feeling which have previously characterized the verse of Negro poets. Mr. Johnson brought, indeed, the first intellectual substance to the content of our poetry, and a craftsmanship which, less spontaneous than that of Dunbar's, was more balanced and precise.

Here a new literary generation begins; poetry that is racial in substance, but with the universal note, and consciously the background of the full heritage of English poetry. With each new figure somehow the gamut broadens and the technical control improves. The brilliant succession and maturing powers of Fenton Johnson, Leslie Pinckney Hill, Everett Hawkins, Lucien Watkins, Charles Bertram Johnson, Joseph Cotter, Georgia Douglas Johnson, Roscoe Jamison and Anne Spencer bring us at last to Claude McKay and the poets of the younger generation and a poetry of the masterful accent and high distinction. Too significantly for mere coincidence, it was the stirring year of 1917 that heard the first real masterful accent in Negro poetry. In the September *Crisis* of that year, Roscoe Jamison's *Negro Soldiers* appeared:

> *These truly are the Brave,*
> *These men who cast aside*
> *Old memories to walk the blood-stained pave*
> *Of Sacrifice, joining the solemn tide*
> *That moves away, to suffer and to die*
> *For Freedom — when their own is yet denied!*
> *O Pride! O Prejudice! When they pass by*
> *Hail them, the Brave, for you now crucified.*

The very next month, under the pen name of Eli Edwards, Claude McKay printed in *The Seven Arts,*

The Harlem Dancer

> *Applauding youths laughed with young prostitutes*
> *And watched her perfect, half-clothed body sway;*

Her voice was like the sound of blended flutes
    Blown by black players upon a picnic day.
She sang and danced on gracefully and calm,
    The light gauze hanging loose about her form;
To me she seemed a proudly-swaying palm
    Grown lovelier for passing through a storm.

Upon her swarthy neck black, shiny curls
    Profusely fell; and, tossing coins in praise
The wine-flushed, bold-eyed boys, and even the girls
    Devoured her with their eager, passionate gaze;
But, looking at her falsely-smiling face
    I knew her self was not in that strange place.

    With Georgia Johnson, Anne Spencer and Angelina Grimké, the Negro woman poet significantly appears. Mrs. Johnson especially has voiced in true poetic spirit the lyric cry of Negro womanhood. In spite of lapses into the sentimental and the platitudinous, she has an authentic gift. Anne Spencer, more sophisticated, more cryptic but also more universal, reveals quite another aspect of poetic genius. Indeed, it is interesting to notice how to-day Negro poets waver between the racial and the universal notes.

    Claude McKay, the poet who leads his generation, is a genius meshed in this dilemma. His work is caught between the currents of the poetry of protest and the poetry of expression; he is in turn the violent and strident propagandist, using his poetic gifts to clothe arrogant and defiant thoughts, and then the pure lyric dreamer, contemplating life and nature with a wistful sympathetic passion. When the mood of *Spring in New Hampshire* or the sonnet *The Harlem Dancer* possesses him, he is full of that spirit and power of beauty that flowers above any and all men's harming. How different in spite of the admirable spirit of courage and defiance, are his poems of which the sonnet *If We Must Die* is a typical example. Negro poetic expression hovers for the moment, pardonably perhaps, over the race problem, but its highest allegiance is to Poetry — it must soar.

Let me refer briefly to a type of literature in which there have been many pens, but a single mind. Dr. Du Bois is the most variously gifted writer which the race has produced. Poet, novelist, sociologist, historian and essayist, he has produced books in all these fields with the exception, I believe, of a formal book of poems, and has given to each the distinction of his clear and exact thinking, and of his sensitive imagination and passionate vision. *The Souls of Black Folk* was the book of an era; it was a painful book, a book of tortured dreams woven into the fabric of the sociologist's document. This book has more profoundly influenced the spiritual temper of the race than any other written in its generation. It is only through the intense, passionate idealism of such substance as makes *The Souls of Black Folk* such a quivering rhapsody of wrongs endured and hopes to be fulfilled that the poets of the race with compelling artistry can lift the Negro into the only full and complete nationalism he knows — that of the American democracy. No other book has more clearly revealed to the nation at large the true idealism and high aspiration of the American Negro.

In this book, as well as in many of Dr. Du Bois's essays, it is often my personal feeling that I am witnessing the birth of a poet, phoenix-like, out of a scholar. Between *The Souls of Black Folk* and *Darkwater,* published four years ago, Dr. Du Bois has written a number of books, none more notable, in my opinion, than his novel *The Quest of the Silver Fleece,* in which he made Cotton the great protagonist of fate in the lives of the Southern people, both white and black. I only know of one other such attempt and accomplishment in American fiction — that of Frank Norris — and I am somehow of the opinion that when the great epic novel of the South is written this book will prove to have been its forerunner. Indeed, the Negro novel is one of the great potentialities of American literature. Must it be written by a Negro? To recur to the article from which I have already quoted:

"The white writer seems to stand baffled before the enigma and so he expends all his energies on dialect and in general on the Negro's minstrel characteristics. . . . We shall have to look to the Negro himself to go all the way. It is quite likely that no white man can do it. It is reasonable to suppose that his white psychology will always be in his way. I am not thinking at all about a Negro novelist who shall arouse the world to the horror of the deliberate killings by white mobs, to the wrongs that condemn a free people to political serfdom. I am not thinking at all of the propaganda novel, although there is enough horror and enough drama in the bald statistics of each one of the annual Moton letters to keep the whole army of writers busy. But the Negro novelist, if he ever comes, must reveal to us much more than what a Negro thinks about when he is being tied to a stake and the torch is being applied to his living flesh; much more than what he feels when he is being crowded off the sidewalk by a drunken rowdy who may be his intellectual inferior by a thousand leagues. Such a writer, to succeed in a big sense, would have to forget that there are white readers; he would have to lose self-consciousness and forget that his work would be placed before a white jury. He would have to be careless as to what the white critic might think of it; he would need the self-assurance to be his own critic. He would have to forget for the time being, at least, that any white man ever attempted to dissect the soul of a Negro."

What I here quote is both an inquiry and a challenge! Well informed as the writer is, he does not seem to detect the forces which are surely gathering to produce what he longs for.

The development of fiction among Negro authors has been, I might almost say, one of the repressed activities of our literary life. A fair start was made the last decade of the nineteenth century when Chesnutt and Dunbar were turning out both short stories and novels. In Dunbar's case, had he lived, I think his literary growth would have been in the evolution of the Race novel as indicated in *The Uncalled*

and *The Sport of the Gods.* The former was, I think, the
most ambitious literary effort of Dunbar; the latter was his
most significant; significant because, thrown against the
background of New York City, it displayed the life of the
race as a unit, swayed by currents of existence, of which it
was and was not a part. The story was touched with that
shadow of destiny which gave to it a purpose more important than the mere racial machinery of its plot. But Dunbar
in his fiction dealt only successfully with the same world
that gave him the inspiration for his dialect poems; though
his ambition was to "write a novel that will deal with the
educated class of my own people." Later he writes of *The
Fanatics:* "You do not know how my hopes were planted in
that book, but it has utterly disappointed me." His contemporary, Charles W. Chesnutt, was concerned more primarily
with the fiction of the Color Line and the contacts and conflicts of its two worlds. He was in a way more successful. In
the five volumes to his credit, he has revealed himself as a
fiction writer of a very high order. But after all Mr. Chesnutt is a story-teller of genius transformed by racial earnest-
ness into the novelist of talent. His natural gift would have
found freer vent in a flow of short stories like Bret Harte's,
to judge from the facility and power of his two volumes of
short stories, *The Wife of His Youth and Other Stories* and
The Conjure Woman. But Mr. Chesnutt's serious effort was
in the field of the novel, where he made a brave and partially successful effort to correct the distortions of Reconstruction fiction and offset the school of Page and Cable.
Two of these novels, *The Marrow of Tradition* and *The
House Behind the Cedars,* must be reckoned among the
representative period novels of their time. But the situation
was not ripe for the great Negro novelist. The American
public preferred spurious values to the genuine; the coinage
of the Confederacy was at literary par. Where Dunbar, the
sentimentalist, was welcome, Chesnutt, the realist, was
barred. In 1905 Mr. Chesnutt wrote *The Colonel's Dream,*
and thereafter silence fell upon him.

From this date until the past year, with the exception of *The Quest of the Silver Fleece*, which was published in 1911, there has been no fiction of importance by Negro authors. But then suddenly there comes a series of books, which seems to promise at least a new phase of race fiction, and possibly the era of the major novelists. Mr. Walter White's novel *The Fire in the Flint* is a swift moving straightforward story of the contemporary conflicts of black manhood in the South. Coming from the experienced observation of the author, himself an investigator of many lynchings and riots, it is a social document story of first-hand significance and importance; too vital to be labelled and dismissed as propaganda, yet for the same reason too unvarnished and realistic a story to be great art. Nearer to the requirements of art comes Miss Jessie Fauset's novel *There Is Confusion*. Its distinction is to have created an entirely new milieu in the treatment of the race in fiction. She has taken a class within the race of established social standing, tradition and culture, and given in the rather complex family story of the Marshalls a social document of unique and refreshing value. In such a story, race fiction, detaching itself from the limitations of propaganda on the one hand and genre fiction on the other, emerges from the color line and is incorporated into the body of general and universal art.

Finally in Jean Toomer, the author of *Cane*, we come upon the very first artist of the race, who with all an artist's passion and sympathy for life, its hurts, its sympathies, its desires, its joys, its defeats and strange yearnings, can write about the Negro without the surrender or compromise of the artist's vision. So objective is it, that we feel that it is a mere accident that birth or association has thrown him into contact with the life he has written about. He would write just as well, just as poignantly, just as transmutingly, about the peasants of Russia, or the peasants of Ireland, had experience brought him in touch with their existence. *Cane* is a book of gold and bronze, of dusk and flame, of ecstasy and pain, and Jean Toomer is a bright morning star of a new day of the race in literature.

―――――――

Braithwaite's unique contribution to American letters was the compilation of his annual anthologies of the best magazine verse. These volumes, expanding over the years, incorporated his Yearbook of American Poetry and a variety of indices and reference aids. A fair sample of the introductions Braithwaite supplied is this one for the 1927 edition.

Introduction
Anthology of Magazine Verse for 1927

With this issue the fifteenth annual volume of the ANTHOL-OGY is published. These volumes, from the slim book of eighty-seven pages in 1913, to the bulky tome of one thousand pages for the Sesqui-Centennial Edition for 1926, and the present volume of nearly six hundred pages, cover an era in American poetry: perhaps, the greatest era America has known in the history of its poetry. Introductions to previous volumes in the series have sketched down, or up, as you choose, something of the character and merits of the poets and poetry which preceded the so-called renaissance beginning in 1912; opinion of the earlier poetry has pretty well settled by now; admiration for the earlier poets, determined by the changes in tastes and outlook, continues or abates independent of critical authority; and if one persists in admiring Longfellow as the greatest of American poets it is for reasons rooted deeply in the personal nature, and those reasons are impregnable against the most incontrovertible critical assault. Likewise, critical appreciation of the highest and most convincing, cannot force the contemporary public to accept at its valuation a poet who has merits and qualities of a high order, if those merits and qualities happen to be through forms and expressions which branch violently from the accepted traditions. This fact has repeated itself too many times in the history of poetry to arouse much controversy one way or the other. Blake is a good example over a century ago, and . . . Wallace Stevens can easily be cited as a present-day American poet upon whom critics have lavished enough sound praise to establish a responsive national reputation — if criticism could be so potent upon human nature as to awaken taste and educate judgment.

Prior to 1912, then, the merits and qualities of the American poets will be just what the reader finds them to be, what the class-room will interpret them as studies in the elements which constitute the character and function of the art; while criticism's only province, in the future, will be to ride on the wave of recurrent popularity as historian. Suddenly, through some inscrutable impulse, there is a stirring, an awakening interest in an author long since forgotten, or only partially remembered; where the interest takes root, no one knows, but with incredible speed it spreads: and everyone is talking about and reading an author, new editions of his books appear, and the old ones are constantly absent from the shelves of libraries. Then some bright, speculating critical mind applies itself to a "study" or a "Biography," and the sum of the author's worth, in the light of *modern research* and *hitherto unavailable material,* is presented *ex cathedra* to a sentimental world of readers.

Already something of the above has happened to Longfellow. There is Mr. Gorman's study. I am sure Whittier, Lowell, Bryant and Holmes will yet break through the wall that rose up and shut out their figures in 1912. Poe and Whitman these last few years have had plentiful critical and biographical attention, not because the world needed more convincing evidence of their greatness, but rather, in my opinion, to pay off the score which made them in the midst

of a hostile taste, play the literary under-dog to their generation. It is interesting, however, to read Professor Saintsbury's article on Poe in the current DIAL, and see to what
futilities these rehabiliments sometimes lead.

Since 1912, an era in American poetry has come to
fullness, and decline. Unlike any other era in English
poetry — I mean by this term poetry written in the English
language — there has been no pattern by which the art can
be named or explained. The only thing in common that can
be said of it is, there was a movement toward poetic expression at the very centre of a great industrial consciousness,
and this movement swelled up and broke over an astonished
and hardened material spirit in transfiguring sprays of song.
As to standards and modes, technique and forms, there was
nothing but riot and confusion, battle and competition. The
Elizabethan Age, the Augustan, the Georgian, in central
purpose and ideals, mean very definitely a certain thing or
development to the student of poetry; even our New England School, is very easy to classify: from Bryant to Lowell
the six poets could be rolled into one individual and there
would be practically no conflict of spirit or form. But the
fireworks that would blaze, and the bedlam that would
break loose, if Robinson and Frost, Lindsay and Sandburg,
Masters and Amy Lowell, Aiken and Sara Teasdale, could
be compounded into one individual! To any critical student
of the period, if the student were honest with himself, the
contemplation of the past fifteen years must appear night-
marish.

It is a singular thing that this era, so gorgeous and bar-
baric in the outpouring of song, is bracketed by two interpretative works on poetry which may be imagined to hold it
in check for future observation and study. It was in 1912, or
it may have been a year earlier, Max Eastman published his
"The Enjoyment of Poetry," a work that championed no
poet, no school of poetry, but unfolded with the clearest understanding, and with charm and passion, the beauty and
power of the art itself. And this year (autumn, 1927), two of

86

the younger poets, Joseph Auslander and Frank Ernest Hill, collaborated in the production of the story of poetry in a book entitled "The Winged Horse," which traces the beginnings and developments of poetry, continuing their narrative of the art in presenting the lives and works of the most famous English and American poets. Though primarily intended for the introduction of poetry to the young, and to those adult readers who have not read widely nor intelligently in poetry, this work serves a much more exalted purpose and brings to the well-acquainted reader a fascinating assemblage of information and appreciation which makes it indispensable.

Professor John Livingston Lowes' "Convention and Revolt in Poetry," came along about the middle of the period, and was a kind of intellectual shock-absorber to the wild license of the new movement. An able and scholarly work, it stands above the limitations of any particular period as a study of the art of poetry.

Between these two works on the general art of poetry there have been published four books dealing with the subject of particular interest to a study of the period. One of these books does not specifically apply itself to the subject, but it is a critical doctrine of a poetic product of the period, and as such reflects one representative quality of the contemporary poetic mind and character. This work, "The Sacred Wood," has been set up as a sort of Bible by followers of the contemporary metaphysical manner, and though the book had a scant circulation, its influence has been wide and impressive. The other three books deal almost entirely with American poets and poetry since 1912: Louis Untermeyer's "New Era in American Poetry," Conrad Aiken's "Skepticisms," and Clement Wood's "Poets of America." I call attention to these works here because all three have been useful because of their forging in the very furnace of the period white-heated reactions to the immediacy of the achievements. All three of the books are prejudiced in certain directions, and to certain figures, and with the exception of Aiken's, are often inconsistent. In Aiken's case, it is the inability to see and understand the work that is beyond his immediate interest. Untermeyer is flippant, with a cheap and smart manner of epigrammatic expression, often weak and insincere in facing a critical dilemma; Wood is too often intoxicated with brilliant paradoxes to give clear and logical analyses the opportunity to be observed, and thereby loses the full credit to which he is entitled for good judgment and sound taste; while Aiken, with a narrow, but curiously limited sympathy, with a tightly woven style and nervous sensibility, drives a ponderous dictum to an irritated and ineffectual summary. In his prose, as in his verse, Aiken produces an elaborately decorated shell, from which proceed murmurs that have blown mysteriously through his mind without leaving the faintest signature of the far-off turmoil of human passion which they echo.

The most recent book summing up the period is Miss Harriet Monroe's "Poets and Their Art," which despite its emphasis on the "modern" note such as Miss Monroe has embodied in her editorial guidance of her magazine, treats more detachedly than the other critics mentioned, the general constitution and glory of the art. That there is a continuity in the art she assents by her study of Chaucer and other early poets, who differed only in time and place from the contemporary poet in truth and reality of vision and a disciplined sincerity of expression.

Amy Lowell's "Tendencies in Modern American Poetry" belongs collaterally with the group above, but specifically dealing with only six poets — four of which illustrate and advocate her own sympathy and practice, the other two being included to give weight and significance to the book by virtue of their accomplishment — lacks the broad survey of the period, which however faultily, is true of the three books referred to above, and which I recommend for the general scope and importance of American poetry in the last fifteen years. The future critical historian of this period has an immensely rich field to work; and only in the future will the confused and conflicting character and quality, the high and individualistic achievement, be resolved into some sort of critical order and perspective, be presented, and win for the poets of this era the appreciation and understanding which they deserve.

The period, as a period, of Robinson and Frost, Sandburg and Masters, Amy Lowell and Sara Teasdale, is over; as definitely over as was the period of the New England School when Stedman, Aldrich and Stoddard, were gaining recognition as the new poets. This is true in spite of the fact that Robinson's greatest success has come within the current year with the publication of "Tristram," which at the time of this writing has sold nearly sixty thousand copies, and has been hailed by many sound critics as the greatest poem written in America. Amy Lowell is dead, and her posthumous volume has done little more than balance the idolatrous and sentimental praise which is given an author who dies, and especially one, as in her case, who had dominated by her personality the world of journalism. Masters and Sandburg have further put their best work behind them by substantial accomplishments in prose. Of the poets who have made this era most notable, Frost is the only one, excepting Robinson, who is likely to give us again the joy of full achievement. He has been sparing of his gifts, and has not allowed them to run unrestrained into uneven expression. But these poets, Robinson and Frost, are of that first order of genius whose power and ever refreshing supply of poetic vision and imagination, gives them a supremacy that overlaps time and their generation. The others have fallen away, even the moral troubadour Lindsay. The newer singers have neither risen so high nor kept for any length of time popular attention. The most promising among them, Elinor Wylie, showed in two slim books, a rare and precious, if somewhat narrow gift; but soon turning her energies to the writing of a highly sophisticated fiction, she has lost that first fine careless impulse for the strange and enchanting verse which captured us. Of Edna St. Vincent

Millay, who belongs with the first flushing of the renaissance in 1912, I have said nothing. Many eminent critics have regarded her as the supreme lyric poet of this era. She, in my opinion, has said very little of any significance; in her first poem to attract attention, "Renascence," she showed a fresh mystical wonder in contemplating the physical world, and in its setting the soul of man was burnished with an heritage which he had only to claim to be dignified and beautified. The poem struck an exotic note, and its triumph was like the triumph of the heavier-than-air flying machine. But like Keats and Shelley, youth put her in touch with the beauty of mystery before the world could obscure it. It was an imperfect poem in many respects; but criticism overlooked the imperfections, dazzled by the youth of the poet. Her advance was a triumphant journey, and critically speaking, she did not always respect the smoothness of the pathway. For sheer musical quality and lyric simplicity there is no doubt she is unapproached by any living American poet. More than any recent American poet she has captured the imagination of the public, as well as of the critics, and in every gesture, every movement, every rapture, they have heard the enchanting strain of song. She shares with Robinson . . . the greatness of the period which they helped to establish fifteen years ago. . . .

Given time, what will the more recent poets do to sustain the national achievement in the art of poetry? Those overcrowded years between 1912 and 1918, were not more articulate than the last five or six years when the numbing effects of the War began to wear off, and human feelings and affairs were getting back to normal. The advance of a new period is well defined in the summations that of late have checked a number of poets. Collected editions have been published of John G. Neihardt, a poet never given his just and full recognition, Arthur Davison Ficke, Lizette Woodworth Reese, Witter Bynner, and William Rose Benet. Those who have not "collected" their works, have made "selections," which indicate the achievement they wish to be judged by. In the meantime, younger and until recently unknown singers are crowding around the springs of Helicon. If I were to enumerate by names the number behind the current year it would take many pages. But keeping to the current ANTHOLOGY year we find sufficient warrant to respect the vitality and variety of present-day poetry.

During the year some of the most important books of poems are by poets who recently have accepted the responsibility of carrying on the significance of the tradition begun ten and fifteen years ago: George Dillon's "Boy in the Wind,". . . . Scudder Middleton's "Upper Room," George O'Neill's "White Rooster," Countee Cullen's "Copper Sun," Lizette Woodward Reese's "Little Henrietta," Harold Vinal's "A Stranger in Heaven," Sara Bard Field's "The Pale Woman," Mary Carolyn Davies' "Penny Show," Rosa Zagnoni Marinoni's "Behind the Mask," Glenn Ward Dresbach's "Cliff Dwellings," David McCord's "Floodgate," James Weldon Johnson's "God's Trombones" and John Hall Wheelock's "The Bright Doom." Of these authors of new books during the year, Mr. Wheelock advances from a little earlier period . . . through a slower recognition to a place beside the first poets of the era commented on. Like his peers he has been a self-disciplined singer with predestined heights to climb, and he is rapidly nearing the top enveloped in flames of ecstasy. . . .

A poet whose first book introduces one of the most promising of the younger men is E. Merrill Root. His volume, "Lost Eden," has a high purpose in its romantic embodiment of contemporary life. To this ideal he gives the glow of a natural magic. Spiritual force and understanding give the collection its most distinguishing quality. Perhaps the best of the recent balladists is Marjorie Allen Seiffert, whose "Ballads of the Singing Bowl" is a notable volume. Woven in these ballads are implications of a high order, and the symbolic fabric tells its story with poignantly swift music. Mr. Robinson Jeffers' new volume, "The Women at Point Sur," has not created the stir made by his previous book "Roan Stallion," but it increases the impression that here is a poet . . . who will slowly arrive at full recognition, but such a recognition as will place him high and permanently.

Two volumes of great significance published during the year have added immensely to our knowledge of two famous English poets; these are Professor Lowes' fascinating study of the sources of Coleridge's great poem "Kubla Khan" in "The Road to Xanadu," which is considerably more than a research into the origins of a strange dream, and is as well an enchanting and romantic adventure into the complicated workings of imaginative psychology; the other work is Professor Peck's monumental and definitive biography of Shelley. Another volume of especial interest is Countee Cullen's anthology of Negro poets, "Caroling Dusk." This work, while it contains selections from Dunbar, is chiefly a record of the amazing progress made during the past three or four years . . . by the poets of this race. . . .

The Pulitzer Prize for the current year was awarded to Leonora Speyer for her volume, "Fiddler's Farewell." Thomas Hornsby Ferril won the Nation's Poetry Prize for 1928. Announcement has been made that the contest will be discontinued. Finally, the Lindbergh Prize contest, in which three awards were made, was won, in order, by Nathalia Crane, the young poet of Brooklyn, N. Y., Thomas Hornsby Ferril, and Babette Deutsch. The three prize-winning poems, with one hundred others selected from among the contestants, have been published in a volume, "The Spirit of St. Louis." General dissatisfaction has been expressed over the prize-winning poem, the feeling being that much better poems were written. Be this true or not, the heroic achievement of that splendid youth deserves a finer tribute in song than the sample so conspicuously selected as an honor to the deed.

Braithwaite's identification with Jessie Fauset's subject matter, background, and values led him, in this essay that *Opportunity* published in January, 1934, to see in her fiction more merit than other critics detect in it. Some of his opinions about class and race changed considerably in later years, but he held to the view that her four novels are a notable achievement.

The Novels of Jessie Fauset

I don't at all mind looking back — a statement I am bold to make, in face of the implied challenge of some of my readers — over thirty-five years, and publicly embrace an era, the *first* era, of creative literature by Negro writers. We have crossed a turbulent, roaring, treacherous, aesthetic Stream of Time between 1898 and 1933: between Chesnutt's "The Marrow of Tradition" say, and Jessie Fauset's "Comedy: American Style," in the growth and development of the Negro novelist.

Our creative literature, chiefly poetry and fiction, has carried the Race across this stream — a bridge, girder and cable and solid granite piers and towers, suspended fairylike in the mist of misunderstanding and calumny, dazzlingly unsubstantial in the sunlight of sympathy and encourage- ment — from the shores of a "backward," "inferior" people of the eighteen-nineties, to, well, to the shores of cultural and spiritual equality with our fellow-citizens of today. A magic structure and an alluring journey! Yes, by all the precepts and paradoxes of an elusive and deceptive oppor- tunity: no, by all the confluent, Promethean flames of bio- logical urgencies and gifts which the bloods of Europe have poured into the original stream-source from Africa. The "gay nineties" was a tragic era, the "mauve decade," of the critical fancy, was a jaundiced vision, where the Negro was concerned; and in them, the Negro was a passionate root, that sent its first fragile stems above the aesthetic soil along the borderlands of the old and the new century.

There was a girlhood at this time whose wistful dreams must have sent her bright, brown eyes staring in the direction of far horizons, where lay hidden the secrets of a people's pride of spirit, secrets that were miraculously endowed with *beauty;* a girlhood that was to grow into womanhood; a searcher after the lure whose priceless possession made her a bright, enchanting blossom on the literary plant that has grown so magically in the last decade.

Within a few months, a decade will have been reached since the publication of Jessie Fauset's first novel "There Is Confusion." In 1928, appeared "Plum Bun," in 1931, "The Chinaberry Tree," and in November of this year, "Comedy: American Style." Four novels in not quite ten years. Only one Negro novelist has equalled this output, Dunbar. Our other novelists, Chesnutt, Du Bois, McKay, Nella Larsen, Walter White, Rudolph Fisher, Wallace Thurman, G. S. Schuyler, Langston Hughes, Countee Cullen, and Arna Bontemps, have produced three, two, and one novel, respectively. These eleven writers have described and interpreted Negro life and experience with an art built, with two or three exceptions, to the same pattern. There has not been much variation to the theme nor to the *milieu.*

Miss Fauset has done otherwise, and done it with superb courage. She stands at the head of the procession; and I deliberately invite the objection of critical opinion when I add, that she stands in the front rank of American women novelists in general. Glance at the procession of American women novelists, and their names will register the quality and character of their art, both as an expression, the rendering of human experience, the delineation of human character and nature, and environmental influences. Sara Orne Jewett, Mary E. Wilkins Freeman, Margaret Deland, Edith Wharton, Dorothy Canfield Fisher, Willa Sibert Cather, Ellen Glasgow, Kathleen Norris, Gertrude Atherton, Julia Peterkin, Zona Gale, to name a few, the most conspicuous and successful of the last two generations. If my claim is extravagant, that Miss Fauset assumes a natural and sponta-

neous association in this company, I am quite willing to take
an immediate chastisement, and leave to posterity the relish
of honoring with reiterated quotation this morsel of critical
extravagance.

Can one by any extension of the critical yardstick
credit any of these women novelists with the extraordinary
imaginative perception of discovering a new world of racial
experience and character, hitherto without psychological
and spiritual map and compass, and with poignant surprise
find it buffeted, baffled, scorned and rejected, by the pressure of an encircling political, economic, social and spiritual
society, as with an intangible wall of adamant, through
which it had to break for the means of survival, and more
than mere survival, *progress,* and return from the discovery
with both a tragedy and comedy of manners? No, Miss Jewett's Maine folk in her 'country of the pointed firs,' are fundamentally of the same dramatic substance in motive and
experience as Miss Cather's Nebraska pioneers; Miss Wharton's Knickerbocker aristocrats are essentially one with the
same pride and mellow grace of mind and habit as Miss
Glasgow's Virginia 'first families,' the only difference that,
with the former the *nouveau riche* gave a surface glitter to
the jewel raping its purity, while with the latter a 'lost
cause' took the sheen from the once proud texture of a feu-
dal regime. Also these white novelists could afford to toy
with some solid virtues and traditions of their craft, which
often, and in several cases amongst them, mitigated their
value and sincerity as literary artists. Strange as it may seem
to all except those of cultivated taste and a broad knowledge of the history and traditions of aesthetic values, many
of these novelists, in spite of their reputations and the authoritative praise given them, are scarcely more than deft
craftsmen, manipulating the profoundest emotions of humanity for the sake of capturing their readers' attention and
interest.

When Miss Fauset tremulously stepped across the
threshold of American literature with "There Is Confusion,"

in 1924, she did more than tell the story of a segment of a neglected group of American citizens of color, whose family, social and economic life, on the plane on which she placed it, was new material for the novelist; she unrecognizably made her entrance upon the American scene of letters as the potential Jane Austen of Negro literature. How is one to make clear the subtle distinction between Negro and American literature? Is Negro literature determined by the material or by the color and race of the author who creates it? If by the former, then there are a countless number of white Americans who are *Negro writers;* and yet obviously they cannot be, because by every evidence of proof these authors are known to be white men and women; if by the latter, here we have a paradox as confusing as the other circumstances, because the author of obvious Negro blood is dealing with individuals who, though they are likewise Negroes, are now, after several centuries of transportation and transformation from the native soil of the race — just as the English, the Italian, the French, the Spanish, or German, whose lives went into the colonization of these western lands, and also into the foundations of the American Republic — speaking the common language, and in the custom of living, dressing, eating, working, depend upon the same means and methods as all other Americans; thus it is not merely a question of rationality, but of truth, that the shaper of their individual and collective destinies upon the patterns of creative literature, though racially of Negro extraction or descent, is first and foremost an American author and the creator of American literature.

Thus, if it is convenient to speak of Negro literature as a classification of American literature, it is essential to insist that the standards are one and the same. And if comparisons are made, it is the character and not the quality of the material that is the chief object of appraisal and analysis. With some modification then, I repeat, that Miss Fauset, when she started her novelistic career with "There Is Confusion," as the potential Jane Austen of Negro literature, after many decades of authorship by white women novelists, became the first American woman novelist to wrap her shoulders in the scarf of rare and delicate embroidery that Jane Austen's genius bequeathed to the American woman who could wear it most gracefully.

I daresay, as a novelist Miss Fauset would be credited with many a virtue by certain eminent critics, if she were but obliging enough to ignore the *conventional* ideals and triumphs of the emerged group of the Race. She has been infinitely more honest with her characters than her critics have cared to acknowledge, indeed, to have even suspected. After all, her purpose, whether conscious or unconscious, has been to create in the pages of fiction a society which outside the Race simply did not and preferably, in accordance with granted assumption, could not be allowed to exist. The spirit, the consciousness of pride, dignity, a new quality of moral idealism, was breathed into this darker body of human nature by her passionate sympathy and understanding of its ironic position in the flimsy web of American civilization. Only recently a review of Miss Fauset's latest novel, "Comedy: American Style," in one of the leading Negro papers, resented what the reviewer charged was a lack of climax and philosophy in the recital of Olivia Cary's color obsession and the pain it brought her family. The philosophy in this latest novel, as in the three earlier ones, is not, and never was intended to be, an imposed thesis upon the surface of the story. Miss Fauset is too good an artist to argue the point; to engrave a doctrine upon so intangible an element as Truth, or to array with a misfitting apparel of rhetoric the logic which like a pagan grace or a Christian virtue should run naked as the wind through the implications that color and shape the lives of her characters and their destinies. I am afraid that Negro critical eyes as well as white critical eyes have quite often failed to discern these implications in which are contained the philosophy of a tremendous conflict; the magnificent Shakespearean conflict of *will* and *passion* in the great tragedies from "Titus Andronicus" to "Coriolanus"; for in this Negro society which Miss Fauset has created imaginatively from the realities, there is the *will*, the confused but burning *will*, to master the *passion* of the organized body of lusty American prejudice.

Philosophy, indeed! If we trace the range of American fiction — so spotty in its genuine qualities — we do not find since Hawthorne a similar, and singular, devotion to the philosophy of *rebuke* to an inhuman principle, elevated to an institution and safeguarded by both law and public opinion, as we find in these novels of Jessie Fauset's. Hawthorne's novels were the vehicle for, and presented types of human lives as, a brooding, passionate rebuke to the hard, callous Puritan spirit, which denied earthly happiness and fulfillment, the sense of joy and beauty, to the people. So in the novels of Miss Fauset, we find underlying the narrative, this same philosophy of rebuke, brooding and passionate also, against the contemporary spirit of the American people, who have elevated prejudice into an institution, safeguarded also by law and public sentiment, denying the freedom of development, of the inherent right to well-being, and the pursuit of happiness. It comes as a strange, mysterious echo out of the pages of the great romancer, to hear Miss Fauset's women, Joanna Marshall, Angela Murray and Olivia Cary (is it singular that her men are less given to this articulate yearning?) cry, in Angela's words: "Doesn't anyone think that we have a right to be happy, simply, naturally?" And Joanna, in the first of the novels, at the very end of her story in which she is drawn as a somewhat selfish, ambitious, and unintentionally hard girl, while building her career, after being twitted by Peter her lover, about her desire for greatness, replied, "No, . . . my creed calls for nothing but happiness."

Happiness and — *beauty!* these are the overtones, vibrating from the ordinary drama of men and women, young and old, acting out their tense and colorful destinies in the pages of these four novels, aloof at the core of their interests and intentions from the broad currents of American life.

These people want, most of all, to be themselves. To satisfy the same yearnings and instincts, which God has given them in the same measure bestowed upon other people. When some of their members "cross over" into the white world, to enjoy the advantages and privileges for which they are fitted and worthy, as Angela Murray, and her mother Mattie, in temporary spells of adventure, Anthony Cross, and Olivia Cary did, it was not because they desired to be "white," but because a cruel, blind, and despising tradition had taught them it was wiser and more profitable "not to be colored." So far Miss Fauset has nicely balanced her survey of this extraordinary scene and the people who compose it. "There Is Confusion," the first of her novels, deals with the clear-cut background and its atmosphere of a rising racial social group in New York, the action taking place largely in the pre-war years. It is mainly the story of Joanna Marshall's artistic ambition to fulfill her talents in the larger world of universal recognition and appreciation. The Marshall family is typical of many Negro families of the period, rising by hard work and moral principles to a position of respectability and influence among their own. Peter Bye, Joanna's lover, though he was careless of the distinction, brings into the story the pride of ancestry from an old Philadelphia family. That Joanna, in the end, was defeated in her purpose to achieve greatness — it is interesting to reflect upon the parallel story of Maggie Ellersley, poor and unfavored by opportunity, who strove so earnestly and honestly to be respectable in the sense that the Marshalls were, and who built her own sturdy ambitions upon the materials and services designed entirely along racial lines — she remains a more significant figure in the late realization of her love for Peter.

"Plum Bun," Miss Fauset's second novel is, perhaps, her most perfect artistic achievement, and the most balanced force of interracial experience. Its heroine, Angela Murray, not so profoundly and vividly drawn as Laurentine Strange or Melissa Paul, in "The Chinaberry Tree," nor as that superbly ironic figure Olivia Cary, in "Comedy: American Style," is nevertheless, the most successful protagonist of the white-colored girl who tragically sought happiness in the white world. "Plum Bun," is the apogee of this mode among Miss Fauset's novels, for in Anthony Cross again, she has taken a character "over"; and he is the most unique of her male characters, one who went "white" not by choice, but because of the hatred, which the murder of his father by a southern mob, had engendered in him for white people. If the story hides a moral, it is, that if one masquerades as white because it is expedient in the search for happiness and security and not because one is ashamed, or would rather not possess the dark blood in them . . . the gods ironically punish with spiritual, and often, physical tragedy. Both Angela Murray and Anthony Cross, who were lovers, following Angela's affair with Roger Fielding, the rich white youth, tasted this fortuitous draught at the hands of fate.

With her third novel Miss Fauset returns to the same general theme of racial solidarity on the higher social plane, as in her first story. In this respect it is by far the meatiest of her books. Laurentine Strange drums upon one's consciousness with the insistent and haunting lure for sympathy and understanding that one has for Hardy's Tess, and more recently for Irene Forsyte in Galsworthy's "Saga." Her experience, of course, is not like that of Tess; and she is not quite that "impinging beauty" of symbolic intentions, rebelling against the acquisitive Victorian propensity of a Soames, of Galsworthy's creation. She is, nevertheless, an impinging symbol within the bound of her social *milieu,* the confluent expression in our modern era, of that free, non-obligatory mating of a white father and colored mother. Proud, unconsciously disdainful, Laurentine emerges from the older racial backgrounds by the way of a critical arbiter, who stirs the tempest in the broadening world of which she and her relatives and the people who would be her friends, had she allowed them to be, pass through a process of crystalization.

Melissa, her cousin, accompanies her through the narrative
as a foil, spontaneous, warm-hearted, impulsive, but a little
designing, with the potential stuff in her of a romantic disaster. The duel between these two girls is a comedy whose
spirit is dipped in a vinegar of affection. And disaster, indeed, is what overtakes these girls; a disaster whose effect is
somewhat artificial when revealed, and seems a bit forced
and unreal. In many ways her strongest book on the theme
of racial solidarity in its advanced stage, "The Chinaberry
Tree" alone strikes what seems to me the one false note in
Miss Fauset's artistic equipment. For the sake of the story
we forgive it, however, as we forgive Thomas Hardy that
equally false and absurd climax in which Tess murders her
betrayer. It is a story that will take a long time for both colored and white Americans to appreciate its supreme power.

The fourth of Miss Fauset's novels, "Comedy: American
Style," — with its ironic title, for the story is a tragedy
throughout — is both the most irritating and at the same
time, the most powerful of her books. The story of Olivia
Cary's obsession not to display the dark blood in either herself, or in those members of her family — with the one tragic
exception of Oliver, her youngest son — is one of the most
devastating characterizations in contemporary American fiction. As in the case of Angela Murray, Olivia would not
have cared a fig about being taken for colored anywhere, if
the fact did not rob her of the things which the white world
possessed, and which, she contended, were necessary for her
own happiness and peace, and the happiness and peace of
her children. She built this desire upon an illusion, which
was not of her own creation; but finding it as she did, she
began early as a child and pursued the purpose through the
rest of her life until we leave her at the end of the story,
that purpose to cheat the creator of the illusion. She did just
the opposite, and it is the irony and paradox of her story, that
those she cheated were herself, her husband and her children. Though all of them saw through her, and took the
stand that honest and self-respecting colored people take,

even when it is often possible for one to deceive, they could not prevail against Olivia's heartless and untiring persecution. Her husband she ruined; drove her daughter into a loveless marriage with an insipid, selfish Frenchman with an Oedipus complex; stung her youngest son into suicide; and in the end became the victim of her own unrelenting fanaticism.

Olivia Cary is a tragic figure — one cannot call her a heroine, though that is the role designed for her by Miss Fauset. There is nothing glamorous about her, and yet she fascinates one with that hard, glittering frostiness of purpose, with which she wrecks and ruins. What makes her so disturbingly alive is the paradox of her morality; for she is, according to a misconception of virtue, an impeccably moral woman in the flesh. Like Becky Sharp, after all, she touches one's sympathy, when at the end of the novel we leave her pathetically stranded in the ashes of her own once consuming desires and hopes. She is the symbol of a force that must ultimately be acknowledged and discussed frankly by both races in America, and when that discussion takes place there will be concessions and revisions on the part of white Americans which will make it possible to draw her like again as a warning.

Owen Dodson, playwright, director, poet, and novelist, was once Braithwaite's colleague at Atlanta University. This review of *Powerful Long Ladder*, which appeared in *Phylon*, Third Quarter, 1946, with its applause for Dodson's "hot javelins of determined racial spirit," is in sharp contrast to Braithwaite's earlier responses to the verse of black poets.

Poems of Mood and Substance

An established dramatist, Mr. Dodson offers us his first book of poems with *Powerful Long Ladder*, and I hazard the

suggestion that with it the poet has challenged the dramatist for supremacy between Mr. Dodson's creative gifts.
They work together so beautifully, however, in these pages,
that it may be folly to assign variations of distinction not determined by the medium of presentation or by the aesthetic
laws governing the materials executed. For these poems are
intensely dramatic in spirit, with a glowing dignity it has
not been the custom of our poets to manifest in the treatment of racial problems and experiences, and yet are woven
verbally with the precise and tempered elements of the poetic vision. Thus he commands an objective comprehension
of the pains and anguish of racial strivings and injustice that
is no less appealing in sincerity and conviction since flowing
from a deep, personal sense of the injustices. The too often
exercised privilege of the Negro poets to claim aesthetic in-
dulgence and become subservient in sentiment and exagger-
ation is redeemed by Mr. Dodson in these poems by the
broader human implications that serve as the loom for his
poetic weavings. The *powerful long ladder* of the Negro's
struggles to rise to the full stature of manhood and democratic citizenship is looked upon by the poet with a detached authority which gives courage and strength to the
climbers toward the goal; and the inspiration that the
poems incite is that the *ladder is there* and the climbing
goes on.

Here you have, I think, the mood in which these poems
of Mr. Dodson's are conceived, and the substance which
gives validity to the mood. But to make an art out of the
mood and substance takes the refining process of a sensitive
feeling and shaping imagination; and the appropriate technique for the patterning of words upon a rhythmical design.
From any of the five sections under which the poems are
grouped one may experience an embarrassment in making a
choice where the excellence of poetic craftsmanship is so in-
triguing. These groupings, from the opening "Powerful
Long Ladder" through "Three Choruses from a Verse
Drama: Divine Comedy," "Poems for My Brother," "All This

Review" to "Counterpoint," are taut and tight in execution as well as message. Out of this tight evocation flash images and memorable declarations of truth, as from the titular poem this line:

No hands can build freedom but your own hands.

and the remark of the Young Boy in "Winter Chorus" from "Divine Comedy" —

I am so black they call me nighttime.
When I walk along everyone looks for stars.

The italics are my own to score the startling imagery of which Mr. Dodson's imagination is capable. And to reaffirm this quality of evocative imagery which glitters so often throughout these pages, let us lift this stanza from the first of the "Poems for My Brother Kenneth":

Death, split-second guest, negative magician,
When will you believe you are not final?
After you have touched a heart
And tricked it into silence,
Standing smooth and quiet by your side,
Memory robs you,
Picks your pockets clean,
Then rings her bells
And dances with the years.

Were there space here I would like to sample many another poem, lift some of the tender, brooding, stoical dignity and exalted faith of "Black Mother Praying"; or the hot javelins of determined racial spirit in "Someday We're Gonna Tear Them Pillars Down"; or from the severe, flame-polished spirit of inevitability in the three "Winter," "Star" and "Autumn" choruses of "Divine Comedy"; or from the illuminating tribute to the founder of Hampton Institute, "Samuel Chapman Armstrong"; or from the lilac-scented lyric "Miss

Packard and Miss Giles," honoring the memory of the maiden ladies from New England who founded Spelman College. If I am compelled to send the reader to the book itself for a taste of the excellent poetic vintage offered, I intend to hold him here to drink of the tart but cleansing flavor of a truth outside of whose orbit most of mankind flounder. In "Definitions" Mr. Dodson has debunked a mystery and restored a majesty in man:

> *Everyone says: fate is a bad number,*
> *Should be jailed and put on bread and water.*
> *Fate has drilled into the spirit's bone,*
> *And all our marrow has leaked out.*
>
> *They talk of fate as they talk of God and Devil;*
> *Something like a storm between mountains*
> *Or tigers or whales or tornadoes,*
> *Something like the chemistry of air.*
>
> *Fate is ourselves awake and asleep,*
> *Fighting in the sky or armies in the earth,*
> *Speeches, treaties, elections, hopes of heaven,*
> *Preparations for hell. Fate is the collection plate*
>
> *Of our sins and our loves — variety of coins,*
> *Stored away or stolen by those fakirs*
> *Who blame the plus or minus of our condition*
> *On God or Devil or the sound of the sea.*

"*It takes a powerful long ladder to climb to the sky, and catch the bird of freedom for the dark,*" sings Mr. Dodson of a people wrestling with the angel of aspiration and hope, and visioned by him with a reverent and undeluded anticipation of fulfillment, just as a brother poet, Francis Thompson, witnessed in a dream the wrestling of Jacob and the Angel by the river Thames. That Mr. Dodson has made poetry rather than propaganda out of his vision of a people contending with oppressive circumstances on the ladder of progress is the happy augury for a new dispensation in the Negro's contribution to American literature.

———

This review of *A History of American Poetry, 1900–1940*, by Horace Gregory and Marya Zaturenska, appeared in *Phylon*, Second Quarter, 1947. It reveals Braithwaite's recognition that his labors and accomplishments as critic and anthologist were being slighted in — or omitted from — the records of American literary scholarship.

Review of
A History of American Poetry, 1900–1940

In spite of what the authors of this work assert . . . the present work is not a history of American poetry of the period designated, but what the authors acknowledge it to be in another sentence, a "survey of recent American poetry." The discriminations against history are never those of poetry as an art, or shall we add, as an expression, powerfully provocative, of the human imagination, but that of the critic or surveyor of the art; and it is just as true, to quote the authors' array of the other human activities whether of "politics or poetry, of religion or economics, or of the familiar and sometimes highly deceptive recording of military events." Neither can the authors find a loophole for escape from their historical responsibility by taking as a "precedent" Johnson's "Lives of the Poets," in offering the reader an abundance of "biographical information" about the poets they have selected to deal with in American poetry from 1900 to 1940.

The case here is that the authors have chosen to ignore some facts and figures that have, whatever their intrinsic

importance in light of the authors' predilections as to substance and method in the art, a historical place in the record. No reference whatever is made in this work to Jessie
B. Rittenhouse's two series of "A Little Book of Modern
American Verse," nor to the annual collections of American
verse which I had the honor of sponsoring, beginning in
1913 (the same year Miss Rittenhouse's first collection appeared), and running until 1929, during which time all the
major and important poets on the American scene were included. When the authors state that among the critics and
reviewers of American poetry in the 1920's Untermeyer was
the first to recognize the importance of the anthology in
voicing a critical survey of his chosen field, they are guilty
of misstatement and the distortion of history, for besides
Miss Rittenhouse's and my own "recognition" of this importance there was also *The Lyric Year* of 1912. W. J. Cour-
thope's *History of English Poetry*, Sir Herbert J. C. Grier-
son's recent *A Critical History of English Poetry*, and more
particularly, because it takes a cleaner leaf from Johnson's
Lives, Arthur Symons' *The Romantic Movement in English
Poetry* could have served the authors well as models in
which history, criticism and biography are objectively and
impartially combined.

More is the pity that a truthful and impartial recording
of American poetry of the first half of the twentieth century
has not been made, for allowing for a personal critical sympathy and taste, there are many brilliant pages of writing
and interpretation in Mr. Gregory's and Miss Zaturenska's
collaborated work. The tendencies and achievements they
trace with caressing enthusiasm and sympathy are all too
obvious as one reads their accounts of the works of William
Carlos Williams, E. E. Cummings, Hart Crane, T. S. Eliot,
Amy Lowell, Ezra Pound, and Conrad Aiken, besides a
host of minor radicals. Again, it must be made clear one
does not quarrel with their sympathies, for the authors present an abundance of convincing critical arguments to sustain their dicta, displaying as they do, a deeply perceptive

sense of the form and substance and technique, in the poets of aesthetic and social and intellectual revolt. But again in this, the record as history is blurred, for the very summary of the battle between the old and new during this rousing period of standards in conflict, was made by John Livingston Lowes in his *Convention and Revolt in Poetry*, of which no mention is made in this work.

Beginning with the "Twilight Interval," covering the period that marked the decline of American poetry at the end of the century, and distinguished with the publication of Edmund Clarence Stedman's *American Anthology*, we are taken into dim regions from which the authors disengage some tarnished talents for a critical polishing — Trumbull Stickney and George Cabot Lodge with their leaden weight of intellectualism as exponents of Henry Adams' "Christian anarchists"; the restoration of Santayana with his truly poetic sensibility escaping from the deadly intellectual chauvinism of Stickney and Lodge; and the ruthless stripping of William Vaughan Moody's poetic virtues. Hovey and Carman are made to look childish and foolish in the exuberant enjoyment of their Vagabondian holiday, while what was worthy of respect in their work, the Carman of "Behind the Arras" and the Sappho lyrics, and the Hovey of the fragment in the ruined structure of his ambitiously projected Arthurian cycle of dramas, "Taliesin," are wholly ignored. Another critical oversight is the authors' neglect of Frank Dempster Sherman, who has not so much as a place in the index, for the purpose of setting up Madison Cawein as an example of an uninspired and ineffectual disciple of Keats. There is an affinity between the mood and expression in the works of Sherman and Sara Teasdale, whom the authors with rare critical felicity in their study of her art have elevated into a classic, and rightly I think, which makes the total omission of Sherman a historical mistake.

"Unlikely as it may have seemed in 1900, Edmund Clarence Stedman's 'twilight interval' was to produce its major poet," we read, and this was Edwin Arlington Robinson. On the whole the authors' treatment of Robinson is admirable, and they have caught the significance of the catharsis and philosophy of the comic spirit which holds in a perfect imaginative pattern the twisted visions and shattered lives that have been flashed and drawn by him. . . . The first World War inspired the argument, for they do possess an argument in behalf of Robinson's hope and faith in human nature, which, as Mrs. Barbara Wells showed in her study of them (unpublished M. A. thesis, Atlanta University), Robinson tried to build into the vision of a redemptive and reconstructed human society.

As this important item of Robinson's development escaped the authors, so did the central force of Robert Frost's arts—that internal reality of communication, the quality of words not as visual symbols, but of a speech as sound imposing both meaning and philosophy upon words. Without this key the impact of the mood in its embodiment in nature or human crisis is lost. The escaping presence of it to most readers, as well as critics, is what confuses the discernment, betraying many into the declaration that Frost is a free verse writer. Again the authors have missed a fine summary of phases in the work of Conrad Aiken, whom they have tried to approach with the same seriousness with which they treated Wallace Stevens (the critique on whom I applaud with enthusiasm), Vachel Lindsay (again where I commend heartily), Edgar Lee Masters and others of the innovators, but who has left a shallow vessel of moods; but what they missed, producing this result, is the imitative nature of Aiken's work. In verse he jumped from one fashion to another, to whatever was in popular acclaim—first, Masefield ("Romance," "The Jig of Forslin"), then Masters ("Turns and Movies"); and even when he took to the prose novel, he copied the purpose and complexion of the "stream of consciousness" practices of James Joyce, Dorothy Richardson, etc., and in the short story the artifices of Katherine Mansfield.

Two of the best sections of this work are those devoted

to "The Poetry of Feminine Sensibility," and "Edna St. Vincent Millay, and the Poetry of Feminine Revolt and Self-Expression." We are given a very penetrating account of Miss Millay's art and personality, with the final judgment of its inability to stand the test and wear of time. In the first of these two sections, the art of Elinor Wylie, Louise Bogan, and Léonie Adams is given a sympathetic but dissolving scrutiny of the "metaphysical" substance and appeal with which these poets have been so loudly credited after the discovery in this country some thirty years ago of John Donne and the minor Carolinians. Of these three women poets, I think, Léonie Adams wears best with our authors, and by them is given a fine recognition for the possession of genuine mystical qualities.

That the authors claim as of distinctive importance and virtue an elegiac note throughout American poetry from its vital beginnings in Philip Freneau, may be seriously questioned, as one may question the significance with which the authors reiterate "wit" as a test of excellence in recent American poets.

There is a chapter devoted to "The Negro Poet in America." Apparently the authors have their information of these poets from two anthologies, James Weldon Johnson's *The Book of American Negro Poetry*, and Countee Cullen's *Caroling Dusk*. Nothing new is said about Dunbar, who is presented with liberal quotations from Mr. Howells and Johnson. There is expressed an insight, scarcely more than that, into Claude McKay's unfulfilled powers, and a summary with some strictures on Langston Hughes, and a much too inadequate reference to Countee Cullen and Sterling Brown. To say, as they do, that James W. Johnson is the "only American Negro poet of the twentieth century who achieved poetic maturity," is to speak loosely. The young poets of the so-called Negro Renaissance of 1922 made Johnson over as a poet. . . . The most popular and successful of Johnson's books of poems, *God's Trombones*, is the least original, for, like the Uncle Remus stories of Joel Chandler

Harris, these are but transcriptions of a speech and imagery that needed no creation. No mention whatever is made of Jean Toomer's haunting moods, or of Anne Spencer, whose sensibility and imagination should take precedence over the declamatory verses of Margaret Walker, or the slender delicacy of Jessie Fauset's few and brief lyrics. . . .

The relationship of Braithwaite and Countee Cullen was one of mutual admiration. Cullen dedicated his *Caroling Dusk, An Anthology of Verse by Negro Poets* (1927) to Braithwaite, who looked with special favor on Cullen's traditional lyrics. This review of *On These I Stand* appeared in *Opportunity*, Summer, 1947. Braithwaite often praised Cullen's verse and late in his life wrote this epigram:

Countee Cullen

Like Keats, too soon enrobed in death's damp shroud,
Like Keats, too, he felt Beauty's fatal touch;
His song, too, rang out sweet and subtly loud,
Repressing aches dark poets feel so much.

Review of On These I Stand

Shortly before his untimely death in January, 1946, Countee Cullen selected from his various books of poems those pieces which he thought his best, and with the addition of six unpublished poems, made this volume to which he gave the apt and challenging title "On These I Stand." Whether he felt that this title was premonitory when he chose it, I don't know. Or if he felt, had he lived, that whatever might be produced later in his career could not add to, or enhance, the value of his work as a poet. The fact is we have in this volume the final and definitive selection of poems upon which his talents and reputation must stand for the estimation and appreciation of posterity.

What then, did Countee Cullen stand for as a poet, and as a poet who was also a Negro? He has given a partial answer to this question in that famous and oft-quoted couplet closing the sonnet "Yet Do I Marvel":

> *Yet do I marvel at this curious thing:*
> *To make a poet black, and bid him sing.*

Now some critics have demanded that because a poet is *black* he must sing always with a social and ethnical implication, and that his importance lies in the degree to which his propaganda is vital and colorful rather than in the quality of his work as an artist. A recent review of this volume in an important publication, though not by a particularly discerning reviewer, made this demand, and not being satisfied that Countee Cullen was painfully social or histrionically ethnical denied him the full accomplishment as a poet to which he is entitled. Such a mind and others like it miss wholly both the ideas and evocative emotions of poems like "Heritage" and "The Black Christ," to name but two poems where the triumphant nature and power of the poet transcends racial limitations while at the same time, in treating a racial theme, bestows upon it a universal significance.

Countee Cullen as a poet was a traditionalist in line with the great English poets, and an apostle of beauty with the fountainhead of his inspiration in the poetic philosophy of John Keats. If his imagination was scorched by the injustice and oppression of a people with whom his lot was thrown, like Keats whose sensitive nature was also wounded, he soared, not by way of escape, but by precept and counsel, into the abstract realm of the spirit. He caught the complexities and contradictions in the net of his idealism, as is attested to in this stanza from "More Than a Fool's Song" —

> *The world's a curious riddle thrown*
> *Water-wise from heaven's cup;*

Criticism

The souls we think are hurtling down
Perhaps are climbing up.

No poet we have yet produced was so complete and spontaneous a master of the poetic technique as Countee Cullen. His octosyllabic line has not been more skilfully handled by any modern poet. He has used the sonnet for many moods and themes and carved its fourteen lines of varied temper and structure with a lyrical unity that earns him a place in the company of Wordsworth, Rossetti and Bridges. He possessed an epigrammatic gift and turn of wit that gave uncommon delight as witnessed in the series of "Epitaphs" among which the one "For a Mouthy Woman" is a masterpiece. His translations from Baudelaire, especially the sinuous felinity of cats, rank with those of Swinburne, Arthur Symons, and George Dillon, in the rendering of that feverish and fantastic French poet into English. The fantasy of the "Wakeupworld" from the mythical narrative of "The Lost Zoo," established his poetic kinship in imaginative humor to the delightful foolery of Richard H. Barham's "Ingoldsby Legends."

No one will say that Countee Cullen escaped the aches that come to a sensitive spirit aware of racial prejudice and insult, but he did not allow them to distort or distemper the ideals and visions which endowed him as an artist and poet. He had as deep a sensibility for the human denials and aches which absorbed the lesser racial ones, and strove through the exquisite creation of imagery and music to evoke and communicate the spirit of Beauty as a solacing and restorative power. Time will, I think, accept him on the spiritual terms he set for himself in the poem "To John Keats, the Poet at Spring Time," and know that though he could sing a "Ballad for a Brown Girl" and make a "Litany of the Dark People" the blood and soul of mankind were alike in its passions and aspirations.

His account of a notable black journal does not disclose that Braithwaite, in November of 1903, was trying to raise money so he might buy an interest from Dupree and "take the editorship of it." He contributed both prose and poetry to the magazine. Braithwaite's "The Quality of Color," in the May, 1902, issue, is a story of miscegenation. The love of artist Richard Chelmsford and a beautiful white girl is brought to a tragic end because her mother "would not for a moment entertain the idea of conceding a sanction to Alice's marriage with a colored man, no matter how talented or wealthy or socially lionized he was." *Negro Digest* published this article about *The Colored American Magazine* in December, 1947.

Negro America's First Magazine

In 1899, an inexperienced youth with nothing to recommend him except a sheaf of verses and a passionate literary ambition, I wrote to Charles W. Chesnutt, the novelist, who was in the first flush of his success, asking his advice and support for the founding of a general magazine for Negro readers. In reply, Chesnutt discouraged the idea, expressing his belief that the time was not ripe for such a venture.

At the same time another young man some four or five years older than myself was possessed of the same dream. His came to fulfillment, and in a minor way I had some share in its history. Few of us today observing, and reading with enjoyment, the numerous and attractive periodicals edited and published by and for Negroes, can realize and appreciate the events of nearly half a century ago when The Colored American Magazine was founded.

Before 1900, there had been two attempts by the Negroes to establish magazines of general interest for Negro readers. Only one of these can be said to have been edited for popular circulation and entertainment, The Anglo-African, edited by Thomas Hamilton, and issued monthly for one year, 1859. It is notable for having published serially (and yet unpublished in book form) the novel entitled

Blake: or, The Huts of America, by Martin R. Delany. An earlier periodical had appeared but it was of special interest, a church organ, The African Methodist Episcopal Church Magazine, issued quarterly from September, 1841, to December, 1842, at Brooklyn, N. Y. This backward glance at the periodical literature of the Negro would seem to the average spectator to present a barren field of accomplishment, but to the considerate and sympathetic, aware of the denials of freedom and education to which the Negro was subjected during the first seventy-four years of the republic, this apparently barren and uncultivated field was brightened in scattered spots by these wild, if not brilliant and fragrant, flowers of periodical literature.

The last third of the nineteenth century from the end of the Civil War — when four million Negroes, mostly illiterate, were emancipated — to 1900, witnessed a steady decline in illiteracy, and the race became fertile ground for the growth of periodical enterprises. Newspapers had begun to flourish and multiply since the early eighties, though an earlier weekly, The Colored American, was published in 1837. No new attempt, however, was made to issue a general magazine, edited, illustrated, and written, by and for Negroes, until nineteen hundred.

The eighteen-nineties ushered in a new era of periodical literature in America. The so-called "quality magazines," The Atlantic Monthly, Harper's, The Century, and Scribner's, were in the field, but their subscription prices were beyond the purse of all except the most privileged. Munsey's, McClure's, and The Cosmopolitan introduced the ten-cent magazines whose circulation soared into the thousands, beyond anything known by the thirty-five cent periodicals. The contents of these ten-cent magazines represented the best and most exciting writings from the pens of famous authors in all branches of authorship. These ten-cent monthlies had a strong ally, in bringing the best writings of the period cheaply to the masses, in the two five-cent weeklies, the rejuvenated Saturday Evening Post under the magical shrewdness of Cyrus P. Curtis and his editor George Horace Lorimer, and Collier's Weekly, whose publication was a conquering symbol of the ambitious dreams of a romantic Irish immigrant, Peter F. Collier. These five-cent weeklies soon crowded the more expensive Harper's and Leslie's weeklies from public favor.

This popularization of periodical literature in the eighteen-nineties had its effect upon the imagination and ambition of the young Negro, and one such, migrating from Virginia to Boston four years before the close of the nineteenth century, made a dream come true.

This young man, Walter W. Wallace, dreamed of a general magazine that would publish the creative works of Negro writers together with informative articles which would record the Negro's progress in intellectual, social and political ideals. Wallace made no pretension to either literary or journalistic ability. He was simply possessed of a burning aspiration and it drove him relentlessly into action. He had a charming personality, with a sense of humor made more effective by an engaging smile that played about his mouth like a memory of childhood. If there was not too much "light," appropriating Matthew Arnold's symbol, there was a fund of "sweetness" in his makeup, and it gave a tremendous vitality and significance to his vision. With three friends, who pooled their meager resources, the publication of The Colored American Magazine took shape. The original associates were H. A. Fortune, treasurer, Jessie Watkins, advertising, and Peter B. Gibson, soliciting agent, the latter having charge of circulation which was promoted chiefly through agents appointed to represent the magazine in prescribed territories throughout the East, Middle West, and South. The magazine had to be carried to the people and subscriptions solicited personally.

One serious problem which faced Mr. Wallace and his associates was to find someone with the technical knowledge and experience physically to produce a magazine; the form and design of materials, with the mastery of those mechanical details of layout and makeup in supervising the printer which would present an attractive and readable periodical. No one of their own race at this time was available with experience in these essential mechanical details, and so a white man was engaged, who resigned from a satisfactory position with the well-known Boston publisher, Lothrop, Lee and Shepard, to join them. His name was R. S. Elliott. A quiet, and on the surface a rather agreeable fellow, he quickly sensed an opportunity that might be profitable for himself in this associaton with a pioneer venture, and soon began to exert a dominant influence in the affairs of the magazine.

The first issue of the magazine appeared in May, 1900, from offices at Five Park Square, Boston. In the charge of the original associates who had founded it, the magazine ran for four years. In the third year of publication there were changes in the organization, and the transfer to new addresses in the South End. The contents during the first two years, while he still maintained executive authority due him as founder, reflected Wallace's energy and enthusiasm rather than his discernment of literary standards. With advice and suggestions, which he sought and welcomed from those competent to give them, he managed to sustain a commendable level of excellence with the contributions.

There were poems by ambitious youngsters, among them Benjamin Brawley, James D. Corrothers, Olivia Ward Bush and Augustus M. Hodges, as well as the better-known Daniel Webster Davis; articles of varied interest to the Negro of the day among which those of Cyrus Field Adams were arresting with their facts about the Negro. Adams was an able and interesting man, resident of Chicago, the President of National Afro-American Press Association, and later an assistant register of the U. S. Treasury. His memory deserves a better appreciation than it has received from later generations. A frequent contributor was an African, Prof. C. C. Hamedoe, among whose articles was a report of the first Pan-African Congress held in London, July 23–25, 1900, and presided over by Bishop Alexander Walters. The magazine featured serial fiction, publishing *The Streets of Impulse,* by Maitland Leroy Osborne, and *Hagar's Daughter,* by Sarah A. Allen. The outstanding contribution in this field, however, was the fiction serial *Contending Forces, A Romance Illustrative of Negro Life North and South,* by Pauline E. Hopkins, which was later published in book form by The Colored Co-Operative Publishing Co.

The magazine also gave opportunity to one of the few Negro artists then developing in America. Besides Henry O. Tanner, who was living in France, no other Negro had a standing in the world of pictorial art. This young man was Alexander Skeete, a West Indian who had gone to Boston to study at the famous old Cowles Art School where many famous contemporary American artists had their training before going on to Paris and Rome. Mr. Skeete illustrated many stories and poems for the magazine. To Mr. Wallace belongs the credit for giving him the opportunity to display his talents.

The book publishing venture was an outgrowth of the magazine. It was at the suggestion of Mr. Elliott that it came into being, and was intended as an outlet for books about Negroes and by Negro authorship. Seeking the necessary funds to promote the publishing enterprise Wallace won the interest and support of a well-known colored citizen of Boston, Col. William H. Dupree, who possessed substantial means and an established credit. Col. Dupree had risen through hard work and faithful service to be postmaster of Station A, then the largest sub-station in the Boston postal district.

With the reorganization Col. Dupree became president of the Colored Co-Operative Publishing Co., Wallace vice-president and managing editor, and Miss Pauline E. Hopkins, editor of the magazine, while Elliott, in the background, directed through the exercise of his experienced knowledge of publishing, the whole enterprise, though ostensibly in charge of the practical details of designing and manufacturing the books and the magazine.

Criticism

In the course of the publishing venture four books were issued: Miss Hopkins' novel, *Contending Forces,* Chaplain Theophilus T. Steward's *The Story of the American Negro as Slave, Citizen and Soldier,* with an Introduction by Gen. Nelson A. Miles (Steward had been chaplain to the Negro troops in the Philippines during the Spanish-American War); *Progress or Reversion, Which?* by Rev. Joseph E. Haynes, and *In Free America, Tales from the Southland,* by Ellen F. Wetherell, with an introduction by the Hon. Archibald Grimké.

Miss Hopkins, as editor of the magazine, inaugurated the policy of paying for contributions. She not only wanted the Negro author to feel that his work, if accepted and printed, was worthy of remuneration, but as an editor she felt it gave her an independence of action in making selections, and a dignity in soliciting manuscripts of the best.

But it was not long before friction arose between the directing members of the organization.

The whole set-up was a magnificent gesture of cultural progress amongst Negroes, and the significance of this is not to be underestimated. That the publishing company together with the magazine, then the only publication of its kind in America, were projects of great potential influence and material value, was realized by the little group of pioneers conducting the enterprises, for these publications were serving as agencies to refute the asserted inferiority of the Negro at a time when there were universal arguments and declarations that attempted to prove this charge. Yet at the heart of this enterprise the current struggle was raging to destroy the dream of the young Negro out of Virginia who had given his dream shape and substance at the portal of liberty in Boston.

Col. Dupree was not very happy in his association with this literary and journalistic venture. He was a practical man, and had lent his support and influence, and it had been substantial, to the enterprise out of pride of race and a faith in the ability of the Negro to make progress in restricted fields of activity if given the opportunity. Even

though literature and journalism were beyond the scope of
his personal interest and knowledge, he felt it his duty to
back the ambitions of young Negroes who were blazing new
trails to success. Between a temperamental editor in Miss
Hopkins, the quiet but effective work of Elliott to shape the
policies and purposes of the enterprises to insure the largest
measure of personal benefits, and the insistent efforts of
Wallace, the founder, Col. Dupree had on his hands a set of
irreconcilable elements which his practical nature strove to
fortify against the doubters and carpers who had been
prophetic of its collapse.

As a novelist Miss Hopkins regarded herself as a national figure, in the company of Charles W. Chesnutt and
Paul Laurence Dunbar and as such felt free to impose her
views and opinions upon her associates in the conduct of
both the book and magazine publications. Miss Hopkins resented bitterly Elliott's veiled authority, and was generally
critical of Wallace's literary incompetence though it was
chiefly due to his vision and enthusiasm that her own literary ambition had found its opportunity.

In 1903 the survival of the publishing ventures was seriously threatened. Issues of the magazine were skipped and
monthly numbers combined to maintain the volume sched-
ule. At this time a white man, John C. Freund, visited Boston and gave an elaborate reception in the Legion of Honor
Hall on Huntington Avenue to a large group of the most
important colored citizens of the city to promote an interest in support of the magazine. Freund was the owner and
editor of *Musical America,* a prosperous and well-known
periodical devoted to the music trades. There was much
speculation as to Freund's interest and intentions for he
dropped into town unheralded. His credentials for assuming the expense of the reception were his personal sympathy with the ambition of the Negro to publish a magazine
of his own, and especially as an evidence of the race's intellectual maturity.

Mr. Freund was known to be a great admirer of Booker

T. Washington, and as many supposed in gossip among themselves, he came as an emissary of the great educator to obtain a financial interest in the magazine which was sorely in need of fresh capital. This supposition was not far wrong. Freund had taken a winter cruise in the Caribbean Sea, and wrote a series of articles describing the peoples, customs, and places of the West Indian islands, which were printed in the Colored American Magazine.

For another year Mr. Wallace and his original associates, with the controlling power in the hands of Col. Dupree and Freund, continued to issue the magazine, and then it was sold with the publishing company to Fred R. Moore of New York, who had already gained control of the weekly newspaper, The New York Age, from that stout-hearted champion of race rights, T. Thomas Fortune. It was now openly known that both publications, The Colored American Magazine and The New York Age, under the management of Fred R. Moore, were controlled by Booker T. Washington.

The Colored American Magazine, the dream and ambition of the young Walter W. Wallace, who was shuffled out of ownership and management, continued to be published for another four years, with Roscoe Conklin Simmons, a nephew of Booker T. Washington, its editorial director.

For eight years of the first decade of the century, this brave effort was made to give the Negro a general magazine of his own. Forty years ago the brave effort faded from the sky of racial aspiration, but like a comet it left a luminous path of cultural ambition whose orbit is now studded with the brilliant stars of contemporary periodicals. To Walter W. Wallace, a young Virginia Negro, must go the credit for the realization of a courageous and passionate dream in an era of repressive measures and discrediting public sentiment affecting the Negro's progress.

W. E. B. Du Bois solicited contributions from Braithwaite for *Crisis* and *Phylon* when he edited those journals, corresponded with him about matters of mutual interest, dined with him, and generally testified to his appreciation for Braithwaite's talents. The men were on friendly but not intimate terms. In their late years they were neighbors for a while in a Harlem apartment building and sometimes passed the time with a game of chess. Braithwaite's poem, "For the Seventieth Birthday of William Edward Burghardt Du Bois," appeared in July, 1938, in the *Atlanta University Bulletin*. This essay, in *Phylon*, Fourth Quarter, 1949, was written at the request of the editors.

A Tribute to W. E. Burghardt Du Bois First Editor of Phylon

The career of W. E. Burghardt Du Bois will reflect a light across the memory of man as long as man seeks and reveres the ideals of Justice and Liberty, of Intelligence and Beauty. His birth took place in a locality that was the cradle of these ideals in America; but his heritage was alien, seeded in the Dark Continent, and he made it a battle cry that in the years to come was to echo throughout the world with the authority of Truth that was first transmitted in thunder on Sinai and later reinterpreted with divine melodies on the slopes of Olivet. Du Bois came into the world at a time when nine-tenths of his people were illiterate, having recently been released from two hundred and fifty years of chattel bondage, despised but yet exploited, and with no recompenses, except in the form of constitutional amendments, to aid the development of their future citizenship, materially and spiritually. The mass of these people were leagues away from his boyhood among the Berkshire hills, but the flames and shadows of those hills communicated to him their anguish and disabilities. In that communication was a message, the interpretation of which at first must have been vague and uncertain, though it stirred an ambition

soon to be aflame with passion. It took the force, first, of a
personal aspiration, and the fulfillment of that aspiration became the precept and prophecy of a Race and Nation,
whose progress in service and justice spread as a gospel of
brotherhood to peoples of all colors and heritage among all
the tribes and nations of the world.

He became the exemplar through his own experience in
surmounting the obstacles to obtain and master knowledge.
The ends that knowledge was to serve were to be determined in good time by the philosophies which developed
from the observation and weighing of human relationships
as they were conditioned by racial associations, traditions,
and prejudices. But all that stirred in the world beyond the
hills that hemmed in the New England town where he was
born. When he had learned all that the schools of the town
could teach him, he went over the hills and down the high-
ways to the great institutions of learning. His first dream
was the great university by the Charles River whose traditions of scholarship and culture were made by the greatest
American intellects. But circumstances forced a detour,
those circumstances which emphasized his alien heritage; so
he went to Fisk University, in the Southland, and came
home in spirit to his people. Though here he learned much
from books, he learned more of something mystical in the
heart and soul and features of his kin that had been clouded
for him in the recesses of both reality and history. Those
years at Fisk forged a mental and spiritual bond from which
there was to be no escape — even if he had wished it, or if
by some sophistry he had tried to will it. From Fisk he trod
the golden path of his dream to Harvard University. And
then came studies at the University of Berlin, during which
zest and value were given to his scholarship through excur-
sions to most of the countries of Europe.

In 1896, his vision of the color problem on both an international and local scale bore scholarly fruit. It was the
year in which his doctoral thesis at Harvard, *The Suppression of the African Slave Trade,* was published and he was

appointed to a fellowship at the University of Pennsylvania, where he produced his study of *The Philadelphia Negro.* These two ends of a vast problem — the ideology of Empire, conceived and pursued by the predatory interests of Europe; and its results as typified by the social and moral conditions of an urban minority — tied their frayed ends in the consciousness of the young visionary and scholar. The modern Goliath, in the shape of an oppressive and merciless industrialism, confronted a meditative and dreaming David, and with what power of arms could he fight against it? Would he dare stand against the giant with his sling and pebble? The young David from the Berkshire hills had come to know that in the pebble he had a potent weapon; for in his imagination the pebble symbolized Education, and he knew that no giant of empire, nor of disease, prejudice, discrimination, political chicanery, nor of any of the other abuses of privileges and rights that destroy the dignity and preservation of man could prevail against it.

He must have known then, in this year of 1896, when there had blossomed in his spirit these two achievements of his scholarship, that in whatever way or form in the future his imagination or his desire would urge him to expression, the fiery impulse at the core of his consciousness would inspire him to teach — to inform his race, to lift it through knowledge, and through knowledge to hope and strive, to use knowledge wisely to advance in a hostile world, and to command the discipline to enjoy the benefits of progress.

There was to be a confusion of mediums; the scientific method was often to crowd the intuitional spontaneity of the poetic imagery: the concept of image and impression and the concept of fact and logic vied with each other for priority of assignment and message. The end to be accomplished however was the same. Education was not a matter of means but the end that was to achieve human understanding and the golden rule of personal and group conduct.

It was natural then that he should choose teaching as a

vocation. Vocation is the name men give to the work one does to earn a livelihood. The practical wants of life — food, clothing, shelter — for the majority of mankind, can only be supplied by wages; but the transcendent needs of racial justice and progress had to be purchased at the price of spirit and mind: those abstract qualities with which, in contrast to the skill of the hands, since time immemorial civilization has made its historic progress.

For sixteen years he taught, first at Wilberforce, and for the most of those years, at Atlanta University. The classroom was too restricted, too limited in audience, for his most effective, most inspiring instruction. Disadvantages with which he had to contend, disadvantages that Jowett, Palmer, and Dewey, in the great tradition, were free from, prevented him from being a notable classroom teacher. He had to break with custom because what he taught was not conventional; he had to lay the groundwork for a tradition. So he made the college the center around which he spun a wholly new and fresh educational approach to the investigation and interpretation of racial conditions and problems. The *Atlanta University Studies* are a monument to his genius in introducing the scientific method to the study of complex racial problems; and equally important, with them he was the precursor of a new science in the study of human behavior which seeks to explain the forces in the individual and the group, and which since the early years of this century has come to be developed and known as sociology.

He wrote in retrospect of these early years: "Turning my gaze from fruitless word-twisting and facing the facts of my own social situation and racial world, I determined to put science into sociology through a study of the condition and problems of my own group." And he added in the same strain of thought the following significant statement which holds the key to the misunderstandings that have affected his work and career at their critical turns: "In my own sociology because of a firm belief in a changing racial group, I easily grasped the idea of a *changing society* rather than a fixed social structure." The italics are mine, to emphasize in the man an acute and sensitive awareness of the necessity for re-education to meet the impinging new order. For he differed from others in the recognition of the changes in society; and unlike so many others who had it in their power to take the initiative, he strove to do something about it.

It was out of this impulse that the Niagara Movement was born, a movement that was the parent of the National Association for the Advancement of Colored People. And it can be said that the Pan-African Congresses, in which he was the guiding spirit, were related to both the Niagara Movement and the NAACP in the effort to unify and give weight to the crusade for justice and respect for the darker peoples of the world.

Du Bois resigned from Atlanta University in 1910 to devote full time to the NAACP. From its inception he created his own potent weapon of education with a magazine, *The Crisis*. For subsidy he wrote to the famous philanthropist of that period, Jacob Schiff, the following:

> I want to lay before you a plan which I have and ask you if it is of sufficient interest to you for you to hear more of it and possibly to assist in its realization. The Negro race in America is today in a critical condition. Only united concerted effort will save us from being crushed. This union must come as a matter of education and long-continued effort. To this end there is needed a high class of journal to circulate among the intelligent Negroes, tell them of the deeds of themselves and their neighbors, interpret the news of the world to them, and inspire them toward definite ideals. Now we have many small weekly papers and one or two monthlies, and none of them fills the great need I have outlined. I want to establish, therefore, for the nine million American Negroes and eventually for the whole Negro world, a monthly journal.

Du Bois had to wait five years before such a magazine came into being, and when it did, it was through his own efforts. For twenty-five years under his editorship it served to educate the American Negro and spread into foreign lands Du Bois's program, ideals and his philosophy of the color problem. It gave also the most substantial support to his faith in the Talented Tenth in the encouragement offered through its pages to the young men and women of the race who were struggling to express themselves in art and literature.

It would take many chapters to tell the story of the growth and influence of *The Crisis*. It was Du Bois's personal responsibility and gave expression to his personal principles and doctrine, and as such it gave to the NAACP a status and influence it could not otherwise have obtained.

During this quarter of a century the world had changed with amazing rapidity. The First World War had brought a quick and violent shifting of American Negroes' status, and an awakening of the dark colonials to their exploitations by their imperial overlords in Europe. He had insisted that the roots of the First World War had been planted in Africa, to which the vast populations of brown Asia were symbolically tied in subjection to European imperialism. The political claims of the American Negroes did not separate them socially and economically from the colonial peoples of dark hue who were subjected to white dominion. Through books, articles, and lectures he reported his observations on race problems as a result of travelling about the world; and in issue after issue of *The Crisis* he informed and exhorted concerning the dangers and hopes of this One World of color. And slowly, surely, there evolved a new philosophy, a new challenge implicit in new principles and doctrines to meet the changing order.

And then came the break with the association with which he had labored for a quarter of a century. The NAACP attempted to mend the immediacies while the times called for reforms in procedure and outlook. Self sufficiency and material security were the dogmas of the twentieth century, and they made justice less the object of elo-

quent, and abstract, persuasion than the respondent of
realities. It was inevitable that much work would have to be
done over. New forces and new conditions were propagated
by unpredictable reactions, and a whole process of re-
education had to be endured. Like the prophet of old he
withdrew to nurse the vision.

So Du Bois came back to Atlanta University in 1933 to
teach the subject whose materials he had learned from practical experience and for which he had formulated a scientific method. When he left Atlanta in 1910, he was already
the author of three books, the scholarly works on the slave
trade and the Philadelphia Negro and a collection of essays,
The Souls of Black Folk, which had won wide appreciation
for its brilliant qualities of style and thought. He returned
not only as essayist, but poet, historian, novelist, and dramatist as his masque, *Star of Ethiopia*, entitles him to be called.
He had established his place in literature both as thinker
and artist, and this was given official recognition when there
came to him on the University campus the announcement of
his election to membership in the American Institute of Arts
and Letters. The return to Atlanta brought the completion
and publication of *Black Reconstruction*, which opened up
wholly new speculations about that intensely controversial
era in American history.

Thirty-five years after the letter to Jacob Schiff, he saw
the need for another kind of periodical, a scholarly university journal that would express the higher intellectual position to which the Negro had risen. With the support of Atlanta University he founded this journal, *Phylon*, which
with this issue is celebrating its tenth anniversary. He became Professor Emeritus of Atlanta University in 1944.

This brief sketch of William E. Burghardt Du Bois can
offer no more than a mere outline of his achievements and
services to racial progress throughout his long career. And
in all those services in literature and propaganda none has
been so vital and effective as his contribution to the education of his race, and the respect and recognition for the abil-

ity and manhood of the Negro which he has won from the white world.

Among the many projects Braithwaite tried to promote after his retirement from teaching in 1945 were some that treated English history and literature. It is ironic that what may be seen now as the least "relevant" of his many suggestions to publishers was accepted and accomplished. *The Bewitched Parsonage: The Story of the Brontës* was published in 1950 by the same firm that had issued his *Selected Poems* two years earlier. The book won some approving reviews, though the publisher, Coward-McCann, had worried about the exalted tone of the early draft. The selection presented here is chapter twenty-one of the book.

"Where Did You Get This?"
(A Footnote in the History of Anonymous)

I have retained, from the chapter on Charlotte Brontë's life, a particular incident that seems to me so interesting and dramatic that it deserves a small niche of its own in this biography. It concerns the day when Charlotte and Emily and Anne decided to reveal their true identity to publisher and public, and no longer camouflage themselves under the names of Currer, Ellis, and Acton Bell. No living soul except Mr. Brontë knew the secret of this anonymity. But the popularity of *Jane Eyre*, the critical furore over *Wuthering Heights*, had roused the literary world and the general reader to eager conjecture as to who the authors might be. Were the Bells men or women? Where did they live? What walk of society did they frequent? Were they one and the same person? Were they well-known figures in the literary world, masquerading under assumed names? *Jane Eyre*, in its handling of social problems, its insight into feminine psy-

chology, and *Wuthering Heights,* with its stoical philosophy, its violent human passions, would seem to indicate experienced writers, wise in the ways of mankind and skilled
in craftsmanship. Indeed, speculation was running high,
wide, and handsome, when Charlotte decided it was time to
make themselves known in their true colors. After all, she
had only taken the path of concealment because she felt
women were handicapped, by the very reason of their sex,
in the practice of any art. She had also known that *Jane
Eyre* and *Wuthering Heights* were strong meat for anyone's
dish, reader or critic, and that if it were known in advance
that the authors were "ladies" there would be an uproar of
shocked protest. So Charlotte, whose instincts were always
so unerring in practical affairs, took the precaution of putting men's names to work that would have done any man
credit.

A letter from the publishers, Smith, Elder, received on
July 5, 1848, brought matters to a head. It arrived by post,
protesting a rumor that had reached their ears concerning
the acquisiton of the American rights to the next work by
the author of *Jane Eyre.* Another London firm appeared to
be selling these rights to an American publisher, and the
whole transaction was contrary to the arrangements agreed
upon between the author of *Jane Eyre* and Smith, Elder.
According to the letter, the affair hinted of double dealing
on the part of Currer Bell. That was enough for Charlotte!
She was stung to the quick by a suspicion of this nature, so
completely unfounded. There was nothing to do but act immediately, and in the open. Smith, Elder must not be allowed to doubt the integrity of the Bells or the Brontës. The
authors themselves must journey to London straightway
and set the matter right!

It was decided that Charlotte and Anne would go, leaving Emily in charge at home. In fact, Emily was not in favor
of the idea at all. The other two packed their satchels that
day, and sent them by oxcart to the station at Keighley, several miles distant, where they would pick them up later as

they took the night train for Leeds and London. Such a journey was quite an undertaking for two young women who had traveled so little. Charlotte and Emily had stopped off for a few hours in London, going and coming from Brussels. But for Anne it was a first visit there, and, sadly enough, would prove to be her last. The walk to Keighley, a distance of four miles from Haworth, was taken in the cool of the evening. A thunderstorm broke upon the sisters before they reached Keighley. It is significant that this should happen. The rage of the elements was in harmony with their own spirits, and they were neither afraid nor sought shelter from the storm.

The uncomfortable night ride in the coach from Leeds to London must have been a strange one, filled with thoughts of the past, anxiety for the morrow. Their spirits, as well as their bodies, could only have arrived somewhat the worse for the cramping night journey. They came into the city early Saturday morning, July 6, and went directly to the Chapter Coffee House, in Paternoster Row, where Charlotte had settled that they should stay. Mr. Brontë had taken Charlotte and Emily there for an overnight stay when he accompanied them to Brussels. The Chapter Coffee House had a past, having been a famous gathering place for critics and writers during its heyday in the early eighteenth century. Chatterton had written of it to his mother when he wanted to delude her about his well-being in London since it was the resort of famous men of letters. Now it was no more than a shabby, run-down inn, in the care of a slatternly couple, and patronized only by men. It was not the place for Charlotte and Anne to sleep, but they knew of no other. They were made as comfortable as possible in a long, low room with high windows, on the second story, where book-trade meetings had once been held. After freshening up from the night's journey, they breakfasted, and lingered a moment to decide what to do next in getting to Smith, Elder's in Cornhill.

From Paternoster Row, the narrow street running north

of St. Paul's Churchyard, famed for its memories of the great bookshops and publishing houses, but now crowded with warehouses, it was only a short walk to Cornhill, where the offices of Smith, Elder were located. Charlotte and Anne emerged from the dim, dingy doorway of the Chapter Coffee House into the business bustle and ferment of Paternoster Row. They decided to economize by not taking a conveyance, though it might have been safer to rely on a driver for directions, and made the dome of St. Paul's a guiding star in the confusion and complexity of the innumerable crooked streets and alleys. But St. Paul's was not always in sight. Surely, they must have asked a stranger the way. And how little he knew that he was directing Apollo's anointed. Two young country women, attired in plain black homemade gowns, one of them possessed of strange, compelling, reddish-brown eyes, the other of a pale fragile face touched with the loveliness of a white flower, had asked their way to Cornhill — that was all he knew.

Perhaps a little breathless with haste and uncertainty, but no doubt grateful that they had come thus far with no untoward experience, the two sisters arrived at the offices of their publishers. With what timidity did Charlotte ask to see Mr. George Smith, and with what puzzled amusement did the receptionist convey the request to his employer? Two simple maidens, he thought, but how extraordinarily forward in asking to see the head of the firm! Or was it naïveté? Yet there must have been something in Charlotte's eyes, in her upright carriage and clear voice, that commanded instant respect, for the attendant announced her to Mr. George Smith without more ado. And so they came into the great publisher's presence. He must have gazed at them in wonderment — at the old-fashioned severity of toilet, at the dresses and bonnets that had certainly never been purchased at any Bond Street shop. Charlotte and Anne, as they stood quietly under his slightly austere scrutiny, were alien to anything he was accustomed to meet in the literary world. There was absolutely nothing about these two frail daughters of a Yorkshire clergyman, so out of their physical element in a London publisher's office, that would convey an inkling to Mr. George Smith of the creative fire he was playing with — unless perhaps it was a certain dignity and simple lack of pretension. He stood there, innocently unperceiving, on the brink of a startling discovery for which he was totally unprepared. Then Charlotte, with no word of explanation, handed him a letter. The die was cast. George Smith glanced at the letter, and back at the open faces before him, for he recognized it as a letter he had written. And one quick, half-accusing, half-puzzled question slipped from George Smith's tongue: "Where did you get this?"

And Charlotte must have answered, "Why, you sent it to me!"

Mr. Smith's unspoken response to that one may well have been, "And who the devil are you?" but he undoubtedly restrained the impulse and replied with courteous doubt, "I did? And are *you* acting in behalf of Mr. Bell?"

When Charlotte made it clear who she was, and also the silent sister beside her, as well as the absent sister whom they could not persuade to leave the Haworth moors, and who together made the trinity of Bells, George Smith's ears must have vibrated with Olympian laughter! There was the letter in his hand, convincing evidence of the truth Charlotte had uttered. And George Smith rose magnificently to the occasion!

This article, published in the magazine section of the *Pittsburgh Courier* on May 30, 1953, is a product of Braithwaite's lifelong interest in the Negro as both author and subject and of his efforts, quite unsuccessful, to edit a book on black novelists.

The First Negro Novelist

In the spring of 1853, was published by a fugitive slave, a novel entitled "Clotel; or The President's Daughter." It was published in England where the author was living and lecturing as an agent of the American Anti-Slavery Society.

The fugitive slave author, born in Kentucky, made with his second attempt a successful escape from bondage, bearing the only name he knew, that of Williams. He had been sold to an owner in St. Louis, and from there, with the usual harrowing experiences of the runaway slave, made his way into Ohio where a kindly Quaker family gave him refuge, and whose name, Wells Brown, he adopted out of gratitude. At the time he did not know how to read or write. Moving on in his search for safety from the clutches of slavery he reached Cleveland, Ohio, where he began the foundation of his self-education; after which he went on to Canada, finally returning to the States to settle in Boston.

In Boston, with access to books, and the association of eminently cultured friends, his own proficiency in knowledge and culture broadened and deepened, and he became an effective lecturer in the crusade against slavery. Here he wrote and published the inevitable fugitive slave autobiography with "The Narrative of William W. Brown," which it is safe to say was scarcely regarded as the introduction to a literary career to which a hundred years later we pay this tribute.

During his stay in England, William Wells Brown's pen became prolific. He wrote historical portraits of famous Negro characters . . . a history of the Negro race . . . and a book of descriptive travel sketches and studies of eminent European figures. . . . This latter work was published in 1852, a year before the novel which was to mark the beginning of the Negro novelist in America.

Brown was later to write a drama . . . which adds another first to Negro authorship . . . that was to develop throughout the century following, and produce, under more fortunate, though not always encouraging, circumstances, the works of Dunbar and Chesnutt, Du Bois and Washington, Countee Cullen and Langston Hughes, James W. Johnson and J. Saunders Redding, and the fictional blooming of the last decade or so, of Richard Wright, Willard Motley, Frank Yerby, and Ralph Ellison.

What of the novel itself? Professor Vernon Loggins of Columbia University, in his invaluable bibliography of the Negro author, declares that it contains enough exciting material to furnish the plots for a half-dozen novels. The subtitle, "The President's Daughter," which appeared on the title-page of the original English edition, linked the heroine with the patrimony of President Jefferson who was indifferent, in spite of his human responsibility, to the system that made of her a commodity for sale in the slave marts of New Orleans.

A summary of the narrative as it is told in the American edition of 1864, might here be made with these essential features:

Clotel . . . is a daughter her mother had by a Virginian master, but who was devoted to her, and maintained them in an attractive and comfortable cottage. His own wife was a weak and uninspiring woman, but whose mother was a malicious and vindictive creature, and the cause of her being sent to the New Orleans slave mart. The young girl, suddenly uprooted from her sheltered life and made to share the common lot of slaves, is spiritually comforted by a courageous and noble-minded young slave, Fletcher.

In the New Orleans slave pen Clotel is seen by a gallant young Frenchman of wealth and position, and captivated by her beauty, he helps her to escape, taking her to France where they are married. She lived contentedly until his death with the French army in India. Fletcher, the young slave, in the meantime, made his escape from bondage, going to England where he acquired a polish of mind and manners. Later wandering on the Continent, he finds Clotel and marries her. To this striking climax is added the compensatory note of Clotel finding her Virginian father ill in a European hotel and ministering to his recovery, a reunion that brings happiness to all.

This bare summary gives no idea of the drama and stirring tragedy of the soul that Brown has woven into his story. It is told in a style that is often vivid and colorful. It was an auspicious beginning of the Negro's contribution to the art of American fiction, and we should salute it on this one hundredth anniversary of its publication with pride.

———————

In April, 1953, after the publication of Claude McKay's *Selected Poems*, the Schomburg Collection of the New York Public Library featured an exhibition of his works. Braithwaite, who was occasionally a speaker or panelist at the Harlem branch of the library, spoke at the memorial program. He had in hand McKay's autobiography, *A Long Way from Home*, and the collection of his poetry but no prepared address. He began his remarks with a brief statement about early correspondence with McKay and closed by praising his nature poetry and reading "The Snow Fairy." The selection below was transcribed with some difficulty from the Schomburg Collection's tape recording, which preserves coughs and traffic noises as well as Braithwaite's words.

Claude McKay

❀ ❀ ❀

McKay was many years in Europe and those years . . . made him the most cosmopolitan poet that the Negro race has yet produced. France, Germany, Russia, Spain, and North Africa were indeed as familiar to him and made an impress on him as deeply as this city of New York. . . . The curious thing is that . . . these years in the twenties, the years of the so-called Lost Generation, the years that most of our young literary men and women were expatriates testing out new forms, new ideas, new patterns of expression, when the seeds of the Imagist group were beginning to sprout, when indeed the overflow or the afterglow of the

French symbolist poets [was] affecting these young contemporaries — these had no effect upon Claude McKay as a poet.

Indeed no American poet of any racial strain ever had the experience and the contact with power and with beauty and with traditions — cultural traditions of Europe — as did Claude McKay. That marvelous adventure, I call it, which was his in Russia when the revolution was beginning to transform itself into power and dominance, when they made a hero of him, a symbol of that racial democracy which indeed it was their thought would dominate the world. But of all the experiences and associations that Claude McKay had in Europe during those years, there is one that stands out with commanding significance.

As a young man in Jamaica he had the ambition to know two great Englishmen, as he records in his autobiography. One was George Bernard Shaw and the other was H. G. Wells. And with a letter of introduction he was invited to meet and spend some hours with Shaw. I want to read you a passage from his autobiography in which he relates this meeting and this association, because I think it was significant of what was deeply rooted in the imaginative spirit of Claude McKay . . . that consciousness of color which he has dramatized in so many ways and often, I think, more impressively in his prose than in his poetry. This is a passage from that visit to Bernard Shaw:

> When Shaw discovered that I was not particularly interested in Irish or world politics, because my social outlook was radical, and that I was not expecting him to say something wise about colored people in a white-controlled world, he turned to an unexpected subject — cathedrals. He spoke of their architectural grandeur, the poetry of their spires and grand arches, and the prismatic beauty of their great windows. He said there were fine cathedrals outside London, structures full of poetry and music which I ought to see — Salisbury, Lincoln, Canterbury, York, Winchester — as interesting in their style as St. Sophia,

Rheims and Cologne, although people did not talk so much about them. And he informed me that the best way to get at the essential beauty of a cathedral was to stand in the center and look up.

I was enchanted with this monologue on cathedrals. . . . And as I stood in the nave of those concrete miracles of the medieval movement of belief and faith, transported by the triumphant arches of Gothic glory, often I felt again the musical vibrations of Shaw's cathedral sermon.

I hope I may communicate to you the analogy between this cathedral sermon, in which McKay was admonished to look up, with that problem which concerned him always and which he controlled in such a way as to liberate himself from any single standard of criticism. . . . The essential beauty of the cathedral is in looking upward. The essential beauty of Claude McKay as a poet is that he could send his spirit wayfaring back through the centuries to those roots in Africa, upon which he had mythically stood and looked up out of the depths of that spirit into this controlled white world, as he puts it.

He was not, as he confessed, an agitator. Yet he advocated organized movements for the colored people, a means whereby progress . . . could be made because of combined strength. . . . He was amazed to find how much praise a certain poem of his won from his own people. He was a subjective poet, intensely subjective, and yet at the root of that subjectivity was the expression and the manifestation of all those impulses which made the universal world. Therefore, in many respects, he could withdraw. And again he could become amazed that a sonnet that he had written, which is indeed in the rhetoric of anger, from a purely aesthetic point of view, should have expressed the mass sentiment. . . .

I suppose one might say that there is only one other American poet with whom McKay can be compared. . . . That other poet is Poe. What Poe made of beauty, McKay made of color. All those poems in which are expressed these various facets of his consciousness about color seem, indeed, to be angry poems. But they are not angry poems; they are defiant poems, but anger and defiance are not the same things. When he said he was not the poet of a mass movement he meant that he was exemplifying . . . that fundamental truth of human nature which had the right to be and fulfill itself. . . .

["The Harlem Dancer"] is a very appealing description of a place and atmosphere, of a human being living by the beauty, the rhythmic beauty of her body, admired by a great many men and women, whose body, he said, swayed like a palm leaf and yet whose soul was not in that dim place. Her soul was not there, mind you. I wonder if this may not be taken as the symbolically typical poem of McKay's attitude towards this world, in which he found so much that was disagreeable and unfair and unjust and yet . . . his own spirit [was] fortified by that isolation of the imagination which made him triumphant over these conditions.

There is an aspect of McKay's poetry which is extremely interesting to one who takes note of the manner in which poets express themselves. As I said formerly, he was untouched, unaffected, by those influences which were in the air during his European sojourn, when poets, or those who are charitably called poets, were trying to extract out of words that which did not exist in the imagination or in the emotions. And we go through McKay's poetry and find that in the great tradition of English art he has . . . confined himself to practically one or two metrical systems. There are no innovations; there are no technical experimentations. He kept to the iambic measure and usually within the four or five . . . accentual measures.

It is curious to know of a poet whose imagination and whose emotions ranged over so wide an expanse of human interest [who] should confine himself to the sonnet. Of the eighty-odd poems in this selected collection of his poetry forty-two are sonnets. And among them, as in "The Harlem Dancer," are some of the finest sonnets written in the English language.

❃   ❃   ❃

This tribute Braithwaite contributed to "The Passing of Alain Locke," featured in *Phylon,* Third Quarter, 1954. A formal statement of Locke's professional accomplishments, it omits expression of Braithwaite's grief at the loss of a close friend with whom he had shared many interests.

The Passing of Alain Leroy Locke

I do not agree, as has been said, that we have lost a friend, just because he has crossed the boundary that separates our world from Eternity. Our memory of him but deepens that friendship; we cherish his worth in memory, making his friendship a greater treasure than mere earthly experience can provide. So it is with Alain Locke to whom we pay tribute here.

I knew Alain Locke for over forty years, the roots of our friendship and associations being embedded in the year of his studies for his doctorate at Harvard. He had returned from Oxford and his Rhodes scholarship, flushed with the spirit of European culture. Having chosen philosophy as the instrument of his intellectual survey of human conduct and aspiration, he decided upon teaching as the profession in which to put his enlightened spirit to service. The cornerstone of the philosophic ideal was the determination of values and by them the estimation of conduct which affects human lives and relationships. Through teaching Alain Locke, during the long tenure of his professorship at Howard University, became a force and inspiration in the lives of young people for more than two generations. But it is as a man of letters that his most enduring reputation will rest. I would say a few words in regard to this aspect of his shining career because it was unique.

His philosophy developed into a study of aesthetic values, and he applied these values to confirm racial integrities. His aesthetic sensibilities might well have prompted him to manifest his ideals in the creative forms of verse, the drama, or fiction, if his intellectual necessity had not urged him to correct long-standing fallacies by applying a critical and interpretative wand to their misconceptions. He saw beyond the local, and detached the universal spirit of man, and sought to bring these segments of social and economic racial differences into a universal spiritual balance.

Alain Locke's aesthetic philosophy became a compelling influence upon the young Negro writers who were striving to break the barriers of literary isolation and escape the limitation of their material and experience. He preached the objective point of view that would enable them to transcend the scope of their racial interests and to destroy the false critical standards assigned them. His work, *The New Negro,* was both a protest and an assumption — a protest against the imposed limitation of the spirit of the Negro artist to the false values of experience, and the assumption of his membership in the wide realm of human vision and imagination. The force of his aesthetic philosophy emancipated the creative imagination of the Negro artist. His annual survey of Negro authors and their works, first in *Opportunity* magazine, and later in *Phylon,* over a period of years, confirms the triumph of this service to the literary talents of the race.

He leaves behind him the fragment of work in which he was exploring a wider, an international field, of Negro culture and his equality in the common heritage of vision and idealism. A fragment, it has the purity and implied design of a classic structure from the antique Grecian world, and symbolizes in his career the philosophy which he had put to the service of truth and the homage he had paid to the harmonious spirit of beauty in mankind.

The silent form of Alain Locke resting before us here bequeaths us the legacy of one who in blood was kin to Alexander Crummell, and in culture and aesthetic philosophy akin to Goethe and Croce.

———

Braithwaite hoped to write a biography of Alain Locke, but neither a publisher nor a foundation would provide the necessary funds. This address, delivered in New York in 1955 before the Memorial Workshop of the Alain Locke Memorial Committee, appeared in *Phylon*, Second Quarter, 1957.

Alain Locke's Relationship to the Negro in American Literature

You will note that in the title selected for this address there is an emphasis on Negro authorship rather than on Negro literature. There is intended a subtlety of implication which reflects, and I hope convincingly to the discerning mind, the spirit of Alain Locke. He was a scholar in philosophy in which he took for his chief concept the theory of values. The doctrine of values, which Thoreau pursued with such dismay to the Puritan skeptics, has always seemed to me the keystone of philosophic thinking, for if the function of philosophy is to estimate and appraise the worth and inevitability of human thought and action, then only by determining values can standards be established for the guidance and operation of human conduct and relationships. These standards serve the interests of society, interchangeable as they are with heritage and tradition which are the props of conformity; but it is the individual that counts in the maintenance of standards, for out of reason and emotion, the imagination and intuition, with their interactions of reality and illusion, is compounded the kind of society that prevails in one era or another. I never have been able, though I confess that better Hegelian minds than mine can, to separate aesthetics from philosophy — philosophy to my belief being the science of Truth, if I may use the term science as connoting method rather than formula or finality, and aesthetics being the science of Beauty. Thus we have the two motivating energies, as Henry Adams would say, sustaining the spirit of man.

How, one may ask, do these observations concern Alain Locke's relationship to Negro authorship? Very decidedly, and effectively, I would reply. And to confirm the reply, we will have to glance cursorily, as the limitation of time and occasion imposes, at the history of Negro authorship.

From the beginnings in the 1760's to the ante-bellum period there was produced some verse, verse of moral reflections and indignant protest against the conditions of slavery, in techniques wholly imitative of English models; there were slavery-songs which we call "spirituals," and work-songs which gave vocal expression to the unremitting and exploited labor on the plantations of the South. These spirituals and work-songs are the first genuine folk-expression in America. From 1800 to the close of the Civil War there was a continuous stream of prose writings, crowned with the unique production of slave-narratives, autobiographical records of fugitive bondsmen, out of which materials of harrowing and dramatic escapes were fashioned the first attempts at creative expression, the novels of Martin R. Delany, Frank J. Webb, and William Wells Brown. One cannot read the narratives of Gustavus Vasa, Frederick Douglass, and William Wells Brown, the most impressive among the large body of these writings, without deep respect and admiration for the character and spirit of a handicapped people who for two centuries and a half had been assimilating slowly and agonizingly the mores of Western civilization. It was more truly during this period than at any later period that the Negro passed *per aspera ad astra,* and reached that glory through the sheer and indomitable exercise of his will.

As a contemporary historian, Richard Bardolph, of the University of North Carolina, says of this period, from 1831 to 1865:

> [It was]° in the nation's social history preeminently the time of the rise of the common man, effectuated by wide-ranging reform efforts increasingly channeled into the anti-slavery movement. The Negro leadership adjusted itself easily to this formula and, convinced of the futility of slave-revolts on the Turner model, worked now in close association with a growing army of northern folk who espoused positive programs.

Through this period, not in single and isolated instances, but in a group consciousness the Negro expressed and gave clearance to the articulated impulse of his nature as a human being. That consciousness was wholly dominated and tempered by the institution of slavery and its far-reaching influence upon the civil, political, and social character of American life both in the North and the South. The spirit of the Negro was fueled but from one source, Christianity, in whose hope lay the single promise of his escape from the suppressions and discriminations hedging in his participation as a member of a democratic society. In his effort to escape he wrote furiously and voluminously, and created a body of discursive and subjective literature out of a natural aptitude for self-expression. Indeed, the period historically can be compared to the Saxon period in Britain, when the conversion to Christianity was the all-absorbing inspiration for literary expression. It is true there were no alliterative verse Beowulfs or Caedmons but the prose writers to whom I have just referred were inspired by the hope of freedom as the Saxon writers were inspired by the exalted

° Brackets supplied by Braithwaite.

visions of Christianity. Those Saxon writers were the fertile soil in which Chaucer flowered, just as surely as the slave narratives were the fertile soil in which flowered the talents of Dunbar.

The name of Dunbar brings us to the third period of Negro authorship — the period from 1896 to the death of Dunbar in 1906 — with a scattering of minor and ineffectual rhymesters revolving satellites in orbits of the major figures, Dunbar and Chesnutt. In Dunbar and Chesnutt was first expressed the sensibility of an aesthetic form in Negro authorship that found evocation in the adequate techniques of specific artistic mediums. It was this matter of form that up to the second decade of the twentieth century was the undiscovered continent for Negro authorship. The Negro, however, has not been alone in regarding form as the structure of language in all its variations of prose and verse; or in the plastic arts, modelling of clay as it is cast into bronze or polished in marble, as exemplified by a Phidias or a Rodin, or in the pictorial arts as exemplified by a Raphael or a Rubens, by a Picasso or a Matisse. Form is a compound of abstract elements that make up the thoughts and feelings of mankind — his desires and dreams, his joys and sorrows, his hopes and despairs, and which imbue the materials of his experiences, as the spirit imbues the flesh and makes of those experiences a manifest in the materials and techniques serving as a witness to man's troubled or serene consciousness.

The literature of the Negro that I have alluded to in the foregoing was a legacy handed down to serve as a springboard for re-conversion for some perceptive twentieth century mind. Please be reassured that what I am about to say is wholly in the aesthetic sense. There was, indeed, this flood of literature, a body of splendid content; but it lacked a soul, and again, I remind you that I am speaking in the aesthetic sense. The mind that gave it a soul was Alain Locke's. At first it was a timid soul, either unaware of, or a bit mistrustful of, its sanctions. But it developed with confi-

dence and conviction under his gentle and encouraging urgency. And suddenly, at the end of the first quarter of this
century it blossomed in *The New Negro* that he fathered.
Negro authorship had come of age and received the inheritance his wise mind and transcendent idealism had prophe-
sied.

That evolutionary work — and mind you, I do not call it
revolutionary — was the expression of a mind and spirit that
had been tutored in the universal law of humanity — that law
of "unity in diversity," as Locke called it. A law whose highest doctrine, he adds, may be, to quote him, "carried out to
a practical degree of reciprocity." This was the demand that
Locke made of Negro authorship, and along with it, the
concomitant demand for its recognition by the white world.
We can interpret the writings as contained in *The New
Negro* as specifically of literary interest, and, perhaps, its
greatest importance lies not always directly on the surface,
but indirectly in the potentiality of a new literary concept
in the intellectual and imaginative development of the
Negro in authorship. For Locke's discerning spirit elevated
the worth and significance of Negro life, and he included in
the work essays dealing with the subjects of social, economic, artistic and civil importance woven into the fabric of
human relations which give design to the patterns of American democracy.

One of the essential requisites for an emancipated
Negro authorship, was, as I have hinted, the possession of a
soul. Locke did not demand, nor would he have had any
sympathy with, the divorce of Negro authorship from the
interest of Negro life. He repeatedly extolled the richness
and variety of Negro life and character, but his passionate
concern was that the Negro as an artist should treat them
on the same high level of interpretation and execution as
the best artists of other races. One of Locke's great masters
was G. Lowes Dickinson, the English Platonist, who had declared in his Ingersoll Lecture at Harvard that there was no
difference between the races of man, except in the growth

of the soul. And that affirmation was echoed by Locke, particularly in its application to Negro life when he stated in his Foreword to *The New Negro,* that "Negro life is not only establishing new contacts and founding new centers, it is finding a new soul."

With this acquisition of a new and developing soul, there is another observation which Locke made, of tremendous importance to Negro authorship. His leadership in cultural aspiration, in the breaching of barriers that obstructed the paths to a full participation in the aesthetic expression of Negro authorship was established inevitably with this assertion:

> It was rather the necessity for fuller, truer self-expression, the realization of the unwisdom of allowing social discrimination to segregate him mentally, and a counter-attitude to cramp and fetter his own living — and so the 'spite-wall' that intellectuals built over the 'color-line' has happily been taken down.

In this, the refusal to be segregated mentally, and in a counter-attitude, to be cramped and fettered, he previsioned a result that was the main responsibility of Negro authorship. It laid a difficult, but not impossible, burden upon that authorship.

That Locke was confident Negro authorship was capable of bearing the burden is attested to time and again in his writings. Unlike any of his contemporaries, he knew that the roots of the American Negro's imagination were fertilized in the primitive arts of Africa. All the Negro intellectuals were stirred only by the political and economic significance of Africa and deplored often in undisciplined invectives her exploitation by the European overlords. But Locke discovered a cultural heritage that may have given the American Negro his basic attributes for artistic expression. The heritage as a factual record of continuity was severed by slavery. Wrote Locke:

We will never know and cannot estimate how much technical African skill was blotted out in America. The hardships of cotton and rice-field labor, the crudities of the hoe, the axe and the plow reduced the typical Negro hand to a gnarled stump, incapable of fine craftsmanship even if the materials, patterns, and artistic incentives had been available. But we may believe there was memory of beauty; since by way of compensation, some obviously artistic urges flowed even with the peasant Negro toward the only channels of expression left open — those of song, graceful movement and poetic speech.

The memory of beauty! What an exalted declaration of a heritage that was to sprout impoverished as a plant for nigh three centuries, until under some miraculous bestowal of fertilization it was to blossom and flower — and that flowering due largely to the beneficial spirit of Alain Locke.

That is too much to claim for this man, you will think, whose memory we are this day honoring. But show me another who had the intensified and cultural dedication to exercise the shaping influence that was his. In saying this, I do not intend to minimize the knowledge and the desire of many who sought to encourage and inspire their compatriots, but their efforts ran in less exalted channels, channels that ran through the temporary realities of material things and affairs. Locke's was that enduring field of the imaginative representation of human emotions and actions, symbolized and pictured in narrative and rhythm, which constitute a flowering of the human soul that approaches nearest to the divine. Behind all this was the shadowy tapestry of a race whose most assertive identities were tangled in a wave of civilization that would distort and devalue its most precious self-expansion of physical growth and an imposed delusion of spiritual serenity. The transient and confused conditions of human life make it imperative that some transcendent quality of faith be found, above the routine practice of prayer and sacrament, to assure man of his spiritual integrity, of his collaborative sense as a child of nature.

Beyond his physical observation and relationship exists a realm of immeasurable, abstract, and everlasting Reality. It has been the unceasing aspiration of man, both in the mood of reverence and defiance, in all ages, and by all peoples, however divergent in racial origins, to penetrate that realm by some measurement of his consciousness. The most effective effort has been made through man's imagination. The border-line of that penetration exists in Sir Arthur Eddington's dictum that the greatest thing in the physical universe is the brain of man. But this is only an arrival at the bourne. To cross it we must accept the concept of that rebellious Puritan, and great American novelist, Nathaniel Hawthorne, in all of whose romances was pursued one imaginative doctrine, the throwing of man's soul against Eternity. Here was a measurement, however infinitesimal, of man's worth and destiny, adumbrating his inheritance both as a child of God and of nature.

What a circuitous way, may well be your charge, that I have taken to declare that this was Alain Locke's profound purpose in his philosophic-aesthetic writings and promptings on Negro authorship: that the soul of the Negro be thrown against Eternity!

In an essay Locke wrote on the "Orientation of Hope" for the *Baha'i World*, he set down this pregnant phrase: "For those of us who are truly dawn-minded." In its context it has an application to his attitude towards Negro authorship. Further, in the same essay he wrote this: "It is the occasion and opportunity of convincing many who were skeptical because they could not see the impending failure of the old order." Here in a differing concern was Locke's re-affirmation of his insight into the literary progress that was to function freely without psychological restrictions, when the 'spite-walls' were demolished, and the mentality of the Negro artist was uncramped and unfettered by the wasteful intensity of a counter-attitude.

This dawn-mindedness of Locke's broke the new day of Negro authorship. It was he who introduced the phrase that described the first group-flowerings of writings by Negro authors. It was the "heralding sign," an "unusual outburst of creative expression," which enabled him to say in the final sentence of his Foreword to *The New Negro* that, "justifiably, then, we speak of the offerings of this book embodying these ripening forces as culled from the first fruits of the Negro Renaissance."

It was a period of enlightenment, too, this proclaimed Renaissance of creative expression, of which Locke was the propelling spirit as surely as was Erasmus the propelling spirit of the Northern Renaissance in the early sixteenth century. Locke glowed with the same humanism which made Erasmus quicken the thirst of optimism and faith among the multitude. As with Erasmus humanism ceased to be the exclusive privilege of the few, so with Locke his humanistic philosophy was based on the common acquaintance and appreciation of the Negro's creative works by his own as well as by the peoples of other races.

There is one more principle in the hierarchy of Locke's program for the liberation and recognition of the Negro author, which he insisted upon as essential, and to which I shall refer briefly. In a sense it was the most important, for it was the keystone of the aesthetic edifice he built in all his writings and teachings. This was the doctrine of objectivity. He was aware, and painfully so, as many of us have been, of the physical proscriptions of Negro life — he had himself tasted them in spite of his intellectual triumphs — and it was his passionate devotion to the effort that the Negro artist should not be depressed and hindered by mental and emotional proscriptions. How many times in the old days of our association and discussions when he visited me at Arlington did he with that delicate but penetrating dialectic and logic of which he was a master insist that the Negro author, if he was to become fully emancipated, must of necessity work in a mood of objectivity. And what, pray, did he mean by being objective? Simply, the release from self-pity, from the illogical conviction that the Negro was the only people to suffer indignities, that the need for sympathy should be made imperative by the exposure of sore wounds, rather than by the therapeutic healing by the inner spirit, and that the imagination alone, however encased in the shell of ethnic varieties of human flesh, was subject to the same determinations. This objectivity of Locke's demand for the Negro author reminds me of the quintessential summation made by dear old Colonel Thomas Wentworth Higginson, when he solved the whole racial problem, and especially for the enlightenment of the American nation, by declaring that like all other people "the Negro was intensely human." This was what Locke meant by the objective mood, and through its exercise and manifestation by the Negro author the latter could destroy the stereotypes and produce instead of lifeless automatons and clichéd experiences a vitality of characterization and the mutations of human experience.

In this way would the Negro author, especially in his fiction, achieve a comedy of manners. The models were a Jane Austen, a William Dean Howells, an Edith Wharton, or an E. M. Delafield. Jessie Fauset in four novels, published a quarter of a century ago, was an example of the unity in diversity which was Locke's artistic credo for the new era. In Miss Fauset's *There Is Confusion, Plum Bun, The Chinaberry Tree*, and especially in the devastatingly ironic *Comedy: American Style*, was Locke's credo practiced with distinction. I mention this author and these novels because they fulfill the aesthetic theories Locke preached for the spiritual marriage of race and art. And I shadow the mention with the regretful knowledge that they stand alone in this particular genre of the Negro's literary activity.

I want to close by bringing to your attention an episode in a novel by Wallace Thurman, entitled *Infants of the Spring*, because it shows how directly Locke announced, in one instance, and to those most concerned, his gospel of aesthetic liberation. In brief outline, the story is this: A Negro lady of intelligence and means, without gifts of artistic expression herself, but devoted to the cause of Negro culture, gave her somewhat pretentious home to a group of poets, musicians and composers, painters and novelists, where they could live and work in freedom from economic pressures. The group was inter-racial, lived a free Bohemian life, and in all things of cultural intent regarded themselves as intellectual reformers. The dwelling was called Niggeratti Manor. They were drifting aimlessly upon a springtide of emotion, each with his or her individual idiosyncrasy of dream and idealism, without as a community being grounded in the virtuous fundamentals of life and art. One of the members heard of a man who he thought could bring them a message of enlightenment and confidence, and they invited him to come to New York and address them. This man was a Dr. Parkes, who had achieved a notable reputation in the inner circles of both white and Negro intellectualism, and also in the academic world of both races. Dr. Parkes was a thin, but palpable disguise of Alain Locke. Of this there is no doubt when you read the novelist's description of Dr. Parkes' personality:

> He was a mother hen clucking at her chicks. Small, dapper, with sensitive features, graying hair, a dominating head, and restless hands and feet, he smiled benevolently at his brood. Then in his best continental manner, which he had acquired during four years at European universities, he began to speak.

And what, this commentator asks, did he say? There were some things that his audience of Negro artists did not like, and particularly about their psychological roots in Africa by virtue of a remembered beauty. Here is what Dr. Parkes said:

> "You are the outstanding personalities of a new generation. On you depends the future of your race. You are not, as were your predecessors, concerned with donning armor, and clashing swords with the enemy in the public square. You are finding both an escape and a weapon in beauty,

which beauty when created by you will cause the American white man to reestimate the Negro's value to his civilization, cause him to realize that the American black man is too valuable, too potential of utilitarian accomplishment, to be kept downtrodden and segregated.

"Because of your concerted storming up Parnassus, new vistas will be spread open to the entire race. The Negro in the South will no more know peonage, Jim Crowism or loss of ballot, and the Negro everywhere in America will know complete freedom and equality.

"But," and here his voice took on a more serious tone, "to accomplish this, your pursuit of beauty must be vital and lasting. I am somewhat fearful of the decadent strain which seems to have filtered into most of your work. Oh, yes, I know you are children of the age and all that, but you must not, like your paleface contemporaries, wallow in the mire of post-Victorian license. You have too much at stake. You must have ideals. You should become . . . well, let me suggest your going back to your racial roots, cultivating a healthy paganism based on African traditions."

The reference to the African traditions brought forth a volley of protest and rejection from the assembled artists. "What old black pagan heritage?" asked one. "How can I go back to African ancestors when their blood is so diluted and their country and times so far away?" another questioned. And this sentiment was unequivocally affirmed by one who said flatly, "I ain't got no African spirit!"

"I think you have missed the point," responded Dr. Parkes. "I mean you should develop your inherited spirit."

What Alain Locke in the guise of Dr. Parkes was trying to tell this group of young hopefuls was that Western civilization and culture were the fruits of the remembered beauty of the Greeks — a people who had also known slavery — and that similarly, the literature produced by the Negro in modern America should be leavened by the remembered beauty bequeathed by primitive Africa. He did not demand, or even remotely suggest, that the mores, or the landscape, of primitive Africa be used as materials for the body or framework of literature by Negro authors; but that modern life, all its tragedies and comedies, all its romances and social complexities, and racial dramas, was at hand to be informed and made lustrous by the spirit òf a remembered beauty.

And that spirit of beauty which was Alain Locke is before us today leading, as a ball of fire by night and a pillar of cloud by day, to the promised land of literary fulfillment, that we may add a new glory to American culture!

Autobiography and Reminiscence
(1908 – 1962)

Of the autobiographical record that Braithwaite, at thirty, set himself to produce, he seems to have put on paper only the fragment announcing his intentions.

My Journal
An Autobiographical Record

December 6th 1908.
Today I am thirty years old. I intend to begin on this day and record the past years of my life. This I shall do from day to day, in no chronological order, but as I recall events and memories until I have filled in the outlines of my youth. For today youth has left me. It was all my own as every man's must be. . . . Some other pen than mine must record if at the end of my life I shall have left behind me achievements in my art that shall be worthy of remembrance after I am gone.

The part of a man's life the most interesting is when he is preparing himself for that function in life which he has chosen or by parental desire has had thrust upon him. The circumstances and conditions under which he equips himself for his life's task, the influences which help him, the obstacles which impede him, his hopes and despairs, his friends and distractions, these no biographic pen can relate with the truthfulness and intensity of his own. In the story of my youth I shall leave out nothing; I shall set down things that may mean nothing to most men, but to me they mean everything for they had a bearing on my character, they may have contributed definitely to the determination of my ambitions or effected a revision in my methods of attaining them. In this record there will be no account of big events in the world such as altered the youth of kings' sons, or the scions of illustrious families, but there will be crises of my spiritual self in the world of imagination and dream, and these will be important to all men who have lived in the silence of their hearts, and will have value because of an intensely human sensibility. Childhood is fable, youth is romance, manhood is reality, and old age is — comedy. I am going to give the fable and romance — and if at times the fable is full of tears, and the romance with suffering, I would have you believe that . . . I am glad they have come into my life, and not only glad to have known them, but also in the way heaven has been pleased to fashion them. If my chronicle may seem to be made of the stuff from which poetry and fiction is woven, it is not because the facts are unreal, but because Time has thrown over them her veil of Beauty, and experience has given me the power to eliminate regret and bitterness through the annihilation of pain in memory. Though I shall not leave out the bitter things of my youth, I do not — indeed I could not — write about them bitterly. If I was disappointed in some hope at twenty, that defeated purpose at thirty is no longer a disappointment. Time forcing this truth upon me has developed in me an optimism strong as nature's two strongest elements, the mountains and the sea. It need not be that one's final realization is in mortality; the true optimist is he who to the end of life still hopes and expects the final triumph just beyond — somewhere.

At the end of thirty years in taking account of my life in its worldly aspect what is its situation? I am married, a wife, and two children — my beloved Fiona and Katherine. I have no regular income from routine employment — only what my pen earns. My indebtedness is about four hundred and fifty dollars, legitimate obligations which I hope to cancel during the next six months. I have four published books to my credit, a fifth towards completion, and plans for many new ones.

While he was a member of the Atlanta University faculty, Braithwaite wrote the story of his life up to the publication of *Lyrics of Life and Love* in 1904. The autobiography appeared as a serial in 1941–42 in *Phylon,* the Atlanta University quarterly founded and edited by W. E. B. Du Bois. Braithwaite used as title for the serial the fanciful, astrological name he had given to his home in Arlington Heights, partly in acknowledgment of the talents of the previous owner, Mrs. Lenore C. Piper, a famous medium whose trances and seances baffled investigators in England and America, and partly as an expression of the mystical streak in his own nature.

The House Under Arcturus
An Autobiography

✿   ✿   ✿

My father was born, William Smith Braithwaite, on January 29th, 1853, at Georgetown, Demerara, British Guiana, on the northern coast of South America. I have learned the facts of my ancestry in Demerara from my uncle, Edward John Braithwaite, my father's brother who, after a long residence in America, and at the ripe old age of eighty-five, died in September, 1939.

Romance and reality seem to have embodied the first definite images of personality in the dim past of my father's grandparents. His grandfather, a colored man, was a shoe merchant in Barbados, a stern figure with the reputation of being the best Latin scholar in the Colony, and whose son, my grandfather, carried through life the memory of bruised knuckles for failing to parse correctly his lesson in Latin verbs. My father's grandmother, the daughter of a French

nobleman in the island of Martinique, who had been educated in Paris, possessed that indefinable charm and passion
of the Parisian temperament as an urgency in her blood,
and had eloped with her lover, an Englishman by the name
of Smith, to Georgetown, Demerara. This eloping couple
had two children, my father's mother, Henrietta, and her
brother, William. It was intended that the descendants of
this couple should carry their family name by the sons begat
through the female line, as my father did, and as was intended in my own case. . . .

This French grandmother of my father's left him a considerable legacy, in trust, at her death, and it was one of the
aggravations to the unhappy relationships between my father and his father, when the latter appealed to the courts
to control the disposition of this money which my father believed it was his intention to divert in support of the newspaper which my grandfather owned and edited.

My father's uncle was a man who achieved a high career in the services of the British Empire. At the death of
his parents he became the head of the family and directed
its affairs until he left home to assume the important posi-
tions to which he was appointed by the Crown. His first significant official position was as the attorney-general of British Guiana, which at the time was a Crown Colony, during
the régime of Governor Pope-Hennessey and Chief Justice
Beaumont, the latter after whom I was named. This distinction which I bear in being named after Chief Justice Beaumont, was in recognition of my grandfather's gratitude to
the Chief Justice for his sympathy and support in the battles
my grandfather fought in his newspaper, *The Creole*, for the
establishment of a local assembly for the natives of the Colony, a move which was bitterly opposed by the Governor,
Pope-Hennessey. My grandfather won his cause in behalf of
the natives, and a legislative body was granted by the Colonial Office in London with the assent of the British Parlia-
ment. But it was not before my grandfather had been
tempted, a temptation he steadily resisted, to desist in his

crusade, with emoluments in the way of public appointment which would have destroyed his purpose and determination, and which, it is said, if he had accepted, would have led eventually to his knighthood.

What attitude his brother-in-law, William, took in this conflict, I cannot say. His appointment as governor of the Leeward Islands may have been the means of escape from any strict partisanship in the affair, for his own career could easily have been determined by his support of such a political concession by the Crown, to the natives. With the appointment by the Crown of the Governorship, my great uncle was knighted, becoming Sir William Haynes Smith.

My great uncle's career advanced rapidly after the period of his governorship. He went to England and was appointed Lord High Commissioner of the Island of Cyprus, in the eastern Mediterranean, when it was acquired by England from Turkey, in 1882. On retirement from this post, he became Chairman of the Naval Strategy Board, which office was recorded to his credit in Burke's Peerage as late as 1910.

My father's father, to repeat, was a native of Barbados, where his son, John Edward Braithwaite, was born. Here my grandfather grew to young manhood, the friend and companion of Sir Conrad Reeves, the famous barrister and Queen's Counsellor, upon whom Queen Victoria conferred the order of knighthood. Instead of accompanying Conrad Reeves to England, where he distinguished himself in the Inner Temple, though later he returned to his native island as a Queen's Counsellor, my grandfather emigrated to British Guiana, settled in its chief city and capital, Georgetown, and won a comparable distinction as a journalist advocating and winning the rights of the Colonists to a participation in their government. In commenting on the estrangement which arose between my father and grandfather, my uncle has recorded this description of my grandfather: "My father," he wrote, "was a disciplinarian of the old school. There was a great gap in those days between parent and child. There was no companionship. It was obey or suffer. He would never stand for an infringement of his authority."

When John Braithwaite arrived in Georgetown, Henrietta Smith was the belle of the Capital. There are legends of her beauty, charm and wit. The stranger from Barbados met, wooed and won her, though not without some opposition. Had John Braithwaite been a man of lesser gifts his case would have been hopeless. Besides being a stranger, though British to the core as the Barbadian traditions had molded him, his immense distinction of person and brains overcame all sentiment against his color. The union was recognized socially, and though the Governor, Pope-Hennessey, opposed his advocacy for a legislative assembly, he and his wife were invited and welcomed to all the functions at the Government House, the arbiter of society in the Colony.

After a busy life of conflict in behalf of the cause to which he had dedicated himself, my grandfather died in his middle years, the age of forty-seven, in 1874. He had spent his personal resources in support of the newspaper which championed the political reforms in which his beliefs were passionate and determined, and in consequence, died insolvent. The end came suddenly on a visit to his native home where his friends had persuaded him to go for rest and recuperation. The grateful citizens of Demerara have erected in Georgetown, a bronze memorial in recognition of his unselfish public services.

My maternal grandmother's name was Lydia DeWolfe. At the end of the Civil War she found her way to Boston from North Carolina with three young daughters. The eldest of these daughters was my mother who was born in 1860. Who my mother's father was I never knew, and I have often suspected her paternity and that of her sisters was merely another of the South's traditional stories of the lustful master violating the helpless and undefended witchery of the dark maiden.

My grandmother was a remarkable woman, and I remember her gentle and refined nature with great affection.

My father adored her, and she was attached to him with a devotion not common among mothers-in-law.

What religious faith grandmother cherished before arriving in Boston I do not know; nor whether my father, whose inheritance in the Established Church of England was natural, determined her final conformity to the Episcopal Church, I am equally unaware, but grandmother was an ardent member of this faith. I daresay her choice was made before father arrived in Boston, for as a means of livelihood, she cooked for a member of one of the oldest families in Boston, and one who was a devout Episcopalian. This lady, Miss Louisa Gardner, was more like a friend than an employer of Lydia DeWolfe, and on absolute terms of Christian equality they were members of the famous Church of the Advent on Brimmer and Mt. Vernon Streets, at the foot of Beacon Hill.

. . . If my paternal grandmother was by birth and breeding a lady, my maternal grandmother, whose origin was in the dark and tragic house of bondage, whose motherhood was the result of a vicious system of rape, and whose life was spent in the humble ranks of service, was also a lady, because of her personal integrity and through training in the holy Episcopal faith.

I am sure Lydia DeWolfe had known her Odyssey on that adventurous journey with her three daughters from North Carolina to Boston. The distance was made by stages from place to place, as I was told, and not with the meagre comforts, even for those days, of steam or stage-coach transportation. Her arrival in the strange northern city, cold and forbidding, for all its warmth of abolitionist sentiment, must have all but daunted her brave spirit after such a journey. She was to suffer acutely from a persecution by the colored people of Boston, which must have menacingly darkened her way and hopes in the city of refuge she believed Boston to be.

My mother and her younger sisters were very beautiful, with no distinguishable racial features or characteristics, and these good people of Boston could not believe they were the daughters of Lydia DeWolfe. They said she had stolen them, where or when seeming to have made little difference. This belief, I suppose was confirmed for them by the secret which my grandmother maintained concerning the paternity of her girls. The fact, also, that she had to leave them daily, with such care as the eldest, my mother, could provide, while away at work, added to their moral certainty of grandmother's irresponsibility. So these people attempted to have the girls taken away and placed in some charitable institution.

Helpless and friendless at this time, Lydia DeWolfe conceived and pursued a bold course of action to keep her girls. She took them and went to see Ben Butler, the famous Union general, who was then governor of Massachusetts, told him her story, pleaded for his protection, and for the possession of her children. How this unknown woman, with such a story as she had to tell, and the appeal she had to make to the nature of the soldier who had been condemned for an unchivalrous act of war in New Orleans, reached the governor's presence, is one of those obscure triumphs of human suffering that are never explained. She did, however, and that her children were not lost to her was due to the powerful intercession of this tragically famous man. . . .

William Smith Braithwaite and Emma DeWolfe married in 1875, when my mother was in her sixteenth year, and my father in his twenty-third. Their first child, Eva, named after one of my father's sisters, was born in 1876, a "centennial baby," as she was often referred to, it being the year of the Philadelphia Centennial, celebrating the one hundred years of the Declaration of Independence. I, their second child, was born more than two and a half years later. There were three other children, Josephine, the third baby, whose illness and death I've already mentioned; a brother, the fourth child, born in 1882 (the year of Oscar Wilde's visit to America, and after whom it was at one time thought of naming him), and Rosie, born in 1885, and who died in 1894.

Autobiography and Reminiscence

My father had many ideas affecting his family that were contrary to the folkways of his American environment. For one thing he would never believe that any children were good enough to associate with his own. We were, therefore, never allowed to play with any of our neighbors' children, and since our immediate neighbors were English, Scotch and Irish, racial and color influences did not inspire his mandate. He did not believe in the American school system, and neither my sister nor myself was allowed to attend school during his lifetime. He taught us at home. My elder sister having the advantage of me in years, he took great care to teach French from the time she began to talk; it is said that up to her third or fourth year Eva spoke nothing but French, which must have created a very difficult problem for my mother when he was away from home. There were certain rules and regulations regarding the conduct and manners, and activities of us children which he insisted must be strictly observed, and my mother enforced his law in these matters without question. He had the first and last word in the matter of our attire, and in this adhered uncompromisingly to the custom and style of English children. I have seen old tintypes of myself taken during those childish years, and a more Fauntleroyish youngster is inconceivable. There was one concession he did make, and that was to my Aunt Sadie, who had a fondness for twisting my top hair into what she called a cuck-a-too. . . .

Though my mother survived my father forty-two years, I am sure I knew him better the seven years of my childhood that he was with me than my mother during the fifty years of life. This does not mean I didn't love my mother for there was never a more passionately devoted and obedient child and youth than I. The young widow she became at father's death excited a sentiment within me that was lyrical with pity and affection. She had to go out to work, for father, like his own parent, had died insolvent, without even an insurance for protection against the immediate expenses and needs following his death, and as I used to watch her going down the walk banked with snow on bitterly cold winter mornings, the tears gushed from my eyes with sympathy and regret. . . .

⚬ ⚬ ⚬

I recall the early September day in 1890, three months before I had reached my thirteenth birthday, when I rode up to the East Boston terminal of the Boston Revere Beach and Lynn Railroad, and took the ferry across the harbor to Boston in quest of my first job. The mellow September sunlight gilded the ochre-colored spears of marsh grass along the way, tinted the muddy, tideless flats, with the gleaming motion of the sea in the background, all the familiar scenes I had known, audibly murmuring in my imagination a sympathetic and encouraging accompaniment to my spirit, embarking upon a new and unknown world of responsibility. My spirit was dimly troubled, the cause of which I could not discern, for I had voluntarily made the decision to leave school; but it must, by some clairvoyant and prophetic means, have pierced the future and tasted the mood and temper of regret and struggle which the denial of an opportunity for schooling was to impose. A gentle depression pursued me all the way to Boston, generated by a sense of loss — the vanishment of my boyhood, could it be? or, of some more vital hope or possession which had to do with my future destiny, the shape and color and significance of which I could not prefigure?

The brief past of my existence was suddenly loaded with something precious that was now beyond enjoyment or possession, and what beckoned ahead was confused and menacing. Out of the confusion and menace I had to shape a destiny, and I had no mental or spiritual tools with which to perform the task. Something was working in me tumultuously toward what end I had not the slightest intimation. Like Eva Gore-Booth's little waves of Breffney, the future was tumbling through my heart, and like a sandy beach my spirit was absorbing the foams of fate without any clear notion of the forces that the sea of life beyond the horizon was driving in upon the present.

Crossing the harbor on the ferry-boat I beheld the huddled city in the autumnal morning sunlight; the gray shaft of the Ames Building towering beside the gilded dome of the State House on Beacon Hill, a symbol, I imagined it, of my spirit, lofty in its direction and reach, but unable in its repulsing granite surface to absorb and effulge the radiance of the morning sun. There was my native city, the city that I loved, veined with memories, though shadowed as they were with the sorrows of death and the shadows dissolving in the illuminated activities of play and school; and now I was to ask, nay, not ask, but demand of it, the right to labor in a man's world.

❀   ❀   ❀

I obtained a position as an errand boy with T. Noonan and Company, the leading barber supply house in Boston, situated then at 35 Exchange Street, a narrow thoroughfare between State Street and Adams Square. My wage was two dollars and a half a week. It was the only job from which I have ever been dismissed. The boy I was could not be easily tamed into a machine, and I am afraid that ever since, my inability to conform to mechanical patterns of either activity or thought has been decisive. I will give, and have given, in measure excessively more than is asked or expected of me, often priceless energies or services, and am loyal to every intrinsic value of the spirit — but individualistic in every sense.

The lure of the Common, the moment I was deprived the freedom to go there and engage in my favorite pastime of hockey, became irresistible, and rather than stay in the store and eat my lunch at the noon hour, I, after a week or so at work, would rush off to the Common to play hockey. The early fall months were the height of our hockey season, and though school was in session, there was always a sufficient number of boys on the Common to make up two teams for a game. My interest and absorption in the game made me oblivious to time, and often the realization that my hour was up would come to me when "dribbling" the ball, or receiving a terrific whack across the legs when in an

off-side position I was trying to prevent the opposing side
from making a goal. Thus I was often late in returning to
the store. The manager of the store, whose first name,
Frank, is all I remember, warned me to no avail, and after
the holiday rush was over, gave me my dismissal. He was
reluctant to do this, he said, for he liked me, I was never
late in arriving at work in the mornings, and did my work
well, and would cheerfully stay overtime if necessary.

I next went to work for Springer Brothers, a ladies'
cloak house, at the corner of Washington and Bedford
Streets, where it was my duty to open and shut the front
door for customers as they entered and left the store. The
Common was now a lost paradise. I began to taste the competition of a commercial world. My duties as aforemen-
tioned, were reserved for a colored boy, but there were
some fifteen or twenty boys working in the establishment,
stock and errand boys, in ages from sixteen to twenty years,
and though my wage was a dollar more a week than I had
received at Noonan's, the prosperity of the other boys, especially the errand boys, aroused my curiosity and ambition. . . .

The stock-boys were not always prompt in returning
the garments . . . that had been shown and tried on the
customers, and frequently they were piled in disarray on ta-
bles, chairs, and cases, to the annoyance of Mr. Fields, the
superintendent. I secretly learned the sizes and racks and
during an unusual rush of business would replace the stock.
Though it took me from my duty at the door, it pleased Mr.
Fields who considered it more important to have an orderly
stock for the quick selection of the saleswomen and sales,
than to save perfectly able-bodied women from the exertion
of opening and shutting the door for themselves. This
thoughtful, willing, and voluntary service on my part won
the admiration and appreciation of Mr. Fields, and through
him the opportunity I longed for to deliver packages.

The opportunity came when every errand boy in the
establishment had failed to deliver a cloak to a customer,

whose street had been incorrectly taken by the saleswoman. Every one was sure the street was located in the Roxbury or Dorchester district, and boy after boy had been sent to find it, and all had returned unsuccessful. . . .

Late in the afternoon Mr. Fields, accompanied by Mr. "P. M." — the senior Springer brother — came to me and said, addressing Mr. Springer, "Willie will find that street if any boy can!" Mr. "P. M." then asked me if I would like to try. And of course, I was eager.

And so with a dollar which Mr. Springer told me to obtain from the cashier, for car fares, and the confident good wishes of Mr. Fields, and with an encouraging pat on the shoulder by Mr. "P. M." himself, I left the store amidst the suspense and good will of the sales staff and errand boys.

My intuition which has been the vital and revealing element in both my creative and critical career as a writer, made its first manifestation to my conscious solution of problems, on this occasion.

As I walked through West Street towards Tremont and the Common, I planned my campaign which was to work from the nearby Back Bay, through the South End to Jamaica Plain and Roxbury. Intuition had convinced me that the first step to take in each district was to go to each Branch Post Office and inquire for streets that looked or sounded like the one on the address of my package. Fifteen minutes after I had left the store I was at the Back Bay Post Office and had secured the names of half a dozen streets; and five minutes later I was ringing the bell at a number 7 Durham Street, off St. Botolph Street, located not more than a twenty minutes walk from the store. I delivered the garment and then went home. . . .

I had been the means of solving a perplexing problem for the firm, a problem though of minor proportions, that concerned the goodwill and the financial security, however infinitesimal the sum compared to its total capital, of the largest business of its kind in Boston, and I had done it not by any large-scale activity, but by a little *thinking!* And the little thinking had out-maneuvered a whole battalion of minds whose intrenched racial superiority was historically established, and whose caste system was manifested in the inferior employment reserved for my kind in their business. I told the story of my successful delivery of the garment and embroidered it from a dictation of the sense of Power which the achievement expanded, as I realized my employer was under a vital obligation to me in sustaining the reputation of his business. I realized also, in some dim way, that beyond a mere expression of appreciation in words and coin, there would be no official concession to my status as an employee, but I resolved on attaining an equality with the other boys by assuming that equality, whether it was agreed to or not — and await the consequences.

Mr. Springer gave me a dollar as a reward, thanking me heartily, for my success, and with Mr. Fields I left his office. I had the feeling that Mr. Fields thought me worthy of promotion as a regular errand boy. The spring had arrived and with the warmer days, the door was kept open. On my own initiative I went to the shipping clerk asking for packages to deliver. I became a full-time errand boy, and thus earned my first advancement in the world by creating the opportunity for it. . . .

✿　　✿　　✿

I obtained a position with Ginn and Company, the school and text-book publishers, at their press which was then located at the corner of Pearl and Purchase streets. I was engaged by a Mr. Wienshank, superintendent of the composition room, and it was my duty to make four trips a day, two in the morning and two in the afternoon, between the press and publishing offices on Tremont Place, taking proofs and other matter from the press and returning with authors' corrected proofs, correspondence, and other items for the various departments at the press which I distributed.

Between these regular errands to the editorial offices, I had nothing to do. A chair and table were mine just outside

Mr. Wienshank's office where four or five women were bus-
ily engaged reading proofs. Seated in the chair I idled for
the first two weeks, watching the compositors as with nim-
ble fingers they picked the type letters from the case following the copy before them, and setting up for printing the
manuscripts of many books. There were thirty or forty of
the compositors, mostly Germans, handsetting the type for
the text-books used by practically all the leading colleges
and most of the public schools in America, for at that time
Ginn and Company possessed almost a monopoly of the college and school book business.

Observing how quietly I sat at my table unoccupied,
Mr. Wienshank asked me one day if I did not like to read.
He thought it a good way to pass the time between my errands and taking me into his office showed me the shelves of
books with the privilege of reading any that might interest
me. He did not attempt to suggest any selections or to guide
my reading. I remember the first book I read was Church's
Greek Gods and Heroes. I must have read some ten or
twelve books when Mr. Wienshank came to me again with a
proposal which had a profound effect upon my future. "Willie," he asked, "would you like to learn the trade of a compositor?" Before, in my surprise and pleasure, I could reply,
he continued, "I've noticed that while you are out here between your errands to the office, you are studious, and do
not annoy the compositors as the other boys I've had working here used to do."

I told him "Yes, I would like to learn the trade of a
compositor." He then told me to get my mother's consent to
become an apprentice. She gave it, and I began laying the
foundation for both my education and the vocation I was to
follow.

I was first set the task of learning the "case" by distrib-
uting the type from the page-forms that had returned from
the foundry after the "plates" had been made. The case,
now that the linotype and monotype machines in modern
printing have rendered it useless — was a square, shallow

box about three feet long and two feet wide, with spaces of unequal sizes, holding the alphabetical letters in type cast in lead. The alphabetical boxes did not run successively, but like the keys on a typewriter, were arranged so that the letters most frequently used in words were nearer the hand of the compositor, as he stood at the center of the case, for rapid pick-up.

When I had mastered the case Mr. Wienshank gave me my first text to set up, and I have never lost the savor of this triumph, for the mechanical skill which won it was glorified by the acquaintance I made with the story of England's greatest naval hero. I was given a reprint of Robert Southey's *Life of Lord Nelson,* to set for a new edition of that famous work.

It was in early December that I began setting type, and in January the press moved into its new home the firm had built in Cambridge, on First Street, which was then but a river road along the banks of the Charles River basin between the old Longfellow and East Cambridge bridges. The Athenaeum Press was the name of the manufacturing branch of Ginn and Company, and it was the first of the many large structures in the industrial development of those marshy regions, which Mr. Howells has so picturesquely described in a familiar essay, along the banks of the Charles River in lower Cambridge.

When I began setting type I was given the additional duty of taking the galley proofs of the type set by all the compositors. My interest in books was beginning to develop into a passion, and to possess reading matter which I could not afford to buy, I used surreptitiously to make an extra impression of every galley of straight text that I proved, taking them home when I left work. I accumulated a good many works in this way, those galleys forming the first library I owned. The most precious of that early reading which I recall, was La Fayette's *La Princesse de Clèves,* the galley proofs of which I read with fascinated interest.

Mr. Wienshank made use of me in a variety of odd

tasks until the composition room was equipped and in
order; new mechanical devices were installed, the first linotype machine, a new-fangled proof operator, new cases, etc.,
and when all was in readiness, I was given a case by a window (we were on the top floor of the building) overlooking
the Charles River basin, and across the river Beacon Hill
with its terraced houses rising to the State House and its
gilded dome.

The morning I stood by that window before my case
waiting for copy, I did not know it was a day of annunciation, and that my spirit would magnify the Lord for making
me a chosen vessel! Mr. Wienshank came with an innocent-
looking sheaf of printed pages in his hand and left them
with me with instructions as to the character of type and
size of typepages. I set to work, and with an instantaneous
transformation wandered into a world of magical beauty!

When I had fixed the pages in the copy-holder, seized
the stick, and began to pick the type-letters from the case, I
was setting the line

Thou still unravish'd bride of quietness

beginning a poem that ended with lines that broke upon
both my sense and spirit with the flush of a sunrise —

*"Beauty is truth, truth beauty," — that is all
Ye know on earth, and all ye need to know.*

Here was the spirit of a man flaming with a strange, new
mystery of life and nature!

Keats' poems were followed with reprints of selections
from Wordsworth and Burns, and from both these poets I
received communications, impressions, and revelations,
which transported me into realms, and awakened sensibilities, that remade my world in terms of poignant imaginative

desires. Keats had created in me an aspiration that became the most passionate urgency in my life, and Wordsworth and Burns nourished it into an ambition that developed into a fanatical determination.

I began composing verses, pitiful attempts, as I have since known them to be, but which nothing could restrain, for the need of expression was as inevitable as the natural force of birth following conception. Croce's aesthetic concept of the identity of intuition and expression had a confirming experience in my case, however mediocre the character of the product.

As I composed these early verses I would put them into type, and again surreptitiously place the type on the end of a galley of composition, and striking off the proof beheld the first printings of my poetic effusions. I made scores of these "privately printed" verses of mine, which in the shuffle of time and movement were lost as was also my first "library" made of the galley proofs of the Ginn publications. No printing of anything I've written, with few exceptions, has given me the thrill and excitement of these early verses, for whatever the verbal and rhythmical merits they had, there was the odor of fresh ink and damp paper in making the impressions, which transferred to the words and the memory an indefinable but persuasive flavor abiding with the senses and the memory forever.

The passion which I now was driven by for a poetic and literary career, made me sensible of the cultural training necessary for an artist before he could hope to realize his ambitions. Keats was my master, nay, more, I worshipped him as a god! From his poems I turned to his life and read such biographies and studies as I could obtain from the Boston Public Library. The deeper I read the more, and often discouragingly I realized the difficulties confronting me of time and opportunity to acquire the knowledge and to cultivate the faculties necessary in mastering an education for the pursuit of a literary career.

✿   ✿   ✿

The fall of 1899 mother returned to Boston for the winter, and with the great resources of the Boston Public Library, I continued with my studies. We returned to Newport again in the spring of 1900, and I went back to work at the Business Men's Association. By the end of that summer I had another manuscript of new poems completed.

I felt more confident of the merits of these new poems than I had of the one Susan Coolidge had rejected. And I also felt they demanded a higher authority than Susan Coolidge to examine and pass judgment on them. So taking advantage of mother's intention to move to New York for the winter of 1900–1901, I wrote to William Dean Howells, informing him of my personality and ambitions, asking if he would receive me to discuss my writings.° As the man who had graciously and generously introduced Paul Laurence Dunbar to the universal knowledge and appreciation of the American reading public, I was confident of his sympathetic attention to my letter, and possibly, harassed and importuned though he was by the demands of nearly all the obscure literary aspirants of the day, might consent to receive me. I daresay it was due to his curiosity, and perhaps his hope of discovering another poet of significance of the colored race, that I received a prompt and cordial reply inviting me to call on him at his apartment at an appointed day and hour where he was then living at 49 West 59th Street.

Mr. Howells had just returned to town in advance of his family, from their summer home at Kittery Point, Maine. He was alone when I arrived, and invited me to sit beside him on a slip-covered couch in the shaded drawing-room.

I don't know whether he looked first at me as a figure, or at the wrapped package I carried. I have no precise knowledge of its exchange from my hands into his, but the image I have always kept was his sitting with the package on his knees.

He asked me a good deal about myself in the friendliest

° Braithwaite sent this letter to Howells, from New York, on October 7, 1899.

and most sympathetic manner, and while talking would turn the package over and over on his knees. Once or twice his fingers touched and played with the knot of twine that tied the package, as if he would undo it, but with a quick and resigned motion would withdraw them.

After little more than half an hour, he expressed his regret at not being able to read my verses, but he had made a rule never to look at unpublished manuscripts which were, in a manner, thrust upon him, though he had felt he might make an exception in my case since receiving my letter. But he now realized, it might be unfair to the many others to whom he had given his refusal. Besides he was getting along in years, he added, and his conscience would bother him if he couldn't give what was expected of his interest and admiration. "But I will give you a card of introduction to Paul Dunbar's publishers," he said, and taking one of his own cards wrote on the reverse side a few words of introduction.

The purpose of my meeting with Mr. Howells had failed, but it was infinitely richer in what it won for me — his friendship and appraisal a few years later when he had seen and read my writings in print.

◦ ◦ ◦

Three months after my visit to Mr. Howells I reached my twenty-first birthday. We were then living on Fifty-seventh Street, New York, a few doors from Tenth Avenue. I make note of the day because I made of the anniversary, the cyclic date in a man's life, when his probationary days are over, and he assumes in the eyes of the world his manhood and his obligations towards society, something more than a chronological milestone — it was a covenant! I turned the day into a sort of confessional, closing myself up in a darkened room, where I remained all day and evening undisturbed, taking stock of my past and planning the future with obscure, and perhaps muddled, anticipations.

I had that winter in New York, sought employment on

the newspapers and in the book stores. I haunted Park Row, where the *World,* the *Tribune,* and the *Sun* were then located, seeking work as a reporter. I think there was not a book store of importance in the city, to which I had not applied for a position as a book clerk. The interviews I had with the various executives of the book stores were always critically interesting, and left a debit entry in my memory which a few years later I made them balance on the credit side of the ledger of my literary advancement. Invariably I was told at the conclusion of the examinations for the position as book salesman, that my knowledge of books, of literature in general, current, or standard, or classical, was extensive and superior to that of any other applicant, but — and this was the usual procedure — the conclusion was interrogatory: "You don't mind if I ask you your nationality, not that it makes any difference?" When I would answer, as invariably I did, with the truth, that I "am an American Negro," the invariable evasion would follow. "Of course," began the way of escape, "I'll have to give all the applicants a fair consideration, though I've been most favorably impressed with your ability, and if you'll give me your address, I am certain you will hear from me." Of course, I never heard from them, but I did not forget, and paid them the compliment of hearing from me later, sometimes to discover what bad memories men have when they make mistakes.

My birthday meditations in the darkened room on Fifty-seventh Street, forged a resolution to which I adhered with determined zeal. I had not been conscious of color, for though I had recognized the limitations and restrictions of both the social and economic relationships of the white and colored worlds, the former had not yet impinged upon the active pathway of my ambitions. I had a taste that winter in New York of what the difficulties and injustices were for one of color who wanted to be accepted at his worth and on terms of equality in the vocation of his choosing. I was forced to face problems which somehow, I had deluded my-

The William Stanley Braithwaite Reader

self would solve themselves upon the higher, the universal, the spiritual plane of art. It was my belief that Beauty and Art were the leveller of all distinctions, and that the source of this transfiguring power was in the common unity of all men, sharing and participating in the same interests and the same privileges.

When I heard the famous English Platonist, G. Lowes Dickinson, some years later, deliver the Ingersoll Lecture at Harvard, on the immortality of the soul, he began by telling his intellectually and socially exclusive Brahmin audience, that there was no difference between men; "nor race, nor wealth, nor social position, makes any difference," he said, "it is only in the *growth of the soul.*"

And in my artistic ambitions I had dimly formulated this belief, certain that the truth of it would dissolve the obstacles that presented a diverted pathway in the practice of one's idealistic vocation. The racial conditions which closed the doors to the opportunities for employment of the kind I sought in New York that winter convinced me that whatever may be the quality and distinction of achievement in literature, if that literature was confined to racial materials and experiences, it would be appraised and judged by a different standard than the literature of American writers in general. For the good of the artistic sincerity, for the cultural values, which must be purified and sustained in a country so much below the standard of European achievements, this double standard of criticism must be destroyed. This purpose became the dominating influence upon my efforts in the career I dreamed for the future. My inclination might have turned toward a field where it might have been easier for recognition, where sentiment and sympathy on the part of press and public, might have been lavishly and profitably remunerative. But I had no such inclination, and the lack of it only served to strengthen and enrich the opportunity to challenge and discredit the illogical and dishonorable attitude of American criticism.

The resolution I formed in that darkened room was to express myself on the common ground of American authorship, to demonstrate, in however humble a degree, that a man of color was the equal of any other man in possession of the attributes that produced a literature of human thought and experience, and to force a recognition of this common capacity and merit from the appreciation of the reading public and the authority of critical opinion. And I resolved with equal determination, not to treat in any phase, in any form, for any purpose, racial materials or racial experiences, *until* this recognition had been won, recorded, and universally confirmed.

This is the first recorded explanation of a course which had invited some criticism from my own people who had accused me of retreat from, and discrimination against, racial materials and interests. It did not occur to these critics that I was taking a way unique, and single-handed to help solve their problems, which were essentially my own personal problems as well, and which were insidious and perplexing. These critics did not know how, in those weaker and earlier days, I was advised by subtly-tempered advocates of racial differences and economies, to devote my talents in behalf of racial experiences. Ray Stannard Baker, then one of the editors of the old *McClure's Magazine* (and later the official biographer of Woodrow Wilson), investigated the "problem," resulting in a book entitled *Following the Color Line.* He interviewed me in Boston, and after his departure, wrote me a lengthy letter, pleading for a consecration of my talents in literature, to purely racial interests. I replied, acknowledging the need of a purely aesthetic voice, to express and interpret the manifold interests of the Negro's life and experiences, but however well, I said, it might be achieved, such an author would still be judged as something apart from both the human and cultural standards applied to *American* authorship in general. He would still be outside the fold of that complete function of equality because he would be regarded as representative, a special phenomenon, rather than competitive in the sense of the rendering and interpretation of human nature and experience.

In this attitude of a special quality and significance, representative of superficial distinctions in human experiences, was the manifestation of a patronage which declared the traditional assumption of the inferior status of the Negro author and his people. Was I not told by a journalist friend, which gave me a shock, that it was common in literary and publishing circles, to refer to that superb and tragic artist, Charles Waddell Chesnutt, as "Page's darky!" because Walter Hines Page, as editor of the *Atlantic Monthly*, had discovered and printed Chesnutt's earlier stories in the magazine, and persuaded Houghton Mifflin to publish his books?

To the resolves I had made concerning the shaping of my literary career, was added the final intention never to permit myself, whatever the practical gain, to be patronized because of my color. That this might have been so, and profitably so, was revealed to me just before the publication of my first book of poems, when the poet Frederic Lawrence Knowles, one of my earliest poetic friends, said to me, "Ah, Braithwaite, when your book is published, you can become the rage of the Back Bay!" I caught the implication immediately and set him right.

"No," I replied, "I would scorn the condescension that would falsely exaggerate the value of my verses because of a sentimental interest in the race of the author. Yes, I might profit materially for a while, but it would destroy the character and respect of my efforts for a sound and sincere growth and reputation." And when some years later, Edward H. Clement, a fine gentleman of the old school, for a quarter of a century editor-in-chief of the *Transcript*, remarked one day apropos of nothing, "I admire you, Braithwaite, for you owe your success to no one — you have paddled your own canoe!" I felt happy and justified in the resolves I had made.

What Mr. Clement really meant was that I had not

been the special recipient of any favors or support in the dark and uncertain days of one's beginnings, as is so often the case with artists in any medium. The only reliance upon which I could depend was the inner urge and determination which could not by any conceivable means envisage failure. The practical question of living and holding on until the foundation was laid for the building of a career, substantial and secure of its own self, this was indeed, to "paddle one's own canoe." But without friends, their sympathy and encouragement, their constant urging of a belief in one's own powers, and the certainty of circumstances to shape opportunities, with the judgment and alertness to take advantage of them, progress and fulfillment were often likely to be dubious. And such friends I had!

When I left New York in April of 1901, and returned to Newport, I looked forward to but one achievement, and that at the earliest, — to publish a book. I returned to the Business Men's Association, where I could work the year round, and where I had ample time from my duties to study and write. Continually revising, omitting and adding pieces, I was shaping the manuscript that was to make the book. Some years before I had printed my first poems in the old Boston *Courant,* then edited by George Forbes, who later became associated with Monroe Trotter in establishing the radical Boston *Guardian;* and a little later, Roy Martin, then editor of the Boston *Journal,* afterwards manager of the Associated Press, accepted some pieces for the *Journal.* Following the New York winter, the *Transcript* began to print my verses regularly through the cordial appreciation of Charles E. Hurd, its literary editor.

I had met the young lady at Newport in 1902, whom I married in 1903, and with this domestic responsibility — though in a sense, I had known nothing but domestic responsibility ever since I first went to work — I felt it imperative to get started in literature. Had I not known the responsibility towards mother to which I have referred, I daresay, I would not have had the courage to do what I did

some four or five months after our marriage. For returning
to Boston in the autumn of 1903, I decided to devote myself
wholly to a literary life. It was a momentous step to take,
but I was ready for complete disaster if it came, so strong
was my passion for a literary career. . . .

Finally they * consented to publish my manuscript, but
at my own expense, which was a common arrangement
then, as it is now, and at the mere cost of manufacturing,
quoting me a price which, if it had been less by one
hundred per cent, I would not have had the money to meet.
I was convinced that the book must be published and the
ways and means found. I thought the matter over for a few
days, conceived and worked out a proposal which I asked
Mr. Turner to consider. The proposal was for me to obtain
the promise of two hundred persons to buy a copy of the
book in advance of publication thus guaranteeing its expense.

When Mr. Turner heard my proposition, and had
called Mr. McCotter into consultation, he sympathetically
accepted it with the comment: "Even with the signature of
the individuals to buy the book it would be impractical to
enforce their purchase if they refused to do so, but I would
like to see you get started, Mr. Braithwaite, and we will
proceed and take the risk."

The responsibility was now mine to make good. It took
me seven months to do so, weary months of tramping and
interviewing people. For the most part I felt that only literary people would be interested in a book of poems by an
unknown poet, and that not all of these whom I would so-
licit would care to buy. In this my experience proved me
right. Fred Knowles, who had a genuine admiration for my
verse, and who had grown to like me personally, and who
was himself preparing to publish his second book of poems
that year, *Love Triumphant*, was of signal service in my efforts.

He was an active member of the Boston Authors' Club,

* Herbert B. Turner & Co.

a member of the Whitman Fellowship, and never failed to attend the weekly *salon* of Louise Chandler Moulton at her home in musty old Rutland Square, where all the Boston literati of the time assembled. He gave me notes of introduction to these authors, and spoke to them personally, commending my poetic promise.

I pasted clippings of my best contributions to the *Transcript* into a little booklet, and prepared another folder with blank pages for the signatures of the advanced subscribers for the book which I entitled *Lyrics of Life and Love*.

Knowles, himself, was the first to subscribe, putting his name down for two copies. I then went to see Colonel Thomas Wentworth Higginson, at his house on Buckingham Street, Cambridge, whom I had met when he spoke at some gathering in Boston. Colonel Higginson, who at this time was advancing in his eighties, was an eminent figure in the golden era of New England romanticism, as abolitionist, soldier, and man of letters. He was intimate with all the great New England authors, and was himself poet, novelist and essayist; and he was among the first to give enthusiastic appreciation to the beauty and high imaginative quality of the Negro spirituals. He had joined the mob — indeed, was one of those that rammed the pole against the jail-house door — in the attempt to rescue the fugitive slave, Anthony Burns, and prevent his return South to his master; he had reported for one of the Boston papers the famous reading of his poems by Edgar Allan Poe; and like his fellow-citizen of Massachusetts, and fellow-alumnus of Harvard College,° had commanded and led a regiment of Negro troops, the 55th Massachusetts, in the Civil War.

My hope in seeing Colonel Higginson was to obtain his subscription for the book; aware and considerate of his advanced age, I did not expect his interest to extend beyond this kindness, but instinctively and spontaneously, he gave me more, his counsel, and recommended my project to

° Colonel Robert Gould Shaw.

many of his friends. At his insistence I returned to his home frequently, to report on my progress, spending many hours listening to his recollections of a long life in the service of humanity and letters. The vivid procession of the figures and personalities of his great contemporaries, marched before my vision as we sat in his quiet drawing-room, reminiscent of the Cambridge days that had vanished; his low-pitched voice, aged as he was, without tremor or hesitation, but full, as I imagined, of the faint and subtle echoes of the mighty spirits that had glorified the environs of Cambridge and Boston and Concord in the nineteenth century.

The winter months of 1903–04 were passing and my progress was very slow. I was confident that the subscriptions would be obtained so as to assure the publication of the book in the spring. Most of the people I was to see lived in the various suburbs around Boston, and to conserve the few pennies I possessed, I used to walk out to the distant places and back. In the meantime, Amos R. Wells, who was editing *The Christian Endeavor World,* bought some of my verses for publication in his magazine. I had obtained subscriptions from notable people: Julia Ward Howe, Thomas Bailey Aldrich, Bliss Perry, Nixon Waterman, Cyrus Dallin, the sculptor; George Gordon, of the famous Old South Church; Eugenia Brooks Frothingham, who had recently published an unusually able and successful first novel, and her cousin, Paul Revere Frothingham, the elegant and brilliant Unitarian minister; Arlo Bates, author of those typically Bostonian novels, *The Pagans* and *The Puritans,* professor of English at the Massachusetts Institute of Technology (and incidentally the author of one of the best texts on composition for college students, *Talks on the Writing of English*); Louise Chandler Moulton, the familiar of the English poets of the Victorian era, especially the minor pre-Raphaelites; Phillip Burke Marston and Arthur O'Shaughnessy; Mark A. DeWolfe Howe, a charming and compassionate gentleman then one of the editors of *The Youth's Companion* and since the biographer of New England Culture; and Hezekiah Butterworth, the editor of *The Youth's Companion,* an elemental Yankee, just fresh from a South American tour when I visited him in his disorderly, book-laden bedroom in a lodging-house on Worcester Street, in the shabby-genteel South End, where he did most of his work for the magazine.

There were some incidents connected with these solicitations that are woven into my memory with dramatic interest. On a larger scale, and where my personal sensitivities were involved so deeply and so critically, I was matching the future, a whole pattern of anticipations, against the uncertain sympathies and impressions of a human nature refrigerated in its social and intellectual superiority and pride. There was an innate assumption of something within me, of whose reflection or subtle communication I was unaware, for the manifest interest was more often, and initially, expressed in my personality than in my verses. I was led into discussions of subjects wholly alien to the purpose of my visit, and I could often discern, like a visible movement, their minds wavering around, but never quite touching upon, the subject of which my appearance made them questioningly aware. There was a lack of frankness in this matter, which seemed to save them from an embarrassing commitment, especially if it proved mistaken. They were also sure to ask me where I was educated, as if that in some way determined the merit, or the sanction, of my efforts in verse-making.

Among the episodes that beaded this experience, some two or three stand out against the background of my memory. One gave a disturbing tone to the spirit of the progress which a people were striving for, and rifted their ideals at the whim of a well-meant but ostensible ostracism. I was so sure of this man's approval of the artistic ideal, indeed of his hearty sympathy with any creative striving, that I could not conceive of a disillusionment on any score. I had found it difficult to catch him either at his home or office, and after journeying to Roxbury several times to see him, his secretary finally obtained an appointment for me to meet him at his office. So I called on Edward Everett Hale! He was then the chaplain of the United States Senate, but when at home in Boston, spent most of his time attending to the affairs of the charitable organization he had founded — The Lend-A-Hand Society.

Dr. Hale followed the long line of New England divines who had tempered theology with literary interests, and was the author of some notable works in fiction and biography, his *The Man Without a Country* with its polemical patriotism, becoming an American classic, and his discursive record of *James Russell Lowell and His Friends*, an entertaining chronicle of New England authorship and culture. He was a patriarchal figure, with his huge frame and massive head — giving one the notion of a re-incarnated Homer, for one could not shake the impression, hearing his full-bodied, tumultuous voice, of his Homeric qualities — as he strode along the Boston streets.

Ushered into his private office, I beheld him sprawling at his desk, his leonine head slung between broad, boulder-like shoulders, over his desk, as his side-wise body was supported, it seemed, by a veritable trunk-like leg slanting straight and stiff backward, half the length of the office floor. With a ponderous turn of his head he looked at me briefly, asked my business as if recollecting some expectant affair, and then turned back to the examination of some papers on his desk. I explained the purpose of my visit, placing the booklet of signatures before him. Without hesitancy, he signed his name subscribing for a copy of the book and handed it back to me, his head still slung over his desk, and as he did so, remarked, "Young man, it is no disgrace to hoe potatoes."

Dr. Hale had focussed, in his remark, the Du Bois-Washington controversy about racial ideals and problems upon my unsuspecting head, and there was no doubt as to which he gave his sympathy and support. . . .

So the book was published at last, and I felt like a conqueror before whom lay the world to ravage and rule! I know that all young authors have experienced the same exultation and convictions. But how disillusioned they soon become when they realize that it is only the start of a race, and to keep going means constant and hard work. Surely, I thought, with the book a reality, and thus introduced and recorded in the annals of acknowledged authorship the portals of every editorial office were down, and editors would vie for one's manuscripts. It was in this mood, that I sent some verses to Henry M. Alden, editor of *Harper's Magazine*. Though he could not make use of any of the verses I had sent, Mr. Alden wrote me a cordial personal letter when returning them, commending their merits, and invited me to submit another batch of my wares. By return mail more verses were on the way to him, and by return mail they were on their way back to me with a printed rejection slip.

Negro Digest called this "a memorable account of a boy's youthful impressions of the great Abolitionist." It appeared in the January, 1948, issue of the magazine.

I Saw Frederick Douglass

How long ago it is, looking back from this mid-twentieth century, to that night in 1888, when my boyish eyes and ears were focussed upon that giant of a man, and being swept by him still further backward through time over southern plantations and swamplands, across turbulent seas into the dim, mysterious African centuries, of racial anguish!

I had seen Frederick Douglass! — heard him lecture at the Park Street Church! Heard his thunderous voice go echoing upwards to vanish through the delicately beautiful

Christopher Wren steeple on the church that pointed to heaven above the old Granary Burial Ground where slept in eternal peace the parents of Benjamin Franklin.

My great-grandmother's husband, Mr. Overman, took me to hear the great man speak. He was her second husband, and everyone in the family, elders as well as children, addressed or referred to him as Mr. Overman. I don't think I ever heard his wife call him Sandy, which was his given name. He was a tall, gaunt man, with a laugh that was pointed with arrows of derision. He had known bondage, and strangely enough, freedom had not tempered him graciously, but made him brittle with arrogance. He seemed always wrapped in memories which made up, I have since surmised, a parcel of retributions he could not deliver. He made of every anti-slavery hero a god, but Frederick Douglass was *the* Divinity, the word made flesh of a conquering freedom, for to Mr. Overman, he was not simply the symbol of successful revolt against injustice but the foundation rock upon which was built a new citadel of human brotherhood.

Mr. Overman had an eloquence of his own when he expressed himself in worship of his hero, and he filled my young ears with Frederick Douglass' exploits as we walked along the Common malls, dimly lighted with gas-lamps, on our way to the Park Street Church.

We found seats in the balcony, the church being completely filled with members of both races. The balcony had a vantage point that gave me great satisfaction — I could look down upon the great figure of the man. When he raised his leonine head with its shock of white hair, as he often did in dramatic gesture, I could look full into his face as he poured forth his eloquence. That exciting moment brought a thrill never to be forgotten, as I have not forgotten it during the intervening sixty years.

I have no recollection of Frederick Douglass being introduced to the audience by some eminent citizen. My remembered impression is that he simply walked onto the platform and stood briefly facing the multitude, for there still echoes in my ears the thunderous applause that greeted him.

I had been bred on the nourishment of greatness in the individual man. My own father, having been but two years dead at this time, had chronicled the deeds of Wellington, Gladstone, and Parnell, in the background of his British heritage, and of Garrison, Grant, and Phillips Brooks, in the land of his adoption, for me, but here I was in the presence of greatness, my eyes upon his stalwart but aging figure, and my ears listening to the voice that had charmed and persuaded the peoples at home and abroad with a fiery eloquence in the cause of truth and justice. Oh, how indelibly etched upon my boyish imagination is the image of the man who had been the Moses of a shackled race and who, after his self-liberation, had by his intellect and the superb power of his faith, conjured out of their disabilities and denials the vision of a promised land of democratic citizenship.

The history of Frederick Douglass' deeds as related to me at this time, like the deeds of all great men for boys, was less important for their character and purpose than in the manner of their performance. The romantic and glamorous, however much of pain and sorrow may lie beneath the surface, these elements are what make the strongest appeal to the boy's mind. Mr. Overman had told me, in preparation for our attendance at his lecture, some facts about Frederick Douglass, which gave a meaning to the scraps of conversation in which I had heard his name mentioned in reference to some sequence of events. However, my boyish imagination could supply what background it might, of his daring and tempestuous career, but the reality of the moment was absorbed by an electric tension, whose central force was the Man himself, standing, a bronze gladiator, receiving with aloof majesty the spontaneous plaudits of the audience.

I have, of course, since, become acquainted with his life and deeds, and the stirring problems and activities of his times. The moral pressure had never before been so strong and insistent upon a young nation, young by the standards of history, to live up to its ideals and purposes. The nation was under the stress of three disturbing problems: to heal the wounds caused by a bitter internecine war, with chattel slavery an inevitable factor during the progress of the war, and after its abolition through the terrible sacrifice of blood, the adjustment of the freedmen into the civil and social pattern of the reunited Republic; and then, during the three decades following the Civil War, a third problem rending the nation, of political corruption and industrial piracy in mutual connivance.

There were titans in those days of the young Republic: there had to be titans if the Republic was to survive its internal ills, the civil, political, and industrial ills, which were the growing pains of the young nation. And the times produced them, the titans, William Lloyd Garrison, John Brown, Walt Whitman, Ralph Waldo Emerson, Edwin L. Godkin, and Frederick Douglass, upon whose shoulders was draped the mantle of an inspired new concept of government and society.

I cannot now recall the words that Frederick Douglass spoke that night in delivering his discourse. That is too much to expect, after all these years, of a boy in his ninth year. But there was something more important which makes, in retrospection, the experience rare and momentous. It was the emanation of an oratory vitalized with the living mythology of a personality that had scaled a modern Olympus in pursuit of the North Star of Freedom. It was the sound of his voice, saturating my memory, that began like a murmur floating from the springs at the foot of Olympus, gathering force and color as it ascended to the crest where with volcanic power it broke into a roar of thunder, pouring out a message of wrongs and hopes.

The dramatic gesture of hands and white-crowned head, flashing like lightning amidst the storm of words, held one in a spell of admiration, in which one easily surrendered to his unfolding drama of personal and racial history. The voice was impregnated with the aching hopes of man, and not only was it generated with visions from the dim recesses of the African heritage, but alchemized with aspirations that Greece and Rome gave of their passionate and lucid philosophies and laws; Italy, France, Germany and England, in their modern awakening of the common man tempered it with their arts and sciences, to prove that in the hearts of all men was one universal ideal of liberty.

The mobile features of his face — the aquiline nose, the firm, square jaws, the glowing eyes — framed by the blocked heavy mass of white hair, made a very document of spectacular human experience. The head shook at times with an appeal for understanding, at others with an ecstatic revelation, and if these moods failed of their effect, there followed a sudden and resonant burst of angry imprecations. It reverberated throughout the church like a physical force — a whirlwind that swept on its wings the agony of years of oppression mingled with the mysterious sighs of faith and hopes. My boyish emotions must have reacted involuntarily, and caused me to move disturbingly in my seat, for I remember distinctly Mr. Overman putting a restraining hand upon my knee. I remember also, that what impressed my boyish mind and senses, and had made me restless in their response to the magical drama of the speaker, composed itself into a serenity of voice and figure as the final words of his address faded into silence. The outburst of stormy applause from the audience dropped the curtain on a memorable performance in which the actor was himself the hero of a tragedy history had written, but to whom God had given the virtues and powers to conquer and ennoble.

Mr. Overman and I left the church, in my spirit eternally woven the image of Frederick Douglass, and crossed the gas-lit Common homewards. The Common was silent and spectre-like, and the surrounding streets, Boylston, Tremont, Park, and Beacon, yet untouched with the modernity that has since altered their aspects. Up the sloping mall on the northern side where hilly Beacon Street rose to its crest, stood the State House with its famous Bulfinch front and

golden dome. And opposite, on the Common side of the
street, was the site where ten years later they were to place
the great St. Gaudens monument which in bas-relief immor-
talized Col. Robert Gould Shaw leading his Negro troops
(the 54th Massachusetts Regiment, which Frederick Douglass had been instrumental in organizing) against the ram-
parts of Fort Wagner. Its beauty and historical significance
could not exist without a related tribute to the heroic memory and figure of Frederick Douglass, whose living greatness
I had that night of my boyhood seen and heard.

———

Among the many books Braithwaite planned to edit but did not
get into print was one to be composed of articles and reviews
from the Boston *Transcript*. For this project he completed, on
December 16, 1950, the draft of an introductory essay, from
which the selection below is taken.

Memories of the Boston Transcript

In 1704, *The Boston News Letter* became the first newspaper to be printed in America, and in 1830, began the publication of the *Boston Evening Transcript*. The latter began
as a social sheet after the pattern of *Town Topics*, edited by
a "Man About Town," whose delight it was to satirize and
caricature the social figures and foibles of the town. The
sheet ran into debt, and changing its character, the long and
brilliant history of the paper began that was to make it a financial and cultural institution in New England life and an
influence upon the literary taste of the nation.

During most of the *Transcript*'s one hundred and ten
years of publication it was issued from an old building at
the corner of Washington and Milk streets; the Milk Street
entrance was on the site where Benjamin Franklin was
born. At the Washington Street entrance one walked up a

steep flight of stairs to the editorial offices; the luxury of an elevator was to be had only if one entered the building on Milk Street. The elevator, ancient as the building, was a perilous affair operated by a cable, and used mostly by members of the mechanical staff working on the top floors. The only editorial office to which it was convenient was the literary editor's, and for over a quarter of a century it carried me up and down almost daily with my books and copy.

The *Transcript* was unique in that it was a family paper with a national reputation, serving specifically the domestic, financial, and cultural interests of Boston and its suburban population. Its daily circulation during the most flourishing period, from the eighteen-nineties through to the first third of the twentieth century, was around thirty-five thousand copies, but the Wednesday and Saturday editions when the magazine section was added and it carried special features and reviews on books, music, and the drama, rose to between eighty and ninety thousand copies. A weekly edition, reprinting the best contents of the regular daily editions, was issued on Fridays and sent to subscribing Bostonians all over the world.

The most notable among the early editors was Epes Sargent, a literary figure of considerable prominence during Boston's golden age of letters. And the paper had the distinction among the nation's major newspapers of having at one time a woman as its editor-in-chief.

The financial pages were a source of great influence and power throughout New England. A young financial reporter graduated from its staff in the person of C. W. Barron, to establish the *Boston News Bureau* and the *Wall Street Journal*, among the most successful publications of their kind in America. It had the most comprehensive and extensive *Notes and Queries* department of any daily newspaper. *The Listener* column, of the familiar essay type, chatty and personal on topics from nature to holidays, from hearthside affections to public affairs, was originated by Joseph Edgar Chamberlain, and conducted by him until he left to join the editorial staff of the old *New York Mail and Express*. The column was continued by Edward H. Clement, an idealist of insistent convictions, a passionate anti-imperialist following the Spanish-American War, an attitude in opposition to the paper's editorial policy . . . which then, and down to the day when it ceased publication, supported every Republican administration. Mr. Clement was the last editor-in-chief of the *Transcript* with authority to engage and dismiss editors of the various departments. . . .

In addition to the regular features mentioned above, the *Transcript* ran a department devoted to the interest of the school and college. Henry T. Claus, who later became "editor of the *Transcript*," was in charge of this department and had as his assistant John P. Marquand, the popular contemporary novelist. Another column of wide importance was *The Librarian*, in the capable hands of the late Edmund Lester Pearson, who afterwards joined the staff of the New York Public Library and gained a substantial reputation as an authority on crime and its literature, a subject on which he bestowed a fine scholarship and imagination. Nor were rare books . . . neglected, for George H. Sargent devoted a regular column to them weekly, called *The Bibliophile*. Nor did the interests of those who collected or traded in antiques . . . lack expert service, for Charles Meser Stowe wrote a weekly column of authoritative information and advice. Mr. Stowe left the *Transcript* to join the staff of the *New York Sun* where I believe, for the first time the interests of the antique collector and buyer were served in a New York paper. Also there was the column called *The Churchman*, devoted to the interests of religion . . . from the layman's point of view as well as the cleric's.

References to the foregoing columns and departments of the *Transcript* are made with particular significance, for I believe it was the first daily newspaper in America to cover by specialists in the field, and regularly, such a variety of interests exclusive of the current news and the subjects of literature, music and drama.

The three departments that gave the *Transcript* its national influence and international reputation, were the magazine section, the literary section, and the section on music and drama.

The magazine section, developed under the brilliant editorship of Burton Kline, became one of the most interesting and instructive periodicals ever to become a part of the daily newspaper. It was not a separately printed unit such as the *New York Times* inaugurated as a supplement to the paper, and now commonly adopted by newspapers across the land. The contributors included notable names, not only in the journalism of the day, but in literature and public life here and abroad.

Even before Burton Kline's brilliant régime at the helm of the magazine, it ran serially a number of essays and articles on various subjects and experiences. Mr. Kline himself had contributed a series on his own experiences as a young man meeting the great literary figures in and around Boston during his assault upon the citadel of Boston's literary recognition. Bradford Torrey for years ran a weekly essay on nature in the hills, streams, and valleys, the woods and lakes of New England, and the seasons that paraded across them, with a spirit akin to Richard Jeffries' description of the wild life around London. Bliss Carman — the poet of vagabondia, of rare mystical insight and a laureate of the magic and fascination of the sea and its adventures and mysteries — contributed over a long period a series of essays called *The Modern Athenian*. From this material he made his sensitive and enchanting book *The Rhythm of Life*. Mark Sullivan wrote sagaciously on political affairs and personalities, forming the material for those volumes which he later published to record the political and social history of America at the turn of the century. . . .

Mr. Kline wrote me recently and referred to the "literary material buried in the files of the old *Transcript*." He said that, in recollection, he "was amazed to recall all the notables who wrote for the old paper." One of them was

Remy de Gourmont; another Frenchman was "Edouard Herriot, then the young mayor of Lyons, afterwards to be a fixture in history as French premier during one of *the* trying times." And he added, "I want to call your attention to the fact that some of the 'regulars' most richly deserved the 'name' they never, somehow, won. Collins in London, Sanborn in Paris, Thompson in Ottowa, Amy Bernhardi in Rome, all turned in what passed as journalism but really was literature of the top level." These writers that Mr. Kline mentions, were more than mere 'foreign correspondents' dispatching political news, for they kept abreast with the artists and literary progress of the European countries, reporting the characters and impression of the new figures and movements for the early acquaintance of American readers through the pages of the *Transcript*. They helped to produce the "top level of literature" which made the *Transcript* notable among newspapers.

No paper in America ever had a department of music and drama with the unique awareness of presentation and interpretation in coverage as the *Transcript* had under the editorship of H. T. Parker. "H. T. P.," as he was familiarly known, are initials indelibly traced upon the arts that he surveyed, criticized and interpreted, just as the initials "R. L. S.," "G. K. C.," and "G. B. S.," are indelibly traced on the art of fiction, the essay, and the drama. Names famous in American dramatic criticism — William Winter, Franklin Fyles, James Huneker, Alexander Woollcott — have left no such legacy to the profession as "H. T. P." Apart from his written criticisms there were the young men who worked under him on the *Transcript* and who went forth to achievements of their own, carrying the inspiration of the master: Kenneth MacGowan, Hiram Motherwell, Walter Pritchard Eaton, and the radiant Brooks Atkinson, the drama editor of the *New York Times*.

Yearly after the season closed on the theatre and concert halls, "H. T. P." was off to Europe, scouring England and the Continent, to obtain the latest information of works and performers in music, drama and the stage; attending festivals, and gathering the facts and promises of new artists and forthcoming works. Other events and creations unrelated to music and drama which were in the European news also attracted his descriptive pen. He sent back to the *Transcript* articles on his discoveries, for publication in the off season. Many names and figures, now familiar on the stage and in the concert halls . . . first had their talents proclaimed in these articles. . . .

"H. T. P." was unique as a personality, and an empire unto himself on the staff. His knowledge of music and drama was limitless, his perceptions of their significance and aesthetic forms, sensitive; and his judgment of the individual work and performer could be devastatingly dogmatic as well as lyrically appreciative. Mentally and emotionally he was poised between the old and new schools of creation — the classic and modern — and the pressure from both sympathies combined to produce a stylistic expression that was the blended agony and delight of his readers. His sentences had the winding elegance of George Saintsbury's, but not their leisure and urbanity; but rather were swift and rippling with the undercurrent of ideas not always too clear from the intensity of his mood. But as they rippled and dashed down the column, they — like Saintsbury's — carried a tide of musical and dramatic erudition that was amazing and infectious. "H. T. P." is now almost a legend which his own peculiar manners, his quick, bouncing, but rhythmic walk, his short figure draped in an opera cape, his almost isolated air of being, and his caustic tongue helped to create. And now that the *Transcript* no longer exists what he has become as a legend helps to sustain the vitality that makes the paper a tradition.

Edwin F. Edgett was the literary editor, succeeding Charles E. Hurd who had laid the foundation for the distinction which the paper was to gain as an influence in American letters. Mr. Edgett descended from a Tory family, which may or may not have had something to do with the eccentric retirement of his social nature. With great self-denial and hard work he made his way through Harvard after which he spent a year with a classmate, Walter Smith, as a drama critic on a London paper. This he gave up because he objected to the formality of the English custom of donning evening clothes nightly to attend performances.

The drama had been his first interest, and he preceded "H. T. P." as drama editor of the *Transcript*. In the interval between the London sojourn and joining the *Transcript* staff, Edgett worked as press representative for John Craig and his Castle Square Stock Company — of which Alfred Lunt was at one time a member. Staying in town once a week, on Monday evenings, to attend the first two acts of the play (he seldom stayed longer) he always preceded the trip to the theatre with a pot-pie and a mug of ale at the Bell-in-Hand in Pie Alley, one of the few genuine English pubs in America, tucked in between the old *Herald* and *Post* buildings across the street from the *Transcript*. This is the only deviation from routine that I ever knew Edgett to make during my twenty-five years of association with him.

There was a curious duality in Edgett's mental equipment and sympathies; he was a *very* good editor, perceptive of new trends, liberal and respectful of another's point of view regarding books and authors. As a reviewer of books he was always predictable, not always so much as to his opinions, but as to the method of treatment. For every type of book — fiction, biography, essays, travel, etc. — he had a formula for interpretation and summary which he applied consistently. His special attention as a reviewer was for fiction, and whether it was Galsworthy's *Forsyte Saga* or Bennett's *Clayhanger* trilogy, or Eden Phillpotts's Dartmoor novels, the pattern of his comment was the same whatever the circumstance of action, the motives or psychological springs of passion or the characterization of the people in the stories. The sequences of his reviews from the introduction to the concluding summary of praise or censure fell precisely in the same order of design.

Yet Edgett possessed enthusiasms for the most part concealed beneath his personally forbidding social exterior. His life was books, and his activities seldom ranged outside the demands and atmosphere of their interests. Literary figures of national and international reputation, visiting Boston, many of whom he had corresponded with, called to see him. After ten minutes of conversation I have seen him uneasy before the visitor, and remain so until he left. It used to amuse me, for invariably it was unnoticed. Never in all the twenty-five years of my association with him, in his official capacity as literary editor of the *Transcript*, did I know him to invite a visitor to luncheon, or otherwise extend the courtesies that might be expected of one who held the important and influential position that was his.

I said Edgett had enthusiasms — as most people do, I suppose — but his sprang from a perversity that constituted his moral nature. How he developed from his Tory ancestry is hard to understand. He insisted time and again in our talks that the privilege of exercising his private rights and desires must not be denied him.

Beyond the weekly mug of ale that Edgett drank at the Bell-in-Hand, I had never known him to drink or speak of taking a drink. In all my long association with him never had I known anything to arouse his anger and denunciation as did the Prohibition Act. It denied him, he claimed, the privilege of a private and personal *right*, a right which, strangely enough, he seldom exercised and now had a very urgent desire or taste to indulge in. So it was with almost a violent determination he set about to defy the edict. He purchased the necessary apparatus and ingredients to produce intoxicants. From time to time he would with childish delight tell me of his progress. Then came the triumph of having made some gin. He read widely in the recipes, or formulas, for distilling spirituous liquors, and combining the techniques with the artistry of application, he made progress, but slowly. The gin he produced was only a token of achievement, for his goal was to make a palatable whiskey.

He achieved the ambition, which for him was a private nullification of the Prohibition Act. How palatable I have a wry recollection to this day. No conquering Caesar ever invaded Gaul with the mental glory and emotional pomp . . . Edgett displayed the day he brought me a four-ounce bottle of his homemade whiskey. I sampled it and praised, while the ecstasy of his satisfaction at my praise added several degrees of heat to the liquid that was burning my throat.

On apples, Edgett was an authority. In his library were all the standard and special books — the latter those issued by the various states on the kinds grown within their own borders — devoted to the cultivation of apples.

It was quite by accident I discovered the interest Edgett had for this typically American fruit, one that is universally associated with certain delectable dishes made by New England housewives. He secretly worshipped at more shrines than was suspected by his colleagues around the *Transcript* offices. As he was violently anti-Volstead he was violently anti-Catholic, and while he was able to find compensations for the former there was nothing he could do about the latter. And in a way it was peculiar, unless it too, was an atavistic expression of his Tory ancestry, for he was thoroughly anti-religious, all sects and faiths having no efficacy in his view of human needs. Somewhere between the idolization of Johnny Appleseed and the philosophy of Winwood Reade's *The Martyrdom of Man* he found a balance in the consecration of his duties as the literary editor of a great newspaper. His personality gave me the feeling such as one has, standing in a New England apple orchard late in the autumn. The scent of the departed fruit still lingers faintly in the air washed with the mellow sunlight touched with a frosty sting. From the twisted branches of the trees comes a sense of rejection, an outward barrenness that shields a rich and nourishing prodigality of fruit. A New England apple orchard sheltered among the hills, rich with fragrance in the spring, vigorous in the decay of autumn, warm at heart under the bitter icy coating of winter. It is an apt symbolism, I think, of the spirit and flesh of the man who for nearly forty years edited with distinction the book pages of the *Transcript.*

———————

Critics, biographers, and bibliographers found Braithwaite a valuable resource in their studies of Edwin Arlington Robinson. Braithwaite had much to say in print and correspondence about his friend, whose poetry he greatly admired. The selection below is from *The Reminiscences of William S. Braithwaite,* a transcription of interviews taped for the Oral History Research Office at Columbia University. These memories of Robinson were recorded on May 15, 17, and 28, 1956.

E. A. Robinson: "Poor Devil, Poor Devil"

Now I'd like to take up Edwin Arlington Robinson. Robinson's first book was published up in Maine, and more or less privately printed. It was called *Head Tide.* His second book was published by Richard G. Badger, in Boston, one of those publishers that are known as vanity publishers — that is to say, the authors paid for their books. I don't think that any of those publishers at that time or today should be looked upon in the way they are looked upon because authors pay to publish their books. Sara Teasdale paid to have her first book of poems published by Macmillan. Houghton Mifflin has done it. The only firm that I can recall that I'm certain has not done it is Scribner's. Harper's I'm doubtful about. I don't know. But I know it was so at Century, because the marvelous Dr. S. Weir Mitchell of Philadelphia, around the turn of the century, published those two very successful romantic novels, *The Adventures of François* and *Hugh Wynne. Hugh Wynne,* of course, was about the American Revolution, and *The Adventures of François* about the French Revolution. He also wrote verse, which the Century Company brought out, a little volume, for which he had to pay.

Well, Badger was the most famous of vanity publishers at the beginning of the century; he was a very successful one. He published Robinson, Willa Cather, Edith Thomas. The second book of Robinson's was *The Children of the Night*. My first reading of it convinced me that here was a major poet. The qualities that were contained in the poems in that book were such as I had not run across in any other American poet. I won't say any other American poet of the times, but *any* other American poet of any times in America.

That was in 1898, I think, when *The Children of the Night* was published. Then he wrote *Captain Craig*. He was a great friend of Josephine Preston Peabody, who was the darling of New England, and when we come to Amy Lowell, we'll have lots to say about her and her position in New England poetry. It was Josephine who had been inherited by Houghton Mifflin from Copeland and Day, when they ceased publishing. He sent the manuscript of *Captain Craig* to Small, Maynard, where it had a secret and unholy reputation. Robinson didn't hear from Small, Maynard, and he wrote them and wrote them, but couldn't get any answer. Time went on, nearly a year or more, and he was beginning to wonder what had become of his manuscript. So, finally, not hearing from Small, Maynard, it was then at Josephine's suggestion that he sent the manuscript to Houghton Mifflin. They accepted it.

I had this story from Maynard on one side, and Robinson himself on the other. Of course, what I'm going to say about it will have to be modified and put in such a way that the very boldness of it can't be communicated, but I think it ought to be recorded.

It seems that Herbert Small took the manuscript home to read. There was a place where Small and Maynard and others of the firm had been in the habit of visiting; Small had taken the manuscript there, and in a way forgot all about it; he didn't know afterwards he had left it. Months afterwards, Maynard visited the same place, and he was told that his friend who had been there months before had left a package. He said, "Good heavens, let me see it; where is it?"

So the package was brought to him, and there was the manuscript of *Captain Craig*. And of course it was too late for them to accept and publish it, because it had been accepted by Houghton Mifflin.

Captain Craig was published in 1902. In 1908 Robinson published his fourth book. This fourth book was *The Town Down the River*. I reviewed it enthusiastically for the *Transcript*. It was a splendid volume. It had that marvelous poem on Lincoln called "The Titan." I can't list them, there were so many splendid poems in the collection. My review was seen by Robinson. I hadn't met Robinson up to this time. And it was seen by Louis V. Ledoux, whose father was practically the patron of both Robinson and Torrence. Ledoux wrote me a letter thanking me for the review of his friend Robinson's book, and thought I had caught the significance of it and my analysis of the poems was very good. Hermann Hagedorn, in his biography of Robinson, stated flatteringly that I was the first critic to penetrate Robinson's art, and he referred to my review of *The Town Down the River* as being "the most cogent analysis that he had received up to that time."

Shortly after the review appeared, Robinson came to see me and said he only had a few moments but he did want to meet me and thank me for the review, and hoped that later we would dine or lunch together and talk over these things. Then he was on his way to Cambridge to attend the Harvard-Dartmouth football game.

When I next saw Robinson, it was in New York. He had said to me, as he left that day, "When you come to New York, let me know. We'll have dinner together for a talk."

It was a year or so before I did come to New York. He was living on Waverly Place, in a little house in the yard at the rear of this house that was the home of the daughter of

Bishop Potter, Mrs. Philip Schuyler. They had allowed Robinson the privilege of living there. About five o'clock one afternoon, I went down to call on Robinson, and the maid showed me out to the little house where he lived and took my name up where he was in the living room on the top floor with some guests. I can't think of the lady's name (the hostess). In a little while, Robinson came down. I noted something a little strange about him, although for the moment I couldn't tell exactly what it was, because there was something he did more excellently than any other individual except Lucius Beebe that I have ever known, and that was to carry his liquor. He said, "Braithwaite, can you wait a few moments? Mrs. Philip Schuyler has company, and when she heard you were down here, she asked me to bring you up, because she would like to meet you."

We went upstairs. The drawing-room had about eight or ten people in it, and among them was Henry Taylor, the artist whose name I always remembered, and Olivia Dunbar, who later became the wife of Ridgely Torrence. So we sat down and talked. I was asked a number of things about Boston and the work that I was doing on the *Transcript* and about the poets around Boston. It was a general talk about people and places and things.

Time went on, and admitting that I'd had lunch rather early that day, I was getting quite hungry. I noticed that Robinson sat more or less silent across the room. And about half past nine, I said, "I must excuse myself and go."

Robinson got up and said, "I'll go with you; I'll go with you," he repeated.

As we were going down the stairs, "Oh," he said, "thank heavens that you rescued me! I've been around the Players all day with Hermann Hagedorn. I'm afraid we quenched our thirst too much."

When we got outside he said, "Look, let's go find a place to get something to eat." We came over to Fifth Avenue and walked up to 14th Street, and as we walked along 14th Street, I noticed every saloon we passed, Robinson would sort of eye it out of the corner of his eye. We passed two or three. We kept moving over towards the East Side. Finally he said, "Braithwaite, do you ever take a drink?"

I said, "Oh, yes, occasionally."

He said, "All right, let's go in here." We were just passing a saloon. We went in. It was two o'clock before we left that place! And I don't know what I can think of that I would exchange for those hours with Robinson, that night. I had Scotch and soda, and for every one I drank, Robinson drank two or three. So finally, after my second one, I said, "I don't think I want any more."

But those Scotch and sodas loosened his tongue. I knew Robinson intimately for twenty years or more after that, and I never knew him to talk so much about his work as he talked that night. And the most significant thing that he said was, "People do not credit me with a sense of humor — and if my work means anything, it means that I have looked at the tragedies of life, and the tragedies of individuals, with a sense of humor."

That was right, and it's right because, of all the poets I have known — I think of all literary people I have known, whether they wrote poetry, fiction, plays, or whatnot — Robinson's was the most compassionate spirit. I think that is confirmed in the fact that practically all of his figures, his characters, are failures — but he makes heroes out of failures in life, because he can see those forces which brought about the failures, and he had compassion for them.

We came out, and I don't know how anybody could know so many back ways, so many nooks and crannies in New York City where you could get a drink after three o'clock in the morning as he took me to that night, trying to find another drink.

Finally, he said, "Oh, it's approaching election time, and all these places are closed. I guess we'd better give it up. I'll walk you to the subway station and see you on your way home."

Robinson always summered in New Hampshire at the

MacDowell Colony, and on his way in the spring to New Hampshire, he always spent three or four weeks or even a month in Boston, and on his return in the fall, he always spent three or four weeks or a month in Boston. Practically every day during his stay we were together. We'd have either lunch or dinner together, and talk. Other times, he visited friends and there were some like Josephine Preston Peabody whom he felt it obligatory to call upon when he was in Boston. But he was not a social being in that sense of making calls on people, certainly not at that time when his foot was on the lower rung of the ladder of fame. He spent a good deal of his time when in Boston at the old Howard Theater, on Howard Street, which was a vaudeville house of the rougher sort. It was way down on the lower end of Beacon Hill. Howard Street ran parallel with one end of Scollay Square, and then Cambridge Street. They did put on the bawdiest shows down there of any place in America, except at one time 14th Street here in New York. He reveled in the shows they put on down there.

But he was always concerned about his close and intimate friends, and their progress. I know when Josephine Peabody published perhaps her last poetic play, *The Wolf of Gubbio*, I thought it was such a let-down from her standard that I delayed reviewing it for the *Transcript*. She must have appealed to Robinson, because when I was waiting for him one day to go out in his room, on St. Botolph Street — I can see him now standing before the mirror brushing his hair — and turning to me suddenly saying, "For God's sake, Braithwaite, why don't you review Josephine's book?"

I told him the reason why.

"Well, she believes," said he, "that the *Transcript* sets the tone of approach for books of poems throughout the country, and if the *Transcript* is silent, it's like a sentence of condemnation of the work, so do say something about it. If you don't feel that it's up to your standard, if you feel that her powers are weakening, why, you can at least apologize for this weakening, because of the splendid things that she has done."

"Well," I said, "all right. I'll do it." And I did.

*   *   *

I did give it brief notice.

One Sunday I was in New York, and Robinson and I had spent practically the day together. He was living on West 86th Street. We went out to lunch at a hotel near Central Park West. We had a very good lunch, and chatted and talked. Robinson asked me, "Do you want to see some of my new poems?"

"Of course I do," I replied.

"All right, when we go back to the room, I'll let you see them."

So in due time we went back, and sat down, and smoked. We didn't say anything for a while. I don't suppose there's any human being in the world I've spent so many hours with in which there's been so many hours of silence. We must have sat there at least three quarters of an hour without saying anything. Suddenly, he said, "Oh, let's have some light on it," and he jumped up and lit the gas jet.

"Robinson," I said to make talk, "isn't it queer? No matter where a New Englander may be on a Sunday afternoon, he has the blues."

He said, "Yes, it's so. I've never been able to escape them."

Somehow a veil of something comes down out of the New England atmosphere, out of its traditions, out of so many things that are awed and twisted also, out of so many aspirations and energies which have transcended the limitations of that atmosphere, that you carry with you as an aura wherever you go, out of New England, on a Sunday.

"Oh," he said, "let's see what you think of my poems." So he brought out his manuscripts. Those two or three hours that followed! For the first time — of course it hadn't been published — I saw that magnificent poem of his, the greatest portrait that has ever been drawn of Shakespeare, that long monologue, "Ben Jonson Entertains a Man from Stratford." It was handwritten in a stenographer's notebook. He always wrote his poems in a stenographer's notebook. When I finished reading it and the other poems, I said, "Robinson, what do you do with your manuscripts after the poems are typed and published? You ought to preserve them."

"Oh," he said, "when I have them typed, I just destroy them."

I said, "Oh, don't do that."

He said, "Well, who wants them? What value would they be? You like this thing?" he said, referring to the Shakespeare poem.

I said, "Yes, very much. I think it's great."

He said, "When I get it typed, I'll give you the manuscript."

"Oh," I said, "that would be wonderful! wonderful!"

He wrote very easily, no corrections. His handwriting was very small, you see, and there was hardly an erasure; there was hardly a correction, on any of the manuscripts of his that I've seen. He was a man who lived within himself, and that withinness was a world populated not only with his ideas and his images but with his friends, the people he knew. Perhaps this may to some degree give an idea or an indication of what that inward world was. He is the man on whose lips was that smile, the Mona Lisa smile — what Leonardo embodied in the cryptic lips of La Gioconda was embodied in Robinson. It appeared and disappeared, and it was in harmony with something in his eyes, in his glance, as he looked. He drew his upper lip in a little bit, and then something rippled down the corners of his mouth when he smiled. The same cryptic magic that you find in the Mona Lisa, Robinson had, and he's the only man I've ever known who did have it.

I said, "I'll type it for you. Who does your typing?"

"Well, I don't have anybody regularly do it," he said.

I said, "I'll type it for you, if you'll give it to me when you come through Boston on your way to New Hampshire in the spring."

He said, "All right. Then you can have the manuscript."

I'll go ahead to the time when he did come. It was on the first of July, 1919, and to the new home to which I had moved in Arlington, a town about eight miles outside of Boston. It was a very hot day. We lived on top of Arlington Heights, which is about a mile from the foot of the hill where the cars ran down through Massachusetts Avenue to Cambridge. It was right after that terrible epidemic of influenza. There was only one cure for it and that was whiskey. Prohibition went into effect the first of July, and I'd gone into the town and, purely for medicinal purposes, I had bought some liquor. I like wines and I like Scotch now and then, but months and years go by and I don't take a drink. Still, I did think it was wise to have it in the house for medicinal purposes, and so I put in several bottles of whiskey and some brandy.

So when Robinson trudged up that hill and came into the house and went up to my room, where I was going to type "Ben Jonson," just before we started, I said, "Oh, Robinson, I got in something because I was afraid this influenza might come back again, and I wanted some liquor in the house to cure it. Won't you have a drink?"

He said, "Oh, no. No. Did you just get it in?"

I said, "Yes, I got it in yesterday, because you know Prohibition goes into effect today, and the bottles are all on the shelves there."

He said, "You haven't opened any yet?"

I said, "No."

He said, "Well, don't open any for me."

I said, "Oh, come on, come on. What's the difference?"

"Well," he said, "if you don't mind."

So I got some ginger ale and Scotch, and put it on the table with glasses, and I went to typing, and he sat there drinking while I worked on the poem. When I finished, he gave me the manuscript. I walked down the hill with him when he left and saw him on the car to Boston.

Two or three years later, in a financial emergency, I sold the manuscript to Andy McCance, a bookman in Boston, who gave me $12 for it. From that time on, McCance never knew what happened to that manuscript. He never had a record of its sale. On two or three occasions, he tried to find it.

A couple of years later when Robinson was in town, he asked me, "Braithwaite, what did you do with that manuscript of 'Ben Jonson' I gave you?"

"Oh, I sold it," I said.

At first, I thought it might offend him, but it didn't. He said, "Oh, that's all right. I think anybody has a right to dispose of anything they want to, and I'm not at all offended. But if you had it, I could get $500 for you, for it. $500! I know a man who wants it very, very badly!"

Well, I had told him I would see McCance and see if he had it. I knew McCance would sell it back to me for a nominal profit. McCance and I had been on very good terms for a number of years, and if I had been frank and told him what Robinson had said, I knew he would have been very happy to let me have it back — if he had it. But he never could find it.

After Robinson's death, I had any number of inquiries from people who wanted to buy that manuscript. They heard that I had it, and they wanted it, because it was one of the most precious treasures, I think, of that period. Oh, I had other manuscript copies of his poems, but that was the prize.

I'll tell you another episode of Robinson that was characteristic of the man and characteristic of his peculiar subtle kind of humor. Lucius Beebe had done a bibliography of Robinson's poems up to that time, which was 1928. It had been published by Dunster House in Cambridge, which had published a complete edition of Robinson's poems up to that time in a number of volumes — I mean, a collected edition, a very special limited edition, in six or eight volumes. But Beebe had never met Robinson. During my publishing career, Beebe used to come over to the office on Boylston Street almost every day.

Beebe said to me once, "Oh, can't you arrange so I can meet Robinson?"

I said, "Well, Beebe, you know Robinson's friends are very careful about introducing him to new friends. You know how reticent and retiring he is, and he doesn't take on new friends very readily. But I think, in view of the fact — and he must know it — that you did this bibliography of him, next when he comes to town, I'll ask him, and perhaps we can arrange to get together."

So in due time, when Robinson came, I said, "Oh, Robinson, there's a young chap here at Harvard who is very anxious to meet you, and of course you must know that he did a bibliography of you."

Robinson's first response to anything of the sort was always a frown, as much as to say, "Oh, oh, what's this thing?"

But finally he consented. He said, "All right."

I said, "Beebe told me to tell you that if you would, he'd like for you and myself to come and we'd have lunch together at the Touraine."

Robinson agreed.

I said, "I'll get in touch with Beebe, and make arrangements for the date and the time," which I did, and so we met at the Touraine for lunch. Robinson did loosen up to Beebe somewhat. He seemed to like him very much.

During the lunch, Beebe said, "Won't you two come and have dinner with me at Cambridge next week?"

I saw quickly that frown come on Robinson's face. This was carrying it a little too far. Beebe saw it too, and he turned to Robinson and said, "If you come, I'll have a nice bottle of Scotch for you."

Robinson looked up. "You will?"

"Yes," he said, "and it's stuff that's just come over. I have a way of getting it, as soon as it gets here on the boat. It isn't like the usual Scotch that you get, harmful."

"Well," said Robinson, "that seems a good bargain."

So we arranged for the time, and Robinson was to pick me up at the office around half-past five or quarter of six. That had been a particularly hard day for me, and it had been so for Robinson, because, after getting up around noon, he'd made one or two calls. He came in, and sat down until I was ready to leave; and finally we got into Boylston Street and went over to Arlington where the subway goes under the Public Garden and Common to Park Street, where we changed for the subway to Cambridge.

After a greeting and a word or two when he came in the office, until we got to Park Street, I don't think we exchanged three words. There may have been some casual, brief remark lost in the silence. We got on the train, went under Beacon Hill, came out at Charles Street where the train stopped, and yet no word from Robinson. We went on to Kendall Square and stopped, and then on to Central Square and stopped, and yet no word, mind you.

When we left the subway station at Central Square, we hadn't gone more than thirty yards from the station when Robinson leaned over to me and said, "Say, Braithwaite, is your young friend truthful?"

"Yes," I replied.

He never said another word until we met Beebe. "Is your young friend truthful?" Oh, I never forgot that.

Well, we finally reached Harvard Square, and went to Drayton Hall where Beebe had rooms on Boylston Street, and then to dinner. Robinson had made a condition in accepting the invitation that if he did go over to Cambridge to dine with Beebe, that just the three of us be together, and that there musn't be any others. Well, Beebe didn't keep his word, because we hadn't gotten back to his rooms after the dinner when a number of Beebe's fellow students began trooping in. By the time they stopped coming, there must have been ten or fifteen students that Beebe had tipped off that Robinson was going to be a guest in his rooms that evening. But we had a very splendid evening. The boys adored Robinson, for he was a great man in their view. They knew his poetry, and altogether with the aid of the Scotch, it sort of loosened Robinson's tense feeling at having all these strangers come trooping in upon him.

Well, we broke up about midnight, and as we were leaving, Beebe said, "Will you carry this, Braithwaite, and give it to Robinson when he reaches the subway?"

He gave me a bag, and in the bag was not one but two bottles of Scotch. So when I saw him descend the stairs into the subway to take the train for Boston, he was the happiest man you can imagine. It was a very successful evening from the point of view of Robinson's sociability. He was gracious, in spite of that restraint that habitually enclosed him. He saw here youth — youth perhaps with ambitions that he had as a youth when he was at Harvard and couldn't remain to get his degree. All that, perhaps, revived memories which made him so lovely and wonderful.

We found him the same among his close friends; there was never any question of his cordiality. But with strangers he was reserved. I know Amy Lowell said of him once that his spirit was, as Shakespeare put it, "cabined, cribbed, confined." It was a disguise, she said, through which he loved admiration. She charged him with really being vain and conceited — which he wasn't at all. She misconceived him as a man as she misconceived his work, when she wrote about him in that volume — *Tendencies in Modern American Poetry*.

❊   ❊   ❊

We were crossing the Common one day after lunch, Robinson and I. This thought had been in my mind for some time, because I thought he had reached a point in his career where there should be a more universal recognition of his genius, which I was convinced would never be accomplished on his single publications. We passed the Park Street Church with its beautiful Wren steeple, and crossed onto the Mall, when I said to him, "Robinson, don't you think it is time for a collected edition of your poems?"

He threw up his head in amazement and said, "Who would want a collected edition of my works?"

I said, "There has been none of your collections that has ever passed into a second edition except one, and that is *Captain Craig.*"

Up to that time he had published, I think, four volumes. As we walked across the Common, I kept urging him to take it seriously, which he didn't. After a while, he said, "Well, I suppose there is no harm in suggesting it to my publishers."

His publisher was Macmillan. They had gotten him away from Scribner's, simply because Scribner's would not publish his plays. He had written two plays. At that time he was absorbed in the idea that he could do successful plays which would not only read well but act well. Of course, he had in the back of his mind Moody's successes with *The Great Divide* and *The Faith-Healer.* It was his idea that if Moody could go from poetry to acting drama, he could, so with Macmillan he began to issue those narrative poems which won him great success, among which the ones based on the Arthurian legend were the most popular. He never used those words but that was in his mind. He wrote *The Porcupine* which Scribner's, who were his publishers at the time, would not publish, and he went to Macmillan, who did, and who became his publishers during the rest of his career. Later they published his *Van Zorn.*

On that walk across the Common, I made a suggestion. I said, "Will you make me a promise?"

He said, "What is that?"

"Will you ask your publisher to bring out a collected edition of your poems?"

"Who'd want a collected edition of my poems?" he replied.

"Will you do it?" I insisted.

"Well," he said, "there can be no harm in that." We dropped the matter there.

That was in the fall. In March, I had a note from him which read something like this. (His notes were always very brief, almost concentrated with the thought he had in mind, to communicate the news.) He wrote: "Since you were crazy enough to suggest that I should have a collected edition of my verse, I think you ought to be the first to know. I've just come from Macmillan, and they have agreed to bring out the collected edition of my poems."

With the publication of that first collected volume in 1921, his fame skyrocketed. It had a very large sale and in 1922 it won him the Pulitzer Prize.

There was another incident which, to me, was historically interesting. I have related how we formed the New England Poetry Club, in the incident of Amy Lowell and her efforts to become president of the club. Well, that afternoon I had promised Robert Frost, who had returned to America shortly before, and who was very anxious to meet Robinson, that after the meeting I would take him over to Robinson's rooms on St. Botolph Street.

We went over, and I introduced him to Robinson. There was also with us Sylvester Baxter, who was a very interesting man. He was Commissioner of Parks and lived not far from Boston. He took a very great interest in poetry and was, by the way, the brother-in-law of Frank Millet, the American artist who went down on the *Lusitania*.

Robinson was sitting over in a corner near the window. When we entered, he got up and stood there. Frost was beside me as we entered the room; I put my hand out and told Frost to stand still, wait, which he did. Then I said by way of introduction: "Frost, when anybody thinks of poetry in America, he always thinks of Robinson as our greatest poet."

So I introduced them, and I don't think Frost ever forgave me the fact that I, before Baxter, made the statement that Robinson was the greatest of our poets. Up to that time when Frost returned from Europe, most of the critics had acknowledged Robinson as being our foremost poet, in many instances putting him ahead of the most important of the New England school of writers. But after Frost returned the allegiance shifted, especially in the case of Louis Untermeyer, to Frost as being our foremost poet.

Well, I don't think Frost took it very kindly, because he was a very sensitive man in regard to the value of reputation, and I think it was somewhat interesting later on, this episode. When once again Robinson and I were crossing the Common he said, "Braithwaite, have you heard from Frost lately?"

I said, "No, I haven't." After his stay here, in Boston, when he returned from England, Frost settled on a farm in New Hampshire and seldom came to Boston. I think he went to New York more often than he came to Boston at that time.

Robinson said, "I was curious to know if you had seen him and talked with him, because I sent him a copy of my last book. That's been months ago, and I haven't had a word of acknowledgment from him. I wondered if he was in any way sensitive about that introduction that you made when we met."

I said, "No, I don't think so. Frost has peculiarities, which I don't think are damaging to friendship."

Well, I know that Robinson was quite disturbed about it, because he was so punctilious himself. Speaking of his visits, his progress wherever he went, I've never known any man to travel so lightly. His single bag, with his change of linen and other few necessities, he carried. But as to books and papers, especially books, he never transported them from place to place. He always disposed of everything except the necessary contents of his traveling bag, for personal use, when he went on his travels.

He had, like his heroes, very strange experiences. One I might refer to as typical — it was one of those experiences which he never could comprehend. He was dining with an elderly lady one evening, a great admirer of his work. He was the only guest. When the soup had been served him and the hostess, he noticed she was not touching hers. Robinson looked and looked, and the longer he looked the longer the time went on and she did not touch the soup. The entree was brought in. The maid had addressed the mistress, asking if she wished her to remove the soup, and she got no response at all. Throughout almost the entire dinner, his hostess did not show a quiver of recognition or consciousness of what was going on. Eventually, he knew that during that dinner she had lost her mind, and lost it, Robinson later believed, because she had brooded so much about the loss of the *Lusitania*. I don't recall now whether she had any friends or relatives on the boat when it went down or not, but it was such a tragic event that her brooding had worn away her mind, so that from that time on, she was a sort of mindless invalid. The break came apparently in the course of the dinner, because she had received him with all the old graciousness with which she had always received him, and exchanged pleasantries about his work and so forth. They sat down to dinner, and then this disintegration began.

There are any number of such instances which Robinson has experienced. There was the exchange with his friend and my friend and many other people's friend at that time — Joseph Lewis French, who had insisted that Robinson and Hermann Hagedorn, especially these two, were attempting to have him committed to an insane asylum. The man was not rational; there was no question about that. He alternately would praise Robinson as a very great poet and then declare that he was not, but he was himself a good poet. He was a man who produced some twenty or thirty books, mostly edited, on various subjects, like great sea stories, great ghost stories, and so forth, books which did very, very well commercially. But there was no question but what he was not mentally sound. Always, when he came to Boston, he came to see me. He was very fond of Boston baked beans and brown bread, and of course Mrs. Braithwaite and I always asked him to have supper with us, so that he might enjoy his favorite Boston baked beans. Invariably, when he was here, the beans were not satisfactory. He would ask Mrs. Braithwaite if he might go into the kitchen, and of course she'd say, "Yes," and he'd pick up his plate of beans and go into the kitchen and cook them to suit himself.

He was a character, a man who had had a very familiar acquaintanceship with the greats of Harvard during that period, William James and Hugo Münsterberg and George Palmer and Josiah Royce — these were people he knew very, very well. But he troubled Robinson, because Robinson manifested, I think most clearly, that compassionate spirit I have mentioned. And he always had a way of using a phrase when he had that feeling of compassion. It was always the same phrase, no matter to whom it was applied. He responded to tragic instances concerning their doings or their life by saying, "Poor devil, poor devil."

———

Amy Lowell was not the kind of person one would be likely to forget. Braithwaite recalled her vividly when he was interviewed on May 17, 1956, for the Oral History Collection, Columbia University. The selection below is from *The Reminiscences of William S. Braithwaite*, a transcription made by Columbia's Oral History Research Office of interviews taped in May and June of 1956.

Amy Lowell—The Kind of Person She Was

I met her on the occasion of one of the regular Saturday luncheons of the Twentieth Century Club in Boston — perhaps the most noted civic organization in the city and . . . fringed with literary personalities. Mrs. Julia Ward Howe had been the president of it at one time. It was quite an old organization, and at the time Charles Dole, Nathan Haskell Dole's brother, was the president. It was to be a poetry luncheon. Bob Hillyer was there and spoke. I spoke, in the sense that I read the preface to my book, *The Poetic Year for 1916*, which I thought met the requirements of a talk. Odell Shepard, I think, was there too.

In the front row, from the speakers' table, Amy Lowell sat beside Nathan Haskell Dole. That was the first time I had seen her. At the luncheon we had the speaking, and then the breaking up, and chatting. When I came away from the table, Dole called me to where he stood beside Miss Lowell and said, "Braithwaite, Miss Lowell wants to know you," and she said, "Oh, I *know* Mr. Braithwaite, I know him," which meant merely through the *Transcript* reviews she knew me.

We chatted and she said, "Oh, I love to talk about this art in which we are both interested and in a sense both exponents of it — won't you come and have dinner with me? Let's say next Tuesday night?"

I said, "Thank you. I'd be delighted." I might have been hesitant about accepting, because of the pressure of other things. But I did go out on the following Tuesday evening, and thereafter practically every two weeks for two years, from early fall until spring, when she went up to Dublin, to her summer place; with occasional breaks now and then, she was quite insistent upon it.

It was a time of course when she was leading a crusade for what they called at that time "the new poetry," in which her particular medium for manifesting the new poetry was in the Imagist school's technique and substance. She had met Ezra Pound and John Gould Fletcher and F. S. Flint in London, and they had really introduced her to this new movement, or this new school of Imagism, . . . wholly unpracticed at that time by any poetry in America, as a deliberate method or ideal, though Stephen Crane and Emily Dickinson had practiced it without conscious intention. She came back and began her crusade. She published, in 1912, *A*

Dome of Many-Coloured Glass. It wasn't her first volume, because some years before that she'd published a little pamphlet of verse privately, so I suppose you can say that the 1912 volume was her second publication. I had reviewed *A Dome of Many-Coloured Glass* for the *Transcript;* the most notable things that I found in it were some sonnets. The other poems were good conventional pieces. I noted the book had a great deal of vigor. There was no startling imagery, nor any appealing music, though the poems were good, and the sonnets the best.

Shortly after that meeting she published *Sword Blades and Poppy Seed.* It was her second book of poems issued by a regular publisher. I reviewed the book for the *Transcript* and had some very good things to say about it. I wish I could define just what was the quality of her influence. It was exerted very strongly in a personal way, you see. She said that God had made her a good businesswoman, which she was, but that she had made herself a poet, and with that making, she manufactured — yes, she manufactured — an arsenal of influences, of demands — oh, I don't know what to call it — in which she overpowered opposition. It was her ambition to be (and she stated it very frankly to me from time to time) the greatest woman poet that this country had ever produced, and a match for the great women poets of England. She had one challenge in New England for the supremacy as a woman poet, and that was Josephine Preston Peabody. Josephine was Mrs. Lionel Marks, and knowing that I had the *Transcript* preempted for reviews of books of poems, she wrote a review of *Sword Blades and Poppy Seed* for the Boston *Herald.* I'm awfully sorry to say that in doing that review Josephine did not believe in what she said. It was not her kind of art, you see. She was a traditionalist, but she was a traditionalist with a very bright imagination, a bright sense of poetic values, and withal a wistfulness in her poetry that was rather rare, superimposed upon a very solid and determined imaginative quality. She couldn't even sympathize with the kind of art that Amy Lowell was producing, but she had an object in mind, you see. Her husband, Lionel Marks, had been in the engineering department of Harvard for twenty years or more, and had never advanced beyond an assistant professorship. Miss Lowell told me . . . herself, when she realized that there were things that she wanted Josephine to do that she wouldn't do, that the only reason Josephine praised *Sword Blades and Poppy Seed* was because she hoped Amy Lowell would use her influence with her brother, Amos Lawrence Lowell, president of Harvard University, and advance Lionel Marks!

I can see Amy Lowell now saying, "I never make any recommendations to my brother. I do not attempt to influence him in any way" — which wasn't true, because John Livingston Lowes, who then was professor of English at Washington University in St. Louis, had ridiculed Amy Lowell's art, and he did so by taking passages out of a novel by George Meredith and taking his prose without altering a word and breaking it up into lines, to show how artificial this Imagist concept was — to show that you could take any prose, and do the same with it, and produce an Imagist poem. And he supported his theory by saying that the main creed in Imagist poems was the rhythm of silence, or the repeat of phrases to make a continuous pattern of the poem, visually or auditorially.

Well, of course, Amy Lowell didn't like the attack. Before long, John Livingston Lowes was invited to deliver a series of Lowell Institute lectures, and the Lowell Institute was an educational creation of the Lowell family. Amos Lawrence Lowell, Amy's brother, was in charge of it. I say in charge — he was a trustee of it, you see. Of course we began to wonder how much President Lowell knew of John Livingston Lowes outside of his sister's information, and it was a conviction in Boston that it was through Amy Lowell that Lowes was invited to deliver those lectures, and later invited to join the faculty of Harvard University.

I reviewed all of her books up to the volume entitled

Pictures of the Floating World. Then she called Edgett up one day and asked if Professor Lowes couldn't review her new book. Edgett spoke to me about it and said, "Of course you have the decision."

I said, "No, let him have it. I wouldn't want Miss Lowell to think I was petty enough to buck her choice for reviewing this new book."

Well, there again was a conclusion that seemed to develop from the Lowell Institute lectures, the joining of the Harvard family and the personal request she made — because Edgett didn't write him to review it; she wrote him, and he consented to do it. And she got one of the biggest jolts that I think she had throughout her career, because his review was not a favorable one. He criticized her book very much, and she was furious about it.

In regard to Mrs. Marks, Josephine Preston Peabody, when she realized that Amy Lowell was not going to do anything about influencing her brother, President Lowell, to advance her husband, Marks, Josephine became very, very mad about it. Amy told me one day that she called her up about something and Josephine was so furious she hung up on her, which brought out the intimation that she was disappointed because Amy would not do anything in behalf of her husband at Harvard.

Edward O'Brien and I had the idea of establishing a poetry club in New England, which we did. It was called the New England Poetry Club, and we asked Miss Lowell to join us as we were organizing it, which she was very happy to do. But as the plans unfolded and we sent out invitations to poets, the question arose as to who was to head the club. Edward would say, "You ought to have it," and I would say, "No, I don't want it; I wouldn't think of taking it; I don't like such things anyway. I don't like the responsibility. I've got too much to do!"

"Well, whom shall we make president?"

I said, "I know who wants it."

He smiled. "Yes, Miss Lowell wants it. But everybody

else wants Miss Josephine Peabody to be the first president."

So, in response to the invitations to get together and organize and elect officers, some thirty or forty writers had gathered in the rooms of the Boston Authors' Club. Conrad Aiken was there. Edward O'Brien was there. Frost and William Lindsey were there; Robert Hillyer was there, and so was Amy Lowell. All the significant poets, but Mrs. Marks didn't come.

We got through our business of organization, and the nominations for the presidency came up. Somebody — I think it was Robert Haven Schauffler — nominated Mrs. Marks for the presidency. And then began the debate on the candidates. Somebody then nominated Amy Lowell. But the discussion that went on showed her very plainly that she was not the choice of that body, that gathering. And when it became absolutely convincing to her that she was not going to be elected, do you know what she did? The Authors' Club was in the Trinity Place Building on Dartmouth Street, right near the Trinity Place and Back Bay Stations, and you entered from Dartmouth Street in a great courtyard, and on the left were the rooms of the Authors' Club. When Amy Lowell realized that she was not going to be elected president, she dashed out of the room, out into the courtyard, into and down Dartmouth Street. Can you imagine her as a woman? Can you imagine her size — what a huge woman she was? She had gone out of the room and out of the building before we realized what she was doing. When we did, Edward O'Brien, myself, Conrad Aiken ran after her. And she had gotten halfway down to the Copley Plaza Hotel, which was on the corner of Dartmouth and Copley Square, before we caught up with her. Even then she sort of forged ahead and got into the hotel, by the Dartmouth Street entrance, and then, what a tirade! If she couldn't be president she didn't want to have anything to do with the club, and so forth and so on.

We resolved it by doing this. We told her, there, before

she would go back, we'd make her president. We'd make Josephine honorary president; you see, Josephine was much too ill to be very active anyway, and of course Amy Lowell was well and active. And that seemed to mollify her, to satisfy her — that she would be made president and Josephine Preston Peabody would be the honorary president.

So she went back, and we put the proposition before the floor of the meeting. In times following, she tried her best to re-establish her friendship with Mrs. Marks because she knew what the sentiment was about Mrs. Marks, that everybody in New England loved her, that she had brought distinction to New England as . . . the first woman poet who had attained importance. Her fame was established before Emily Dickinson's. There were others — Celia Thaxter, Harriet Prescott, Louise Imogen Guiney, and others — but none that had attained the eminence that she had, because she won the first Stratford Prize, Shakespeare Prize, on the 300th anniversary of Shakespeare's birth and death, with a poetic play, *The Piper*. That, of course, not only increased her national reputation but gave her an international reputation as a poet. Miss Lowell had too good a mind, too astute a mind, to let her friction with Josephine Preston Peabody broaden. She felt it was to her interest to have her as a friend.

Well, I had mentioned that I would do an interview article with Mrs. Marks for the *Transcript*. She was one of the few poets of the day, and especially of New England, that I hadn't interviewed. And by the way, Amy Lowell's first pronouncement of her Imagist creed and of her art was done through an interview article I had with her in the *Transcript*. That was the first time she had been interviewed extensively on the methods and claims of her art.

So Amy heard me remark that I was going to do this article, but time went on and time went on and I hadn't gotten around to it. So one day, in response to the ring of the doorbell Mrs. Braithwaite had answered, here stood this liveried individual asking if I was in. Mrs. Braithwaite came and told me. I went down, and she said, "Jump in. You've been working hard — and let's go for a ride."

I went and got my hat and came out and got into the car. We were living then on Ellsworth Avenue in Cambridge, about five or ten minutes' walk down Cambridge Street from the Harvard Yard. We started up Cambridge towards Massachusetts Avenue and the Square. When you get to Massachusetts Avenue, you turn to the left and cross Harvard Square, and then to Brattle Street, and up Mt. Auburn Street. When we got into Brattle Street, I said, "Where are you going, up to Belmont? Going to take a ride out to Belmont?"

She looked at me and said, "No. We're going to Josephine's and you're going to do that article about her."

"Oh," I said.

Oh, she was an autocrat. Well, Josephine lived in a dear little Swiss chalet on Mt. Auburn Street that was built by the Chickering Piano Company for Arnold Dolmetsch, whom they brought over here early in the century to make virginals and clavichords and harpsichords which they thought they could introduce to America. So she drove on. I didn't say anything. She drove up in front of Mrs. Marks' house and stopped. The car stopped. I didn't say anything after she said, "Yes, you are — you're going to Josephine's house and do that article about her."

So when we got out the footman had come around and opened the door, and I got out and helped her, and then she started up the steps of the house. It was a mean trick — her back was to me as she went up the steps — and as she left me to go up the steps I turned around and walked down Mt. Auburn Street. I'd gone about two blocks before she noticed it. When she turned around and didn't see me there she was furious!

Well, she walked back and got into the car. She didn't go into the house. She caught up with me. "Get in," she said, "and I'll take you home."

"Thank you," I said. Then she took me home, and she was furious all the way home.

Shortly after that I had promised to give a talk to the Authors' Club on criticism. On the original date I was out of town, but it was finally held at Mrs. Marks' house. I had been talking about ten minutes or so when the maid ushered Miss Lowell in, and I never saw such confusion in all my life. You see, Josephine had not seen Miss Lowell since the breach over the review of *Sword Blades and Poppy Seed* — not so much the review, but the constant failure to do anything for Marks as to his promotion.

Amy Lowell phoned me one day. She'd come down from her summer place in Dublin to read proofs on her volume of *Six French Poets* — Emile Verhaeren, Albert Samoin, Remy de Gourmont, Henri de Regnier, Francis Jammes, Paul Fort — and she wanted me to come out that evening while she was working on the proofs. People in many instances would not believe this, but it is true. She said, "I'm so depressed. I don't know how to get hold of things."

I had told her that I didn't see how I could take the time to go out to Brookline. It was summer time, and as usual at that time of year I was terribly busy with the Anthology. I said, "Aren't you going to stay over? Can't I come out tomorrow some time?"

"No," she said, "I've got to get back to the country; get up to Dublin. *Please* do."

"Well," I said, "if it'll brighten your mood, I'll come out."

So I went out and spent the evening with her while she was going over her proofs of the French poets. But the admissions that she needed spiritual comfort, help, encouragement, as people knew her later, would hardly be believable.

That brings up the fact that the younger men who went out to her house after her success didn't know her, and they have written so many complimentary things that her character does not sustain. For instance, Samuel Foster Damon's biography of her is wrong on so many points, and he didn't know her till long after this period — after the period when, one evening, she said, "What can I do? I can't get a poem placed anywhere. I send them out and they come back."

I said, "If you want to use my name when you send them, if you're willing to —"

She said, "Can I? Can I?"

"Yes," I assured her. "Just state, 'Mr. Braithwaite suggested that you'd like to see this poem,' or 'suggested that I submit it to you,'" and I told her the man to send them to, to Robert Bridges of Scribner's and to Thomas B. Wells of Harper's.

Well, she was very grateful, for she had not, up to that time, had a poem accepted by a general magazine. Another incident which shows how I helped her accelerate her acceptance and appreciation was when she published in the *Little Review*, which was edited by Margaret Anderson in Chicago, perhaps her most famous poem, "Patterns." It came out in the July or August number, I'm not quite sure which, and I was in McCance's a day or so after it was on the stands there, and got a copy and read it and said to myself, "Why, this is the best thing that Amy Lowell has ever written."

Now, let's grant that was in July or August. In mid-November I published my annual poetry article in the *Transcript*, and I reprinted that poem and praised it very highly. But between July and mid-November it had not been reprinted anywhere. No paper, no magazine had reprinted it or commented on it. It was, for all its artifice, a striking poem.

She was a woman, as far as art goes, of pure artifice. You can use artifice if it's merely a decoration on a substance, or a symbol, but you can't have artifice as an ingrowing force or energy in your poem if you want to be a pure poet. She never got rid of it, no.

She came down to dinner one night — I can see her coming down the stairs now — excited, exhilarated, because, as she said, she found a poem in a railroad timetable. Found it in a railroad timetable!

While she was not the originator of the Imagist concept, she was the originator of the polyphonic prose poem, in which she did those rather splendid narratives, "Sea-Blue and Blood-Red," "The Story of Lady Hamilton and Lord Nelson," "The Great Bronze Lions Fronting St. Mark's Cathedral in Venice," or Perry's opening of Japan in "Guns as Keys: and the Great Gate Swings." All these are polyphonic poems; they have a certain magnificence. They had magnificence because she had transfused perfectly normal historical events with a fascinating embodiment of sound in the polyphonic prose rhythm, and made easy reading because she broke out of the limits of the traditional metrics and gave you a sense, a quality of those events. They were excellent.

"The Hours of Sister Clotilde" is another one of her poems that I liked very much and also a little thing like "A Bather" and "Lilacs." But "Lilacs" has more mechanism in it than any of her poems, I think, and yet next to "Patterns" it's her very best known poem. And yet she might have written a historical essay embodying the same mood and the same feelings that she put into that poem, which of course was in irregular verse forms.

There was a quarrel between Amy Lowell and Leonora Speyer, which had a limited interest at the time, and which came on the flowering of her success. After her success flowered, the more autocratic she became. She pointed her finger at me one time, because of something . . . I disagreed with her about, as we sat there before her fireplace, and said, "You're the biggest aristocrat I've ever known," simply because I wouldn't bow to her demands, which everybody else did. Everybody did.

The Leonora Speyer affair grew out of the fact that she was jealous of Leonora Speyer. She was jealous of any woman who showed talent in verse. The Speyers came to America after being forced to leave England on twenty-four hours notice because Sir Edgar Speyer wouldn't subscribe to the loyalty oath the Government demanded. After his (as he felt) long residence in England, his financing the Scott Antarctic expedition, his financing Asquith to the premiership, he didn't think it was necessary, so they got out.

When they reached America they settled in Boston, and Amy Lowell took it into her head that Sir Edgar was concerned with espionage on behalf of the German government. This was during the First World War, of course. They were invited by Miss Lowell to dine, and, as Leonora told me later, it was very pleasant, but Sir Edgar saw through Amy. He despised her.

You see, Leonora Speyer was a Mrs. Howard before her marriage to Sir Edgar, and she had been a professional violinist. Amy Lowell did say at one time, "To think of her marrying that dirty little Jew for his money!" It shows her temper. It shows the kind of person she was.

Well, one year I had Leonora's picture in the *Transcript* — I usually printed three or four pictures, sometimes more, accompanying the poet whose poem was featured. I found an exquisite little poem of Lady Speyer's about Pan which she had printed in the *Nation*, and I printed her picture to accompany it. The next time I visited with Miss Lowell we had, as usual, a very pleasant dinner after which we went into the library and lit our cigars. She had a couch at one side of a great, huge fireplace. I sat over by a round table on which was an elaborate lamp. She reclined on the couch and lit her cigar and blew a great puff of smoke into the air, and then rising to a sitting posture, pointed her finger at me and said, "Why did you print Leonora Speyer's picture in the Boston *Transcript* Saturday?"

I'm afraid I was very rude. My response was, "It's none of your damned business."

Well, we had it. I don't know what that woman did, now. We went through that night, with her maintaining sovereignty, as it were, over the poetic women of America, or England for that matter, or anywhere. I usually left about a quarter of twelve to catch the latest car coming down from Chestnut Hill that would take me in to the Massachusetts station where I changed for the car to Cambridge and Arlington, and if I missed that I'd have to wait an hour or an hour and a half for another car. I missed it that night because when I was leaving she came out of the house with me and walked a good eighth of a mile from her house door to the gate. She walked all the way down there with me, begging that I would not let this quarrel break up our friendship, and saying that much had been said on both sides that was in anger, thoughtless and unkind, but the association had been too precious to lose, and that she didn't want to feel that there was anybody who held anything against her because of her rash opinions and comments about some other poet.

I never saw her after that night. I never saw her. She telephoned. She telegraphed. She sent emissaries. I talked with her once over the telephone, when she wanted me to come out.

The Civil War Centennial inspired Braithwaite to write this "vignette," previously unpublished. He was trying to market it in February, 1962, a few months before he died.

Mrs. Washburn

Mrs. Washburn was a colored woman who came with her family to Boston, after the Civil War. She was very fair in complexion with regular features, straight dull brown hair streaked with gray. She was of medium height for a woman, rather frail in appearance, but vigorous in movement for all of her sixty or more years. Her daughters towered above her, possessing solid physiques. Mrs. Washburn was driven by a ceaseless activity in the performance of her household duties, whether it was small detail of keeping trifles in order, or the heavier tasks of cleaning or laundering the family's soiled linen.

Mrs. Washburn and her family were highly emotional and highly superstitious.

They lived in Buckingham Street, that curved in from Columbus Avenue at Clarendon Street, and after some

thirty or forty feet straightened to run the short distance to
Dartmouth Street. On the right, or north side . . . as one
proceeded to Dartmouth Street, was a row of brick houses,
two and a half stories high, if you counted the basement
floor a half story, which was a few feet below the sidewalk
level, where the dining room and kitchen were located. The
kitchen was Mrs. Washburn's habitat.

From the rear windows of the house one looked down
over the railroad tracks of the old Boston and Providence
railroad. Separated from this railway system by a grilled
iron fence ran the tracks of the Boston and Albany. At the
time of which I write the Boston and Albany had a station
off Columbus Avenue close to Clarendon Street, later re-
placed by a more attractive and commodious station at
Trinity Place; the Boston and Providence had a stop on
Dartmouth Street which, when the Boston and Providence
was incorporated by the New Haven system, was enlarged
and modernized, extending its domain the entire length of
Buckingham Street occupying the ground where stood the
row of brick houses on the north side of that street.

Now, for many years the Back Bay symbolized the line
of progress which wiped out the homes of a colony of well-
to-do colored people, one of which was the home of Mrs.
Washburn.

I have given these particulars because of the steel and
noise which formed the accompaniment to an experience I
had when Mrs. Washburn related to me the bombardment
and fall of Richmond.

The recital was unique not only for its dramatic quality
which alone would have captured the imagination of a boy,
but for the power the woman had to make the boy a witness, and at moments a participant in the action and endurance of a people who were subjected to the test of the most
devastating assault of fire and steel made in the great conflict.

The roar of the artillery guns and the flame of bursting
shells had their repercussions and their emotional response

in the vibration in Mrs. Washburn's personal habit of snuff-taking as her description of the assault grew more intense. The practice was common with many women of her race and was performed with a little stick at one end of which was a fibrous brush . . .which was dipped into a can of snuff and put in the mouth where the gums and teeth were swabbed. Holding the snuff stick between her lips, Mrs. Washburn could with facility carry on an ordinary conversation, the stick missing and falling as her jaws opened and shut with the flow of her words. When she became excited in detailing her description of the panic and confusion of the people under the heavy bombardment of Mister Grant's guns and flames mounting from burning buildings and the sky filmed with smoke through which the flames of bursting shells streaked the sky with vivid brightness, the snuff-stick would quiver between her lips as if in harmony with the carnage.

As if to make the spectacle more realistic than her words, trains passing on the railroad tracks in the rear of Mrs. Washburn's house would belch smoke and flame from the engine's bell-like funnels, their brass bells would clang, and the piston-driven wheels scrape the steel rails coming to a stop at the station on Dartmouth Street a short distance away.

Mrs. Washburn's description of the assault upon Richmond came to a climax with a highly emotional outbreak of remembered terror. She merged all those frightening explosive artillery shots into one devastating stream of noise, smoke and flame and then with a dramatic wave of her arm swept it over the city into the night sky, splintering the darkness with flashing beams of light blinding the stars. There was an old remembered terror in her voice that had its effect upon the snuff-stick between her lips. The quivering it sustained throughout most of her recital now turned into a violent wobble, accenting both the memory and the terror it revived.

Mrs. Washburn could no longer restrain the wobbling

of the snuff-stick, and for the first time during her dramatic recital took it from her mouth. The act seemed to calm her agitated spirit. In a calm meditative mood she said: "Mister Grant had won, but we all felt sorry for Mister Lee, for like him we colored people were Virginians." With a sudden concern for the lateness of the hour for a young boy to be away from home she remarked, "Willie, you had better run home, your mother will be worrying over your long absence on the errand she sent you."

I was loath to leave the awesome but fascinating adventure of being present through the magic of Mrs. Washburn's memory at "a battle fought long ago."

I left, moving hesitantly into the dark street, lit only at long intervals by lamplight. Those intervals of menacing blackness were filled in my boyish imagination with all the terror that Mister Grant had rained upon Richmond.

The past is with me today, the last phase of the Civil War, Mrs. Washburn's dramatic recital of the capture of Richmond, her barometric snuff-stick, and the lamplighted streets through which I walked home.

Letters
(1899 – 1962)

Not until five years after writing the fragment below did Braith-waite get his first book of poems, *Lyrics of Life and Love*, in print.

Newport, R. I.
128 Prospect Hill St.

April 3, 1899.

Messrs. L. C. Page & Co.

Dear Sirs:
I send you, dear Sirs, herewith a collection of my poems, with a view that after your perusal and examination of same you may deem them worthy to be issued by your house.

Perhaps a foreword of the author of these verses may interest you, and perhaps it may not.

Do not be surprised therefore should I inform you that I am an American Negro, a Bostonian by birth, and received my M.A. from Nature's University of "Seek, Observe and Utilize" and am now in my 20th year. The pieces in this collection are the fruits of my art up to my 20th year, which I turned December last. Therefore, without advantage of even a high school education and teeming with the faults inherent to youthful poetical genius, I beseech you to be indulgent of the minor imperfections that pervade my work. The road of one who attempts to court the Muses, while daily endeavoring to sustain a mediocre existence, is, you will admit, a very sorry picture. Encouragement at least

should be offered them, especially if their work in youth
gives pro. . . .

———————

William Dean Howells conferred national recognition on Dunbar when he praised his *Majors and Minors* and wrote an introduction for *Lyrics of Lowly Life* (1896).

> 456 West 57 Street
> New York City
>
> Oct. 7, 1899

Mr. W. D. Howells

Most Reverend Sir:
I am an American Negro in my twentieth year who has just
come to New York with a *MS* with the hope of disposing of
it to a publisher. To you as the "Dean of American Literature" I make an application for assistance, hoping that you
will evince the same interest in me and my work (if you find
it worthy of your consideration) as you revealed in behalf of
Paul L. Dunbar.

Beseeching your pardon for addressing you unintro-
duced, believe me dear sir

> Your Ob. servant,
> W. S. Braithwaite

———————

Poet, critic, and Wall Street broker, Edmund C. Stedman was
co-editor of the multi-volume *Library of American Literature*
and editor of *An American Anthology* (1900).

456 West 57th Street
New York City

Feb. 2, 1900.

Dear Sir:

I hope you will pardon me for addressing you this letter
without a formal introduction. I have been reluctant hither-
tofor in intruding upon your time, knowing the manifold affairs your business and literary career combined must have
necessitated, but when reading in to-day's papers your con-
templated resignation from business I thought you might
spare me a little time from the labors on your "Anthology"
to consider my appeal.

In reference to myself I might state briefly my request.
I am an American Negro youth, who has written considerable poetry, and who would ask of you critical advice and
assistance in the literary world. I would ask you the permission to come and see you. I have educated myself and have
worked very hard at this art to which I am passionately devoted. May I hope for a reply? Hoping for your generous
compliance believe me dear Sir, to be

Very respectfully yours
William Stanley Braithwaite

To
Mr. Edmund C. Stedman
Bronxville
New York

Though he contributed verse, fiction, and book reviews to Boston's *Colored American Magazine* (see, in this volume, Negro
America's First Magazine), Braithwaite was unhappy about its
quality. Chesnutt gave cautious encouragement to his ideas for a

journal of his own, but nothing came of the plans announced in the following letter or of Braithwaite's efforts, a year later, to raise money with which to buy an interest in *The Colored American Magazine* so he might assume the editorship.

4 Green Street
Newport, Rhode Island

November 29, 1902

Mr. Charles W. Chesnutt, Esq.

Dear Sir:

I have in mind the issuing of a magazine for the Negro in America. It is my belief that one of the highest standards with a general and popular appeal is a necessity. There is a wealth of material among the colored writers in this country, and it is my aim that these, expressing their needs, ideals, and art through a Race organ, shall create a backbone for a Negro school of writers in this country. I flatter myself that you acknowledge the truth of this matter. We have truly no magazine of a literary standard. I am quite convinced that it is time we have.

Considering you, sir, the very first writer of our race, I appeal to you to lend me your assistance. I count this in that you possess a style quite exceptional, which as a rule is a rarity with us.

I want to ask you to give me your promise of a contribution. Frankly, from what I have stated, you must understand that the idea of this matter is embryo. For this reason, I rely entirely upon your patriotism and hope for the Race that you give my request a consideration. In the realization of the project, I desire something from your pen to give weight and standard to the first number.

Do you suppose, all things working well, you could see your way on assurance to supply copy for a three-part novelette, or three tales connected by incident or character? My hope is to have the first number issued next September first.

Your remuneration for this work I pray of you to place at the lowest figure consistent with that quality of work which I know you to possess.

I hope, sir, that you will be so kind as to acknowledge this at your earliest convenience.

Not knowing precisely your address, I take the liberty to send you this through your publishers.

Respectfully yours
William S. Braithwaite

Braithwaite had a life-long ambition to edit the kind of anthology announced in this letter, but he was never able to find a publisher for it. James D. Corrothers' poems in *Century* were admired for their resemblance to Dunbar's. His *Selected Poems* appeared in 1907.

24 Harwich Street,
Boston Mass.

3d December 1903.

Mr. James D. Corrothers:
Red Bank N.J.

Dear Mr. Corrothers:
I have in prospectus the compilation of a book made up of prose and verse from the best colored writers, and I am very desirous of inserting some of your poems. I have looked, but do not find any volume of verse by you listed with any publisher or on the catalog of the library here. Perhaps you have a volume privately printed, if so I will be glad if you will let me have it; failing this, may I request you to select eight or ten of your best pieces and send them to me?

I have written to the publishers of your book "The

Black Cat Club," and in reply they gave me the assurance that on my naming the selections I would use, they would permit me to reprint from it.

I intend to preface each writer with a biographical and critical essay and would be obliged for whatever data you will be kind enough to furnish me with.

I want to make my book a representative achievement of what the Negro has done in letters.

Hoping that you will give this your earliest attention, I beg to be

Very Sincerely yours
William S. Braithwaite

The Book of Elizabethan Verse (1906) Braithwaite dedicated "to Thomas Wentworth Higginson in recognition of a long life spent in the service of humanity and letters." His poem, "Thomas Wentworth Higginson: On His Eighty-Third Birthday," first published in Boston in December, 1906, was reprinted in *The New York Times* on December 22, 1906, and, with some lines of praise, in the *Tuskegee Student,* January 5, 1907. Quiller-Couch, Arber, and Grosart were English editors.

Dear Col. Higginson:
I was sorry to know that during your first days in the country you were unwell. With all my heart I hope they have changed for the better out of which you have extracted the best of health and spirits.

I am so glad you feel that my book promises to be attractive. I try to persuade myself that the more you see of the proofs the more you will become convinced in this belief: — and this notwithstanding the imperfections and blunders I am sure you are going to discover. The question of the modernisation of the old English in many pieces has been a matter of infinite concern with me. I have realized with Quiller-Couch, Arber and Dr. Grosart that in some instances, especially that of Spenser . . . so much is structural and inflections where the genius of the poet is markedly individual, that the rhythm and color of the poem is likely to lose in being modernised. I have therefore, with the exception of one selection, retained Spenser in his old clothes; which to me is more beautiful than anything of modern fashion. With the case of Shakespeare I think it is quite different in this sense: he is universally known in the later fashion of the tongue — having been so completely regarded by judicious editors that he would not be recognisable in the original — that he would not be Shakespeare to readers outside of scholars and editors were he allowed to be himself. I have used some Scottish poems of the period because of the obvious influence on them of the English masters; these with the exception of Drummond of Hawthornden — who in fact was more English in . . . style, feeling and expression than Scotch — and likewise, the Earl of Stirling, I have retained in their vernacular. Such a piece is the one you mentioned, "The Night is Near Gone" on page one of the sheets. However I am very glad to follow your suggestions on this point, if you think the book will gain in balance and attractiveness by uniformity of spelling.

Mrs. Braithwaite begs me to thank you for your kind solicitations and would have me tender her respects and well-wishes.

Monday July 9th 1906.

J. Max Barber was one of the editors of *The Voice of the Negro: An Illustrated Monthly Magazine,* published in Atlanta. He became sole editor when the place of publication shifted to Chicago and the title became *The Voice.* Braithwaite never published the volume of poems mentioned in this letter.

273 Columbus Ave.
Boston

January 5th, 1907.

My dear Mr. Barber:
I am sorry in failing to have my friend send on his article
"The Supreme Court and The Negro," which has been due
to the pressure of many literary obligations crowding it out
of my mind. For weeks I have been closed up with lots of
new work in preparation for my publisher broken into by an
imperative journey to New York. The *MS* I will have for-
warded to you this week, and hope you will find it an additional contribution to one side of a vexing situation.

I applaud your desire to make the Voice first among periodicals edited by Race men, and in so far as it falls within
the policy I have formed, and maintain, in pursuing my literary career I shall be glad to co-operate with you. I do not
send verses to the magazines as most of my friends do, pre-
ferring to have them appear first between covers. I have
now standing requests from editors which I am in no hurry
to comply with. I am sending you, however, six pieces
which you may have for twenty dollars ($20) with the con-
dition that three of them, which are named below, are published by April, as my new volume of poems, "The Ghost in
the Carpet," a Play with Lyrics, will then be issued and
they are to be included. The poems in question are: A Song
of Living, Messengers of Dreams, and Malaguena. I trust
you will find this proposition satisfactory from the point of
view of my meeting you half way.

What you say about "Lyrics" earns my gratitude and
thanks, and by the enclosed slip you will discover how near
some other eminent men have reached your way of thinking. The demand was so great for the Book of Elizabethan
Verse that my publisher did not send out any review copies
out of the first edition which was entirely exhausted before
Christmas. You will receive a copy of the 2d Ed. which is
expected in a week or ten days. If you desire any matter to

use in your review of it my publisher will be glad to send you extracts from letters in acknowledgment of personal copies, from literary men and university professors, which you may quote.

Very truly yours
W. S. Braithwaite

Ray Stannard Baker's articles in *American Magazine* on the "race question" were published as *Following the Color Line: American Negro Citizenship in the Progressive Era* (1908). The information Braithwaite supplied in the letter below was used in Chapter VI of Baker's book. Braithwaite did publish *The Book of Georgian Verse* (1908) but not the volume on Howells.

273 Columbus Ave.
Boston, Mass.

October 3d 1907.

My dear Mr. Baker: —
I expressed to you yesterday a copy of each of my published books: Lyrics of Life and Love, and The Book of Elizabethan Verse. Enclosed, also, I send you the review clippings of my book of lyrics which I thought you would like to see as they will give you some idea of the opinion my verse has won from the critics. These and the two or three clippings unpasted I would ask you to return me when you are done with them as they are the only copies I have.

In answer to the questions in your letter of September 23d, beside the two books I have presented to you, I am now at work on two books which I have contracted to have finished by January 1st, 1908: "William Dean Howells: a Critical Study," and The Book of Georgian Verse which my publishers are issuing in the spring and autumn of 1908.

The last named title is the second volume in a series of four — of which the Elizabethan Verse was the first — designed to cover the entire range of British poetry from the publication of Tottel's Miscellany, 1557 to 1910.

My father did not, as I have discovered . . . attend Oxford but received his degree from an Oxford examination; he then studied medicine at King's College, London.

I am a member of the Boston Authors' Club.

Dr. Courtney, I find, did attend the Harvard Medical School, but for some reason which seems to be generally obscure did not receive his diploma. Raymond, the Cambridge real estate dealer is a colored man, who I am told succeeded his father in the same business.

While talking with you the other day in New York, it was in my mind a number of times to inform you of Robert Hemmings a painter of Boston birth — the family is one generation from Virginia — who is undoubtedly the most remarkable colored artist next to Tanner. He has been home this summer for a visit after four years of study in Paris. He returns to complete in another year his five years of instruction, after which his intention is to open a studio in Paris. Hemmings is now about twenty-five or -six years old: his earlier studies here in Boston were at the Eric Pope art school, where they report him to have been one of the most talented students known in their school, taking in his latter years there all of the first prizes at their annual exhibitions.

I am glad you liked the verses you were good enough to have me leave you. The question you ask concerning a racial note in my verse is one that I have often had put me. I confess that in my earliest days of poetic expression I had a great ambition to do that sort of thing — and I tried it to a realization of failure. I discovered limitations in my temperament, as well as a certain undeveloped material in the race's history that prevented in me . . . spontaneous expression. There has been only one way — and this method will hold priority yet for half a century or more to come — to express the Negro in verse, and that is the manner in which

Dunbar made his appeal. If you recall a passage in Mr. Howells' "Silver Wedding Journey," you will be convinced of the attitude the poet who sings the "Souls of Black Folk" must take.

. . . Now, as I grew in artistic conscience in those days, I found that this sort of thing was not in me, but something which seemed to me higher in the universality of human nature, something in the vision of the soul, in the aspirations of the heart toward God, toward nature, that was a general meaning in the consciousness of human brotherhood, and I dedicated what power I possessed in poetic expression to this service. This was something I discovered to be holier than patriotism and race — the perfect goodness, the absolute beauty, the divine evolutions of spiritual and physical growth towards the perfection of God's conception of man. Art seemed to me finer than morality, since God conceived neither religion nor politics in his creation. He wrought this world out of his imagination, and if humanity was the result therefrom the form and intuition was an artistic achievement from which he sought a kind of . . . entertainment and pleasure to occupy his lonely moments. Sorrow, disease, slavery, kingship, sufferings and responsibilities were revisions of the original draft of his work, by which discord was to effect through invented melody a grand harmonic finale. The Negro has his place in the silence of this symphonic existence. Like every other race the salvation of the mass is in the individual. And these individuals of all nations and races are a community unto itself, and I must confess it is my ambition in song to voice the spiritual federation of men.

Yours etc.
W.S.B.

This unsigned draft of a letter about the William Howard Taft *vs.* William Jennings Bryan presidential campaign must have been written in 1908. By the "Brownsville incident" Braithwaite might have meant either rioting that occurred in an Atlanta suburb in 1906 or, more likely, an outbreak of racial violence in that same year in Brownsville, Texas, involving black soldiers of the 25th Regiment and white civilians. Eugene Debs, who helped to found the Industrial Workers of the World in 1905, was the Socialist candidate for president in 1908.

To Editor, New York World
New York City
New York

My views of the approaching Presidential campaign are the views of an American citizen. It is only as an American the administration of either Party can affect the individual to whom it grants the right of franchise, levies taxes, and demands personal sacrifice in its defence. The attitude of what is termed the "race" should be the attitude of the Irish, German, and Italian citizens in labor agitation against industrial oppression; of the Scotch-Irish-English merchant interests against the protective tariff laws which make immune tyrannical trust control of commodities; of the American families in New England and Virginia whose Saxon blood through three centuries has been the least contaminated with alien mixture, in their prejudice against the political theories and religious beliefs of continental families of not so many generations back. Consequently this attitude of political self-interest which signifies liberty and has been given the modern synonym of "American" is the attitude that promises to be followed in the coming campaign by the thinking members of the Race. Mr. Taft told them in an address in Kentucky last year, that when they learned to vote "intelligently," they would secure all their rights, and to vote intelligently was to vote in their own interests.

Now whether they should favor Taft or Bryan ceases to be a question of sentiment for Republicans and prejudice against Democrats. It is a question of voting for the man who will concede them as American citizens full civil rights and governmental participation according to their fraction in the total population. This is a justice more likely to be gained through the Americanism of Mr. Debs. It is not necessary therefore for these Americans to favor either Mr. Taft or Mr. Bryan if the principles of both these candidates are less than their (the Race's) conception of what the American spirit in politics should be.

Political platforms are . . . drapes upon which to hang party pledges. The first consideration regarding this, to be examined by all Americans without respect to class or race, is the economic effect party policies are to have on industrial conditions. To have a single plank touching race issues in the platform of American party politics is to admit a fatally weak link in the chain of the American Institution. The more complimentary insertion of a Race plank in the Republican platform does not delude thinking members of the race, nor the lack of it in a Democratic platform convince them that the entire principle of the Democratic party is without sentiments of political justice. To grant political justice collectively to any of the heterogenous races in this country is all that can be asked; equality in all other aspects depends upon the individual — and can be attained.

The Brownsville incident will have the same effect of any act, whether right or wrong, where a body of men consider pride and honor to have been wounded by the assumption of an uncompromising attitude in the creator of the act, when ultimate evidence shows it to have been at least partially mistaken. Consequently a considerable vote is going to be lost to the Republican party this fall. It is not going to Bryan, for no self-respecting member of the Race can vote for him. Where it is going one can not say; it may stay at home, for the leaders have never instructed it concerning Mr. Debs.

The anthology of Victorian verse discussed in this letter to Temple Scott was never published. One blow to Braithwaite's hopes was the refusal of a publisher to allow him to include copyrighted selections of crucial importance by Tennyson, Arnold, and several other writers. Across the face of the letter from London, dated September 16, 1910, Braithwaite scrawled, "Go to hell. WSB."

59 Museum Street
Cambridge, Mass.

June 9th 1909

Brentano's
New York City

My dear Mr. Scott: —

The last installment of the advanced royalty on the *Book of Victorian Verse* has reached me; the amount I find inadequate to carry me through the preparation of the manuscript. The experience was similar with the other two books, but I tried to make the best of it — as my expenses were then smaller than now, I find it impossible to repeat the experience.

The Victorian Verse is much more difficult to prepare than the other books of the series. The selections demand more deliberation in choosing. . . . There is extensive corresponding with English authors and publishers to secure copyright privilege, especially so there will be no hindrance in the way of an English edition. I could not possibly finish the book before November, as I am compelled to do all the copying — which is in itself a tremendous task — besides making all the indexes, and the biographical index in this last book, especially of the later and younger poets, is going to demand search and correspondence. While I am working on this book I have absolutely no other source of income — and with a family on one's hands it is an imperative necessity — and as it will take me four months longer to finish the book, I am going to ask you out of my necessity, to further advance me two hundred dollars ($200. —) payable . . . in weekly installments of fifteen dollars ($15.00) each. I am willing in consideration of your compliance to waive the royalty on the first thousand copies of the *Victorian Verse*. This last concession will leave me without royalties on the first thousand of the three Verses — a concession of six hundred and fifty ($650. —) which I have voluntarily sacrificed in consideration of your allowing me nine hundred and fifty dollars ($950. —) of advanced royalties. I think, you will permit me to say, I have tried to show a spirit generous and grateful and just in return for your firm's courtesy in cooperating with me in printing these books through and hope that now that the labor, which has taken me over three years to accomplish, is nearing completion, you will not fail me at the end. I trust you will take the matter up with Mr. Brentano immediately and let me know at your earliest opportunity.

You will be glad to know that Prof. Barrett Wendell, as I have been told here, is contemplating using my anthologies when the series is completed at Harvard in place of Ward's English Poets.

I have not yet received proofs of the *Restoration Verse*.
Hoping to hear from you soon, believe me
Very faithfully yours,
William Stanley Braithwaite

A Southerner once as well known for his campaigns in support of civil rights for blacks and poor whites as he was for his stories and novels, George W. Cable complied with this request from Braithwaite. Another contributor to the *Transcript* tribute was W. E. B. Du Bois, who wrote in praise of Howells "As a Friend of the Colored Man."

523 West 122^d Street,
New York City —

February 17th 1912,

Mr. George W. Cable,
Northampton, Mass: —

Dear Sir: —

Mr. William Dean Howells is seventy-five years old on March 1st. *The Boston Transcript* on February 24th is publishing the tributes and appreciations of Mr. Howells' contemporaries in honor of his birthday. These tributes are requested to be from three to five hundred words. Would you be kind enough to join Henry Van Dyke, Margaret Deland, Alice Brown, Bliss Perry, George Edward Woodberry, and many others in contributing to this collective expression of the esteem we have for Mr. Howells as man and author?

I regret the time is so short, but hope, in case you accede that you will let me have the manuscript by Feb. 22d.

Faithfully yours,
William Stanley Braithwaite

Miss Emma Kelly of Baltimore, Md., whom Braithwaite met in Newport, R.I., in 1902, became his wife in 1903. The checks he mentions in the following letter might have been due from the Los Angeles *Times* for one of the reviews it printed in 1912 or from *Lippincott's* for an essay and a poem the magazine published in 1913. The stationery bears this letterhead: The Sharon Series of Contemporary Authors/ Edited by William Stanley Braithwaite.

2 Central Street
Winthrop, Mass.

August 4th 1912.

My dear Emma: —
I suppose you were expecting me today; but I have been wondering if things went on alright. I couldn't come because I didn't get the money in, and you didn't forward the letters I expected — as I told you to in case they came. Did any come, and you held them expecting me home? If they did, forward them just as soon as you get this, by Special Delivery, to go out on the one o'clock train, so I can get them here by four or five o'clock. I am as you know, expecting the *Times* cheque and one from Lippincott's — the latter it will be easier to cash here.

I went out to Mrs. Hart's Saturday forenoon and saw the house. Will tell you about it when I come.

I hope you and children are well. Kiss them and lots of love. If you send any letters that hold the cheques I'm looking for and I get them by five o'clock I'll be home tomorrow night.

affectionately,
Willie

Laurence J. Gomme, twice mentioned in this letter to Amy Lowell, published the *Anthology of Magazine Verse for 1916*, which reprinted some of Amelia Burr's poems. "The 'Spoon River Man' Takes Our Measure," Braithwaite's article on Edgar Lee Masters, was in the Boston *Transcript*, August 21, 1915. Braithwaite did circulate the picture post cards he planned as promotion for the anthology.

27 Ellsworth Ave.,
Cambridge, Mass.

August 22nd, 1915.

My dear Miss Lowell: —
One half of the "Anthology" is about finished with the same
old experience of tight-rope walking a chasm. The book is
going to be a big surprise and knock the country into absolute submission regarding the poetic ability of this era. How
I shall get through the other half I don't dare guess. I de-
pended on the regularity of the agreement with Gomme,
and I know he has done the best he could for this time of the
year, but it upset my calculations for work. He will make
good with the book when it is published there is no doubt;
but I am fearfully worried about getting it finished on time
so it will come out as announced in the middle of October.
I've got just a month to finish six or seven weeks' work; and
that's leaving out of account the time for work to keep the
domestic pot boiling. I am so satisfied with the value and
quality of the selections in this year's book and its more rea-
sonably assured success, that I am moved for the sake of the
work to make an appeal that was suggested by the action of
Louis Untermeyer, who was here the other day. He realized
the problems the accomplishment of the book presented and
said: "Braithwaite, it's an institution; it's for us all, and we
ought all to help. It's been a hard year with us in the jew-
elry business, but I'll send you a cheque for twenty-five dollars, a pittance, but an expression of my desire to help."
And he did. I wished to regard it as a loan till the book
made good, which he refused. Would you like to contribute
the widow's mite, for this cause in which I am but a ser-
vant? I'd be glad to regard it as a loan until the book gets
going. Amelia Burr just sent me an order for thirty copies,
all pushing the work forward.

Now I am somewhat worried about one of your selections. I want to use "The Bombardment" — got it all typed

—but frankly admit I don't know how to approach Houghton Mifflin & Co. because of its inclusion in the "Imagist Anthology" and because they are so unlike Macmillan in their attitude towards my efforts. Macmillan have seen the value of what is attempted in this work and have always been generous and affable in granting every opportunity to make the work successful; and this is also true of all the other publishers. They send me advance proofs and copies of new books to facilitate the work without hesitation; a request for the same from H. M. would have to be enforced with the powers of Divinity. I know it's asking a great deal, but I wish you'd take the matter up with Mr. Greenslet about your poem.

I am using, as you know, "The Fruit Shop" from the Yale Review; and I've just seen "Patterns" in the Little Review which I like immensely and want to use.

Two more features I am adding to the "Year Book" this year: one is to give a complete list of all the essays, criticisms, and important reviews of poets and poetry that have appeared in the magazines, weeklies and quarterly reviews, and such literary papers as The Transcript, N. Y. Evening Post, Times and Chicago Evening Post. You would be surprised how interesting this would be to the poets and the students of poetry. Another is, I shall try and induce readers to begin the building of a private library of modern American verse. And so I am giving a list of fifteen or twenty of the volumes that every one ought to have which have been published since 1900. In conjunction with this I am going to see if the publishers won't agree to have these volumes bound uniformly and sold as a set. I think if I can get five hundred subscribers to start with it can be pulled through; and if it goes to that number there's no knowing but what it may go on into the thousands. Poetry is the only form of literature that has not been presented to the reading public in this way — that is within this country and within the past half century. The time now is ripe for it. I expect a sale of the Anthology of ten thousand copies at least this fall and winter, and it will make a splendid opening for the sale of such a uniform set as I propose.

Gomme is pushing forward a lot of publicity that I have planned for him. Two circulars are about ready and will go out this week.

I have also planned a post card for distribution by the trade in their October first statements. It is to have the portraits of eight or nine of the greatest poets who have poems in the book. It's a fact that the public, though it may know the name and work of a poet, does not know the likeness as with other authors. It's time to do all these things for poets and poetry now. Do you mind if I used the profile of that picture of yours which I reproduced in the Transcript? We are planning to distribute a couple of hundred thousand of these post cards; and they, the pictures, will also go on a poster in the window display of the book that is being planned in all the leading bookstores throughout the country on publication.

Masters was here and I had a very pleasant chat with him and got an interview which came out in yesterday's paper.

Forgive this long letter and its necessities. I hope you've been well and productive. The enemies of Imagism are all about our heads. I shall be in for the shock of attacks when the Anthology comes out. I want to make myself sure in the introduction. I've been begged to leave it alone. In considering this matter it's not a case of merely looking at appearances, there is something deeper that both the public and the critics have got to realize. I think I've got them on that one question of "Magic." I had a test of it the other day. A friend debated the opposition with me, and I held that in reserve until after we had exhausted nearly all the arguments on both sides. On that point he surrendered. "Work that has that," I said, "is poetry, and if you concede that you concede all your other objections which are nonessential." It was surprising how it worked. And another surprise I have for them, is a dictum of Coleridge's which I discovered in re-reading some of his poetic theories. Well, we'll see! I trust Mrs. Russell is wholly well again, and beg you to give her my best wishes.

Cordially yours,
W. S. Braithwaite.

The letter below was written on stationery of *The Poetry Review*, 12 Chauncy Street, Cambridge, Mass. Issued from May, 1916, through February, 1917, the journal was edited by Braithwaite and strongly supported by Amy Lowell. Among the important poets whose work it published were John Gould Fletcher, Richard Aldington, Alfred Kreymborg, Conrad Aiken, and Witter Bynner.

June 29th, 1916

My dear Miss Lowell: —
One of the delightful duties to contemplate in connection with the Poetry Review, is the letters to contributors accompanying the munificent cheques in payment of their work. I hardly know what to say in offering you this cheque for $5.00 for the review of Aldington and Flint. I have gotten so much more than $5.00 worth of instruction and pleasure from it — and I am certain our readers have — that the offering seems very unworthy. It is only that I know you are a good soldier in the army that I at all — yes! — command you to accept in the spirit of ultimate victory for the cause.

Cordially yours,
William Stanley Braithwaite

Maxwell Perkins, the great Scribner's editor, was one of the many people in the publishing world with whom Braithwaite was acquainted. Braithwaite did win permission to include Alan Seeger's "I Have a Rendezvous with Death" and several sonnets by Olive Tilford Dargan in *The Poetic Year for 1916*. The book was composed of his *Transcript* reviews and a series of literary dialogues in which, said Claude McKay in his autobiography, "the characters were intellectual Bostonians with Greek names and conversed in lofty accents that were all Greek to me."

27 Ellsworth Ave.,
Cambridge, Mass.

March 15, 1917

Charles Scribner's Sons,
New York City.

Dear Mr. Perkins: —
Perhaps you did not understand that "The Poetic Year for 1916" is not an Anthology of poems, but a volume of prose dealing with the books of poems published during last year. These poems which I have requested permission to use, are by way of quotation to illustrate the critical point of view.

The "George Crabbe" poem by E. A. Robinson is quoted to show the influence of Crabbe upon contemporary English and American poets — and in this sonnet the obligation is directly acknowledged.

Out of a selected number of published volumes of verse for 1916, it would be a pity to omit a study of Seeger and Mrs. Dargan. I trust you will not deny me the opportunity to spread still further by means of this book the interest in these poets.

Very sincerely yours,
W. S. B.

———————

Lew Sarett wrote pantheistic poems about Indians and life in Canada and the Rocky Mountains. Braithwaite reviewed his

Many, Many Moons in the *Transcript*, May 8, 1920. *The Golden Treasury of Magazine Verse* (1920) was Braithwaite's selection of poems printed since 1905. His *Transcript* poetry reviews began with "The Magazines and the Poets; a Critical Examination of Periodical Files for 1905," February 14, 1906.

> 243 Park Ave.
> Arlington Heights,
> Mass.
>
> October 6, 1919.

My dear Mr. Sarett: —
Please pardon my delay in acknowledging your letter and thanking you for your many courtesies. It is a real pleasure to have poems of yours in this year's "Anthology." I am also delighted to know of the publication, early in the new year, of your book. In connection with the book I trust you will let me have a portrait of yourself to use with my review. Will you also write for me, at your leisure, an account of your experience with the Indians — suggested to me by your note in *Poetry* — and your interest in poetically interpreting their spirit and customs. . . .

I can of course, readily see Mr. Holt's objection to the use of "The Blue Buck" in the "Anthology," and I am taking it out of the proof. The proofs came to me paged, but I am trying to work in "The Philosophic Frogs," which as you will see by the enclosed clipping was printed in *The Transcript*.

Let me thank you most heartily for your generous and reassuring comment on my critical work. Of course we all differ on certain points and values, but that scarcely affects, or shouldn't, the fundamentals. But you understand what I am striving for; a misunderstanding by certain of my critics seems sufficient to confirm a basic lack of critical perception on my part. This really annoys me more than anything else, and as I never answer reviews or criticism, it gives them a certain advantage in distorting the truth. For instance Louis Untermeyer in the New Republic a week or two back reviews the "Golden Treasury of Magazine Verse" eighteen months after it was published and attempts to deprecate my critical judgment by asking why I had not included Lola Ridge who was never heard of before eight or ten months ago. This is but one example — in that single review — of distortion, but *he* calls it criticism. Irony!

What an author wants — especially a poet — is to be *understood* and interpreted. There are as grave faults in Browning, for instance, as in the least significant of contemporary poets. I have found in many an ordinary poet of today as true and deep an insight into man and nature as to be found in Browning — only Browning repeats, the others may not, but that is no reason the single poet should not be given his credit. Well, I miss nothing of the glorious wonders and beauties of life and nature for seeing them through the spiritual eyes of a hundred poets instead of a few, and that after all is what counts in my experience and not what some limited-mooded critics think and say.

Yours very sincerely,
William S. Braithwaite

Braithwaite's "The Angry Voice of a Poetic Rebel: Carl Sandburg" appeared in the *Transcript* for October 16, 1920. He had reviewed *Chicago Poems* on May 13, 1916, and *Cornhuskers* on January 11, 1919. This letter to Sandburg bears this letterhead: William Stanley Braithwaite/ 27 Ellsworth Avenue/ Cambridge/ Massachusetts.

November 14, 1920.

My dear Sandburg: —
I was away in New York and so didn't get your note until my return. Your belated reply to my letter of request made

me wobble about keeping your poems in when I returned proofs to the printer. My experience of other years finally decided me to keep them in as your consent was generally forthcoming. So the pieces went beyond redemption and the book was in the bindery when your note came.

Of course, I saw in it the un-righteous displeasure you had in my review of "Smoke and Steel." And I was a bit sorry to have a conviction shattered — the give-and-take of the man behind the work. The sort of splendid sportsman of which there are altogether too few in American literature. Some of these fellows haven't left me with even a ragged undershirt against the icy blast of critical contempt — but by God, they have never gotten a shiver out of me.

Well, the point is you'll understand my review one of these days. It's rather a tough proposition, I'll admit, at present; but I am working out a theory, and the attitude is the test. A couple of poets have absolutely flunked on it, and it would be a damn pity to count you in. Look out or the "ee-feete" East will put it over on the "virile" West in this respect. The West seems more "touchy" than this strip of coast leathered with damp, salty east winds off the Atlantic. The future of American literature is in your keeping out there — as soon as the West admits it is grown up. You can afford to laugh at us back here, and not grow peevish.

What can I do to satisfy you for letting the Anthology by with your pieces in it short of going to jail or having the lining ripped out of an empty pocket-book?

Yours,
Braithwaite

Braithwaite succeeded in persuading Sarett to let him include "The Box of God" in the anthology for 1921.

243 Park Avenue,
Arlington Heights,
Massachusetts.

September 9, 1921.

Dear Lew Sarett:

I have just received your letter and it has made me feel as if I'd had about a dozen live nerves extracted with hot pinchers. Briefly, the story of the Anthology is this: After I saw it was possible to get the Anthology out this year I worked overtime getting it together to meet the demand of the publisher for the copy. It was shot right to a printer out in Wisconsin and proofs began immediately to come in, which I had to return corrected without delay. Letters of permission to the poets, editors and publishers, could not be attended to during this rush. In the meantime the book was paged and by now is in the foundry.

I am making a strong plea that you will let me retain "The Box of God" in the Anthology. I can assure you from the testimony of a good many poets that the inclusion of their poems in the Anthology, previous to publication in their books, has been a decided help rather than harm. I can cite examples of long poems that I have used, that have appeared in the Anthology first, which have been beneficial to the individual volume of the poet. Lindsay's "The Chinese Nightingale," Frost's "The Death of the Hired Man," Masters' "Bonnybell," Amy Lowell's "Guns as Keys: and the Great Gate Swings," etc. I have come to be convinced that people who buy the Anthology buy it, for the most part, as a catalogue and guide to the poets they wish to purchase. This except the library sales, the readers of which use it as a means of becoming acquainted with poets' works and which has profitable results. I do not emphasize all this to spare myself the trouble and expense in breaking up the foundry plates to take out the poem. I am trying to make it clear to you that it is my conviction, after long ex-

perience in these matters, that it will be for the interest of
your book to have "The Box of God" appear in the Anthology. There are hundreds and hundreds of people who when
they like a poem, want it in its own setting and not accompanied by poems of other authors. Such people, won by
your poem in the Anthology, will buy your book when it is
published.

Of course the peculiar and difficult problem of the Anthology this year makes the taking out of a poem a catastro-
phe. It was my feeling of assurance of the unlikelihood of an
objection as raised in behalf of your poem, that led me to
take such a risk and belatedly push the Anthology through.

Will you wire me collect, after receiving this letter, the
result of reconsideration about letting "The Box of God"
stay in the Anthology.

With every good wish, believe me

Cordially yours,
William Stanley Braithwaite

Braithwaite was an incisive critic of E. A. Robinson's poetry and
wrote many lines in its praise. There were a number of pieces in
the *Transcript* (e.g., "America's Foremost Poet," May 28, 1913,
and "The Arthurian Legend in Poetry," June 12, 1920), but the
review mentioned in this letter to one of Robinson's most important admirers, who was familiar with Braithwaite's comments
about the poet in *The Cornhill Booklet* (December, 1914) and
elsewhere, evidently did not appear. Richard Cary edited
Edwin Arlington Robinson's Letters to Edith Brower (1968).

243 Park Avenue
Arlington Heights, 75,
Massachusetts.

January 18, 1922.

My dear Miss Brower:
I owe you an apology for the delay in replying to your inquiry regarding the Robinson study as issued by The Poetry Review in 1916. I regret to say that the series was not finished, owing to the fact that The Poetry Review suspended publication, after, I believe, only one volume of the Contemporary Poets Series had been published.

I shall have a picture review of Mr. Robinson's "Collected Poems" in The Boston Transcript within the next few weeks. I do not know, at this time, the date it will appear; I will, however, have my secretary make a note and send you that copy — unless you have The Transcript sent you.

With sincere appreciation of your deep interest in Mr. Robinson's work, believe me

Yours cordially,
William Stanley Braithwaite.

To
Miss Edith Brower
15 North Franklin Street,
Wilkes-Barre, Penna.

————

Two of Claude McKay's sonnets in *The Liberator* Braithwaite chose to reprint in his anthology for 1922, in which year Harcourt, Brace published *Harlem Shadows*.

Letters

243 Park Avenue,
Arlington Heights, 75,
Massachusetts.

February 18, 1922.

Dear Mr. McKay:
I want to thank you for your letter of February 9th, and also
for restoring my name to the complimentary list of *The Liberator.*

I have not as yet received the copies you mentioned,
but no doubt they are on the way.

With best wishes,

Yours sincerely,
William Stanley Braithwaite.

Mr. Claude McKay,
138 West 13th St.,
New York City.

P.S. I am very glad to know that you have found a good publisher here, and I wish you every success.

Spurred by the publication of Georgia Douglas Johnson's *Bronze*
(Boston: B. J. Brimmer Co., 1922), Mrs. Mary Church Terrell
wrote to ask Braithwaite's opinion of a book she thought of writing. Sometimes, when soliciting contracts for the publication of
vanity books, Braithwaite found it convenient not to disclose his
identity as president of Brimmer. Nothing came of the correspondence with Mrs. Terrell, a civil rights leader whose autobiography, *A Colored Woman in a White World,* appeared in
1940.

October 6, 1922.

My dear Mrs. Terrell:

I was very glad and interested to receive your letter, which reached me last night.

It is a real privilege to be able to do what I have been able to do through the Brimmer people for Mrs. Johnson. It is a pioneer effort that I have tried again and again to get other publishers, who have published the books of colored authors, to do; have tried often, in fact, to get them to do *something*. It is a dream of mine — the recognition of our writers — the becoming of a world force in literature. I hope all Mrs. Johnson's friends will back her to the limit; it means much to future writers, I believe.

You know, I am sure, how interested I am in your writing. I have long been deeply interested in your lecture work. I know, a novel is not put on the gas burner of brain and paper — as one puts prunes on! No, publishers will not take large risks, as they believe, on short stories. However, I believe that there is a field for just such books. The Brimmer people are bringing out Ralph Bergengren's book *Gentlemen All and Merry Companions*, a book of short stories, arranged in such a way that they are sure to charm.

Of course, you know, there is not, I believe, a publisher in the country that would or could, as they look at the matter, publish your volume of short stories at their own risk. I could get the Brimmer people to take your book if you would pay for publication. I believe that with your following, your influence, and my efforts, the Brimmer's interest and willingness to make every effort to make such a book a successful one, we could bring out a book that would be a source of joy to you. And a source of real pleasure to other hundreds — thousands — of readers. If you want to pay for this I will do all I can to push it along in every way. My heart is in this work, as you know. The Brimmer people, perhaps, charge a trifle more than some publishers I would not name — but the difference in every cent is reckoned into doing something for the author's book. Their percentage of real profit is less; I know; and — they will sell all the books it is humanly possible to sell and that means an effort season after season and year after year. Not a spurt of a week or two — and the "graveyard."

If you want me to give you an estimate, send your manuscript right on, as there are many plans being made and if you do desire publication I'd like to start the logs rolling. The log rolls a way, you know, before it gets to the landing — to be driven down the river, into the mills, into boards and beautiful homes.

With best wishes I am
Yours faithfully,

———

Alain Locke's *The New Negro* (1925) includes a revised version of Braithwaite's "The Negro in Literature," first published in *Crisis*, September, 1924, and reprinted in this volume. Braithwaite spoke on that subject at the Philadelphia convention of the National Association for the Advancement of Colored People, July 1, 1924.

April 13, 1925.

My dear Locke: — I would have answered your letter immediately to give you my deepest thanks for your generous activity and response to my levy upon your friendship, but about the time your letter arrived I was developing a case of poisoning which has tortured me all the week and kept me away from the office most of the time. The doctor said it was a case of exhausted nerves which made it easy for some food to poison my system. Well, I don't wonder! The last four years have been a heavy and steady drain upon my nervous system, and I marvel today that I am on my feet, however wobbly they are from the buffetings of circumstance.

Just after I last saw you I took a terrific downward shoot and landed flat at the bottom of my life. With what was domestically ahead I knew it was suicide to expect to pull up again with the pen; so I took a late date chance of going into business. We started $65. in debt, and in consequence without capital; today after an even three years of the publishing business we have built up a really remarkable asset but are terrifically handicapped for lack of working funds. A few thousand dollars, with the program laid out, would yield handsome profits within the next year or so.

In the meantime my affairs at the house have not been straightened out from the bad set back of 1921. I got deeply in it that year, and have merely been hanging on ever since. Last year I rolled a number of debts into a second mortgage, on which I agreed to pay off at the rate of $500. a year. The first yearly payment fell due March 30, and without the money to meet it the mortgagee said he would foreclose on a certain date. It was in the face of this that I 'phoned you, hoping that with success in making several loans I could meet the demand. I did raise $200, which I paid, with the understanding that the balance would be paid this week. At this writing I have not raised an additional cent.

I have kept, as you know, to a pretty straight line in the game called life. I still believe my theory was and is right; but as youth begins to subside I realize with increasing conviction that the barriers grow more stubborn. There is no doubt, my dear Locke, had I been white, the whole course would have been paved for me, and all I would have had to do would be to travel steadily. Today were I other than I am, I could go to a score of people about here and get all and more than I need for my urgencies. But like Grant, I am going to fight it out along these lines if it takes all the summer of my life.

Bless you, Locke, for your willing friendship.

Ever,

Letters

———

Chard Powers Smith, poet and novelist, wrote *Where the Light Falls: A Portrait of Edwin Arlington Robinson* (1965).

August 13th 1925.

Dear Chard: —

Don't think me ungracious for not answering your letter sooner, and acknowledging your contribution towards the *Anthology* effort; but the past two weeks have been full of meetings and discussions relating to the purchasing of the Brimmer assets. You can well imagine that my part in these conferences was with an empty purse which put us at a disadvantage with the party who showed a strong inclination, backed with sufficient funds to purchase. The Trustee however, was a very decent fellow, and really wanted us to buy, but of course, in behalf of the creditors he had to get all he could. Well, yesterday, he accepted our offer of $875. I gave him $200. and the court allowed us two weeks to raise the balance of the amount. We came through so far, and now it is up to us to raise the $675. and with the success of this Brimmer once more will be ours. Where the money is to come from heaven knows, but I am hoping that it may be done in parcels if I can't find someone to underwrite the total sum.

In the meantime the *Anthology* work has got to be pushed forward without halt to have it ready in October. A big batch — in fact all the *Yearbook* is ready — goes to the printer in a day or two. Then the final weeding of the selections of poems; then a spell for a real, worthwhile introduction which I am quite anxious to do for the book this year. People hardly realise that the past few years have given us almost an entirely new brood of poets, and these I want to present with some sort of intimate and adequate introduction. The past year has produced little or no work by the figures which a few years ago dominated the scene. Robinson

269

has no poem printed, neither Frost; Masters and Amy Lowell nothing of consequence; Sandburg the same; and so it was with all the so-called major figures of the Renaissance. Yet there was a mass of material printed, good stuff, and all by new singers who are developing a newer harvest of verse.

Do you know that your "Ben Hammond" sticks in my memory since I read it so that I am considering it seriously for inclusion if space will permit. Space is what concerns me deeply because there are so many pieces that literally cry for inclusion. I do so agonize over the problems that the poems force upon me in an effort to give every ounce of loveliness I discover.

I do so want to do so many things to help, and the opportunities are limited because of circumstances. I was thinking that if I could carry out plans, for instance, for an *Anthology* poster again, it would give me a chance to give you some publicity for your forthcoming books. Anyway I can use your picture in the annual *Transcript* article with a poem and that will give the books a send-off that ought to count. It will appear early in October.

Sorry I didn't see you when you passed through but my time was so mixed up I didn't dare to be sure of a free space.

Ever yours,

———————

Chard Powers Smith, who loaned Braithwaite $250 in response to the appeal below, published *Along the Wind* in 1925.

October 8th 1925.

My dear Chard: —
For days I've been trying to get this letter off to you, especially since your note gave me such a feeling of the shut-in-

ness of you, — but the days have been, as you will suspect, full to overflowing with the details of the *Anthology* and all of them overshadowed with the anxiety of financing it. It has reached a crucial stage: the composition has gone along splendidly, the book nearly all set-up and the proofs being read and corrected — but the paper has got to be bought if the . . . printers are going to put it on the press the end of next week, and the money for the binding must be in hand so it can go to the binders and be bound so deliveries can be made immediately. I have developed a proposition to meet the situation if I can put it through. I am going to New York Monday and try to find six or eight people who will loan me $250. each — I will need between $1500 and $1800 — and I will assign the amount, with interest, in advance trade orders as security to protect them. I will assign to some individual or bank as trustee who will receive the cheques in payment of the bills, and who will repay the loans. Last year, which was a poor year owing to the lateness of the book, the orders amounted to $2500, and the year before, to over $4000. So you see, it does sound a reasonable proposition, and its success will make certain the publication of the book around the date I have worked for all summer — that is, the last of this month or the first week in November.

Just as soon as I put this through, I will be free to prepare the *Transcript* article which I want to appear the last of this month.

I hope you will see that I get an early copy of your book. As a matter of fact I ought to have it now, or proofs. All of the *Anthology* is finished but the *Introduction,* and I must have this ready for the printer in about ten days. If it wasn't for the fact that the first form of the book is printed last, it should be not only ready now, but set up. So if the book isn't available, do let me have a set of proofs. I am deluged with proofs publishers have sent me of books that will not . . . be ready for a month or more.

I don't know whether I wrote to thank you for the picture. It came safely, and should reproduce well.

Have been rather expecting Robinson to turn up, now that his migratory season is on. Perhaps he returned to New York by way of Worcester.

———

William Lyon Phelps was a Yale professor whose book, *The Advance of English Poetry in the Twentieth Century*, Braithwaite reviewed in the *Transcript*, October 26, 1918. James Southall Wilson contributed an essay on poetry in the South to the *Anthology of Magazine Verse for 1926*.

May 27th 1926

Dear Professor Phelps: —
A gentleman who desires to remain anonymous has donated three cash prizes in amounts of $100, $50, and $25, for the three best poems published in the *Anthology of Magazine Verse for 1926*, to be determined from a list of ten each selected by three judges. It is the wish of the donor, in which I most heartily share, that you serve as one of the judges. The other two are Robert Frost and Professor James Southall Wilson, of the University of Virginia. May I have your consent to honor the awards with this service?
    With many thanks, I am,

Cordially yours,

———

George E. Haynes, of the Urban League, wrote *The Negro at Work During the World War and During Reconstruction* (1921). Alain Locke's "The Negro Poets of the United States" is one of the introductory essays in Braithwaite's 1926 anthology.

Letters

June 28th 1926

My dear Locke: —

I am sending you (confidentially), a copy of the communication from Haynes in which I was named to give reference as to your candidacy for the Harmon Award for Distinguished Achievement in the field of Race Relations. You will see what I have said with perfect sincerity and truth, and I hope the Committee will honor itself by giving you the Award which you deserve above all else for the splendid achievement of "The New Negro."

In the Sesqui-Centennial Edition of the *Anthology for 1926* I am having a number of *Introductory Essays* on poetry in America; and while at first I had only planned six or eight, to give the idea more substance I have added several more subjects, one of which is a paper on *The Negro in Poetry.* I want you to do this essay for the *Anthology.* Two or three thousand words is about the scope. Can you let me have the manuscript around the first of August? Those who I know can use the money I am promising to pay $50 for the paper on the publication of the book. Among the contributors are James Southall Wilson, professor in the University of Virginia and editor of the Virginia Quarterly Review; George Sterling; Marianne Moore, editor of The Dial; etc.

The family's well, and we are all hoping you can get up to visit us this summer.

Let me hear from you as soon as possible about the article as I am soon preparing the announcement for the *Anthology* with the names of writers of the articles.

Ever,

Like Braithwaite, W. E. B. Du Bois admired Nella Larsen's *Quicksand* more than he did Claude McKay's *Home to Harlem,* much of which, Du Bois wrote in a *Crisis* review in June, 1928, "nauseates me." Dorothy Scarborough, poet and folklorist, published a novel, *In the Land of Cotton*, in 1923.

> 243 Park Avenue
> Arlington Heights,
> Massachusetts.
>
> November 29th 1928

Dr. George E. Haynes,
102 East 22nd Street,
New York City.

My dear Dr. Haynes: —
I have examined the materials submitted by the candidates for the Harmon Awards in Literature for 1928, and beg to report my decisions herewith.

> The First Award I should give to
> Nella Larsen   for her novel   "Quicksand"
> The Second Award to
> Jessie R. Fauset   for her novel   "Plum Bun"
> For honorable mention I submit the following

authors and titles:

> "Home to Harlem," by Claude McKay
> "Dark Princess" by W. E. B. Du Bois
> "Toussaint L'Ouverture" by Leslie Pinckney Hill
> In accordance with your instructions I am forward-

ing by express prepaid, the materials to Professor Dorothy Scarborough.

> With best wishes,
>
> Yours very sincerely,

Despite the arguments Braithwaite advanced for his preferences, the 1928 Harmon Award for fiction went to McKay for *Home to Harlem*. Nella Larsen's *Quicksand* won second honors.

Letters

243 Park Avenue,
Arlington Heights,
Massachusetts.

December 26th 1928

Dr. George E. Haynes,
Harmon Awards,
105 East 22nd Street,
New York City.

My dear Dr. Haynes: —
I am in receipt of the summary of decisions for the Harmon
Awards in Literature as submitted by the judges, and note
the results as tabulated by you. These give, referring only to
the two substantial Awards, the first to Claude McKay, for
his "Home to Harlem" supported by his previous work in
prose and verse, and the second to Nella Larsen Imes, for
her novel "Quicksand," and for this performance only. In
my opinion "Quicksand" is in all respects a better piece of
literature than "Home to Harlem"; and one other judge who
voted for "Home to Harlem" seems really to agree with me;
if this judge had on the basis of this opinion (see report of
Dr. J. Melvin Lee, fifth paragraph) voted for "Quicksand"
for first place, the result would have stood three to two in
favor of Mrs. Imes's novel. I also fail to agree with Dr. Scarborough that the first award should go to McKay's "Home
to Harlem" because the judge considers that "he has more
literary genius than any of the other candidates proposed at
this time." That may be true and yet the work submitted in
competition may easily be inferior to the best he is capable
of and also inferior to the other works submitted for consideration. My method was to judge the material submitted
and not the general and potential character of the authors'
ability. An impartial judgment convinces me that of all the
material entered as candidates, Mrs. Imes's "Quicksand" is
the best and should be given the first award.

Yours very sincerely,

The *Transcript* published the article about Willard Huntington Wright that is mentioned in this letter on February 2, 1929. Once an editor of *Smart Set,* Wright turned to the writing of mystery stories after an illness and created the popular Philo Vance novels. There was considerable public interest in discovering who S. S. Van Dine, Wright's pseudonym, really was.

Edwin F. Edgett, literary editor of the *Transcript,* may have given Braithwaite the idea for his annual anthologies of magazine verse by accident. He wrote to Braithwaite on December 9, 1911, to pass along an inquiry from a reader who supposed she could find in book form a reprint of Braithwaite's newspaper article on the year's poetry. Brimmer published Edgett's *Slings and Arrows* (1922).

243 Park Avenue,
Arlington Heights,
Massachusetts.

January 26th 1929

Dear Wright: —

I saw Edgett today and he is printing the article Saturday, February 2nd. He is happy to give Scribners the right to quote whatever they wish from it. I will mail you some copies, and as the literary section is printed Friday evening I'll stay . . . in to get them off so they will reach you Saturday. Shall I mail Perkins a copy direct?

I was mighty glad to see you again after all these years, and was sorry I couldn't have seen more of you. There were so many things I wanted to speak about. I was sorry my own desperate needs had to take the forefront of the brief meeting. And thank you more than I can say for your promise of the helping hand. You'll be glad, I think, of helping an old friend to get over some of the torturous road you have so triumphantly travelled yourself.

Ever gratefully,

Letters

W. E. B. Du Bois wrote Braithwaite about the *Encyclopaedia Britannica*'s policy of printing "Negro" without capitalizing the initial letter.

> 243 Park Avenue,
> Arlington Heights,
> Massachusetts.
>
> February 18th 1929

My dear Dr. Du Bois: —
Replying to your memorandum concerning the contributions to the new edition of the Encyclopaedia Britannica, I beg to inform you that I declined the invitation to contribute the article on Negro poets, otherwise I would be very glad to stand solidly with you.

As a matter of fact I believe it would be strategic for every Negro contributor to summarily withdraw . . . from publication: the Encyclopaedia can less afford to be without a summary of the Negro's activities and accomplishments at this time, than can the Race in being represented under the conditions of its editorial overlordship.

Do you know Willard Huntington Wright's "Misinforming a Nation," which is a searching analysis of the work's pretensions to an offering of complete information? There's destructive ammunition in this book available for use if the editor doesn't surrender to your demand for justice and complete freedom.

> Cordially yours,

E. Merrill Root contributed two essays to Braithwaite's 1926 anthology. One was on poetry of the Middle West and the other presented his notions about H. L. Mencken's opinions in *Preju-dices, Third Series.*

> 243 Park Avenue,
> Arlington Heights,
> Massachusetts.
>
> August 12th 1929

My dear Root: —
Thanks for your fine letter and the greeting once more which it brings to me. You are never for a long space out of my mind, for struggle as I may I cannot seem to start on the reduction of my indebtedness to you; in fact, these past months I've sunk deeper in the hole. I have a book in prospect, recently discussed with a publisher here, which if it goes through, may by spring lift me out of the financial morass. The blessed Anthology has taken its usual toll the past four months, and for the seventeenth time I'm paying the price.

I'm happy to know about your second book. It shall have my service to the utmost. When "Lost Eden" was published I had been off the *Transcript* for several years. Since Brimmer affairs went on the rocks, I've picked up the reviewing again to help out. This has been since late winter, and I suspect I'll be in the full stride of old again this autumn. So I'll be most happy to give your new book the attention it deserves. I'd rather, of course, review it in the Transcript, where I can use a column and a half or two, than in the Christian Century. It will help a lot in both timeliness and preparation if I can have a set of proofs or advance sheets. If the publication date is November it will fall in a time of great rush and voluminous outflowing of books, and often reviews stand in type some time before printed.

I am enclosing proofs of poems I have selected of yours for inclusion in the 1929 *Anthology.* I hope you won't think I have been too greedy. In case you think there might be objections on account of the book — in case all are included — I'll ask you to say what should be omitted. Permission slip is also enclosed for your signature.

With all good wishes,
Hastily and most cordially,

The Miss Robinson to whom Braithwaite sent the following appeal for aid is unidentified. Because he could not raise funds to continue the series, the annual Braithwaite anthology of the year's best magazine verse did not appear in 1930.

243 Park Avenue,
Arlington Heights,
Massachusetts.

January 3rd 1930.

My dear Miss Robinson: —

Thanks for your very kind letter. The situation is this: Ever since the first Anthology there has been a yearly loss in producing the work. This loss has, as you will see, accumulated, until this year it was too much to bear and shattered me. I am eight or nine thousand dollars in debt; my immediate and imperative need is about three thousand dollars to clear the immediate front if the work is going to be continued this year. I have a large family to provide for and I haven't been altogether just to them with the continual sacrifice that has been necessary in serving poets and poetry.

Because no publisher believed in the book or in the value of poetry or the merits of poets, I published the first two volumes at my own expense; then the work was taken over by a young New York publisher who failed; then a firm here in Boston, Small, Maynard, took the work over and published it from 1917 to 1922; this firm handled it very badly; all the time Small, Maynard published it, through six volumes, I didn't earn enough to cover the expense in time and energy that would produce one volume; and when this firm too, went into bankruptcy they claimed I was in their debt $1500. Then I became associated with Brimmer and brought the Anthology out as my own venture; from 1923 to 1927, I edited and published the book at a great loss; then Brimmer went into bankruptcy. Vinal then brought out the book, and here again I suffered loss, for three months after the book was out Vinal went into bankruptcy, after only binding and distributing 2000 copies, leaving another 2000 in sheets which were sold as bankrupt stock from which, of course, I receive nothing when they are bound and sold as they have been. The 1929 Anthology was brought out by Sully in New York, and you write copies cannot be obtained in the Washington bookstores. My difficulties have not been this year in publishing the book. It's from the accumulation of years which came to a crisis this year with the editorial preparation. I sacrificed to make the work possible in its continuance of the service which was its purpose to render, risking everything for its sake, as my letter to the subscribers informed you. I must have at least three thousand dollars as soon as I can get it to salvage the situation; upon the success of obtaining this relief depends the 1930 volume. I cannot go on with the work under conditions which have brought about this smash. If you can interest those you have in mind to contribute, whatever the amount, towards this fund, I shall be very grateful to you; and you and they can be assured that it is for a cause in which all poets share.

> With deep appreciation,
> Yours very sincerely,

To the following letter Lawrence Lee, an editor of Street & Smith publications, replied that Braithwaite's stories were suitable neither for *Excitement* nor *Short Story Magazine*.

243 Park Avenue
Arlington Heights,
Massachusetts.

July 8th 1930

Mr. Lawrence Lee,
79–89 Seventh Avenue
New York City.

My dear Mr. Lee: —

It was very generous and fine of you to write me so hopefully about the stories I want to place in your hands. Turning to fiction after so many long slavish years devoted to the interests of poetry cannot help but be accompanied with a great deal of speculation, as well as hope — hope created by necessity. I shall, however, welcome your frankness, and trust to profit by it. The stories I am sending are: "On the Knees of the Moon," the novelette of thirty thousand words, "Sylvia Tampers With Tradition," "Mr. Gary's Blunder," and "The Upper Field." I daresay, there is variety among these, and I trust, an interest, to warrant the attention you give them. For that attention I am most grateful.

Thanks warmly for the hope you offer that I might possibly obtain a copy of your ballad. I fear you are a bit too modest about its value. As you know a ballad is one of the most difficult of poetic forms to achieve with its simplicity of speech weaving a story of action or passion. I know, I think, your other poetry too well, not to believe that your ballad comes of a rightful heritage. I hope those "few essential pieces," you will not postpone too long before gathering into a book. The front line ranks are thinning of the poets who in the second decade were advancing the traditional standards of the art. A book will place you.

I appreciate deeply what you say about the service the Anthology has striven to render. I did want to carry it on to the twentieth volume at least. My zeal these many years

281

overwhelmed me completely. I must now make good the cost of those years.

With all good wishes for your kindness, believe me,

Yours very sincerely,

—————

Novelist Nella Larsen published *Quicksand* in 1928 and *Passing* in 1929. The book Braithwaite says in this letter he is sending her is *Our Lady's Choir, a Contemporary Anthology of Verse by Catholic Sisters* (1931). On the abortive *Omnibus of Negro Literature,* see my "W. S. Braithwaite's Southern Exposure: Rescue and Revelation," *Southern Literary Journal,* 3, No. 2 (1971), 49–61.

> 243 Park Avenue,
> Arlington Heights,
> Massachusetts.
>
> June 19th 1934

My dear Nella: —

Fate plays us damnably mean tricks for a breach of years, and then repentant, showers its good Fortune with lavish generosity. Hardy's god, Circumstance, as you know, sets the stage, and the actors upon it, for the inscrutable drama of Chance, sweeping our emotions into the pit of experience. The whole thing stings — stings under the indifference, the unremembered, detached and unassociated sliding of the years: but we do not know of the sting and laceration, until that lavish generosity has bestowed the good Fortune. I don't know how it was with you since the Time after Saturday — but the above is a reading of my spirit when I recall your remark: "It is eleven years since I saw you in Boston." I feel the whole complicated web of Time and Chance and Circumstance working its irony upon my emotions. I missed you once in New York, the day I called you up from the old Waldorf-Astoria, just before, or just after, perhaps, you had published "Passing"; and I missed you here in Boston again, while you were hidden in the depths of La Patrie; and your winged words from Majorca shot by the disturbing threshold of my darkened house of misery the first Depression summer.

Then — someone dropped your name into the well of my consciousness last Thursday, startling it with the fact that you were in New York, someone who knew only that you were in New York, but did not know your address nor 'phone, but said Harry Keelam did, and that they would get them from him for me. I called you Friday night — no answer; and again Saturday morning, and Lo! the accumulated memories of eleven years were transformed into the golden thread guiding me out of the labyrinth of mischance and separation into the clear recognition of a destiny no longer to be thwarted, but to build a glorious palace of Art for the Race.

You know I said over the 'phone when you asked me a question that I drink Beauty! And to be rude, how I guzzled it during those hours of dusk and echoes from the Avenue! Lingering on a subsiding departure you'll remember I said, "I have championed you!" I have a special annunciation from Heaven for the Immaculate gifts of Art, and take the angelic manifest of good tidings unto the shepherds who tend the flocks of Beauty and Vision. — I think I had better slide off this cloud upon which I have been floating and take a chair in the mart!

This *Omnibus of Negro Literature* has obsessed me these months and months. I want to get forward with it, and there is hard and laborious work to do in the preparation of it. I've been handicapped because the depression all but wiped me out. I could hardly paint the horror of these recent months. Ten days ago I went off to Philadelphia and Washington to try and get financial help to start me on this work. And I need it today, tomorrow, if I am not to lose valuable time and that vibrant energy which drives one to the achievement of a fine purpose. You gave me a new heart with your great promise to help me to the money that will realize this great purpose. This work will stun the country into a recognition and acceptance of the spiritual and cultural equality of the Race. Its unity and completeness will present a standard and volume of literary expression and embodiment that will do more than all the politics and propaganda that have been in action for a generation towards the solution of the so-called 'problem.' There is no problem where the spirit is concerned, where Beauty burns away all barriers, where desire and passion for the Vision cups a common understanding. For twenty-five years I gave my best for the poets and poetry of America; it was a labor of love that cost me dearly; at the same time I proved something that no other man of the race dared even so much as to attempt; I won something precious for the future hope and aspiration of the artistic and creative youth of the Negro; now I want to add a tower to that foundation, a tower that will stand glowing in the reflection of that heavenly and divine sun of the Imagination, a tower on the hill of our sufferings and repressions, of our denials and persecutions, . . . which will throw its beams far out over the troubled waters of the Racial sea. Do your best dear Nella, and quickly!

When you told me you were a Catholic you will recall that I was silent. Thinking of this since, I was afraid you might have misunderstood the silence and thought I had been opposed to the Faith. It isn't so. My mood was suddenly reverent, because I felt compressed within those brief minutes the finest art of the world, in all forms and mediums, whose roots and developments were in the Catholic Faith. Perhaps you will be surprised to learn that I produced a book three years ago, long neglected by those who should have cherished the honor of sending it forth to the world. I am sending you a copy, as one who lays a lily upon the Sanctuary.

And won't you send me the book and photograph which I left behind when I left? Please inscribe the photograph for me.

Do let me hear from you.

Faithful always,

———————

When Braithwaite wrote the letter that follows, Benjamin Brawley, author of *A Short History of the American Negro* (1913), *The Negro in Literature and Art* (1918), *A New Survey of English Literature* (1925), etc., was teaching at Howard University, of which Mordecai W. Johnson was president.

243 Park Avenue,
Arlington Heights,
Massachusetts.

June 24th 1934

My dear Brawley: —

My stay in New York was much longer than I had expected, and so I did not return home as soon as I meant to after leaving Washington. This explains the delay in writing you and in dispatching the letter to President Johnson. I have written him with this post and am enclosing, as I promised, a copy of the communication. As I said, I trust you will find the opportunity to talk the matter over with him and assure him of the great service he can render the cause of our achievements in letters by giving me his support.

It was a delight to see you again and to spend that while, all too brief, with you and Mrs. Brawley at the lunch to which you asked me. It was all too brief there at your home, and all too brief there at Locke's, to say all that has been storing up through these years since we last met. And for your generous thoughtfulness in giving that helping hand when I left I do not know sufficiently how to express my appreciation. This project of the Omnibus has been with me for long, haunting my desire to get it forward, and yet being so handicapped I knew not how, that it was only by taking a desperate start, that I took my departure insufficiently provided for. I am glad I did, though it seemed too much like trusting to fortune, because I believe a substantial progress on the gigantic effort will be made. It has seemed all along too big a thing, too important to the aspiration of the Race not to take a risk. Any book by a Negro author should be good for a sale at least of ten or fifteen thousand copies, and we have got to make the Race book-conscious to that extent. It is our literary self-preservation, for the publishers have been sadly disappointed in their experience of the last ten years. At this critical time we must stand together and work and fight, not only for ourselves, but for the future creative expression of the Race.

I will write you again soon. Mrs. Braithwaite was happy to hear of my visit with you and Mrs. Brawley, and not having heard of Mrs. Brawley's loss sooner wishes me to convey to her her deep sympathy. I just heard this morning that Jim Johnson is dangerously ill; I know nothing further and am deeply concerned at the news.

Let me hear from you, and I will keep you informed as to the progress and results of my crusade in behalf of the Omnibus. Again let me thank you for your generosity. Remember me most kindly to Mrs. Brawley.

Ever yours,

———————

Florence Read was president of Spelman College in the Atlanta University System when Braithwaite sent her this letter. He had given several addresses at the university at the close of a southern lecture tour. In February he returned, at the invitation of Atlanta's President John Hope, to accept a professorship he was to hold until his retirement in 1945. See my "W. S. Braith-waite's Southern Exposure: Rescue and Revelation," *Southern Literary Journal*, 3, No. 2 (1971), 49–61, and "William Stanley Braithwaite and the College Language Association," *CLA Journal*, 15 (1971), 117–25.

December 2nd 1934

My dear Miss Read: —

I was so sorry not to have been able to stop over at Atlanta on my return from Tuskegee as I had planned, but I arrived at Atlanta at ten-thirty at night and took the eleven-ten train for Washington homeward bound. At Tuskegee I received a disquieting letter from Boston which made it necessary to reach here as soon as possible. My home here has been hanging on the suspensive operation of the Home Owners Loan Corporation for many months, and I believed when I left in October that the details had all been smoothed out and that it would go through securely and relieve me of a disastrous domestic upheaval. But the whole fabric of rescue has collapsed, the Home Owners Corporation informing me on Wednesday last of their refusal to refinance any more homes caught in the tangled web of these depression years. So at present I am staring foreclosure in the face unless I can raise a thousand dollars for the bank immediately, and in these times that kind of currency doesn't flow in on the tides of poetic rhythms. If this breakup should go through I am wondering how it would affect what, since leaving Atlanta, I have been looking forward to with a sort of passionate eagerness?

It seems so strange for me to be dreaming and brooding over a service which a year ago I would have considered impossible. Never before have I come home with a nostalgic yearning for other scenes and associations which in so short a time had been unfamiliar and unknown. I have done a task in this northern and sea-washed corner of the

land; it's finished, a labor of love, that won the appreciation
and stimulated the taste of many for the beauty and wisdom
of poetry, and I feel like a ghost in the field where the harvest is over. Now it is almost with a mystic consecration
that I look back upon the six weeks that I was in the South,
where I looked for the first time into the soul of a race and
saw the wistful yearning for a glimpse of the bright image of
beauty. I am still quivering with the magic of the potentiality that brushed against the nerves of my exposed sympathy. To quicken those sensibilities, is there a more divine
service that one can render one's fellowmen? To wash their
lives, their tasks, their studies, with the liquid freshness of
Arnold's "Sweetness and Light," drawn from those inexhaus-
tible spiritual fountains of the world's great creative souls —
the men and women who looked with Blake's divine eye
through the window of the sun into Eternity. In spite of the
flight these words may seem to take on the wings of emotion, there is a kind of hard reality in the thought. The
mood of the seraphical Saint Teresa (do you remember?)

Live in these conquering leaves; live all the same;
And walk through all tongues one triumphant flame;
Live here, great heart; and love, and die, and kill;
And bleed, and wound, and yield, and conquer still. —

and,

O thou undaunted daughter of desires!
By all thy dower of lights and fires;
By all the eagle in thee, all the dove;
By all thy lives and deaths of love;
By thy large draughts of intellectual day,
And by thy thirsts of love more large than they;
By all thy brim-filled bowls of fierce desire,
By thy last morning's draught of liquid fire;
By the full kingdom of that final kiss
That sealed thy parting soul, and sealed thee His;

By all the Heav'n thou hast in Him
(Fair sister of the seraphim!);
By all of Him we have in thee;
Leave nothing of myself in me.
Let me so read thy life, that I
Unto all life of mine may die!

This rhapsodic tribute of Crashaw's seems to fit my mood for the late experience better than any other. But I feel no martyrdom as I should have felt a year ago. We cannot understand these things can we, those of us who look beyond the horizon for reality? It's that climbing up the slopes, so crowded with broken dreams, with weary hearts that have ceased to listen on the way for those poignant and mystic strains which echo across the hill-crests.

I am sending you a little package of books at the first moment I can get them to the post. I found a copy of my second book of poems "The House of Falling Leaves," which it will please me to send you; with a copy of "Our Lady's Choir," and "The Golden Treasury of Magazine Verse." And if I can find a copy, "The Book of Modern British Verse."

I shall make a manuscript copy of the best of the new and unpublished poems. I shall make, if you want, a manuscript of the best poems in the two published books together with the unpublished poems, for the reprint which you were so kind enough as to want to make. We will give it a new title, and I want you to accept the dedication of this reprint if you will.

As soon as I can re-polish a bit and make a clean copy of it, I will send you the lecture on "The New Emancipation," which you thought you would like to print there at Atlanta.

I shall send you soon the draft of my functioning in creative representation at the University of which we spoke. Please commend me with heartiness to Dr. Hope.

Faithfully yours,

This letter is a reply to an inquiry about the manuscript of E. A. Robinson's poem "Ben Jonson Entertains a Man from Stratford." Gardiner, Maine, where Robinson spent much of his life, was the Tilbury Town of his poems. Carl J. Weber edited *Letters of E. A. Robinson to Howard G. Schmitt* (1943).

Atlanta University
Box 333
Atlanta, Georgia.

December 1st. 1935

Dear Mr. Schmitt: —
Don't mind in the least telling you to whom I sold the manuscript of Ben Jonson: he was Mr. Andrew McCance, the proprietor of Smith & McCance's bookstore, Ashburton Place, Boston, Mass.

I have some copies of the Anthologies which I don't mind selling, but of course, they are at home. A number of the volumes are rare and at a premium, especially the *1913, 1917, 1921, 1914* . . . and *1924.* They all have poems by Robinson included. I shall be home for Christmas when I'll see what is available.

I envy you your pilgrimage to Gardiner. And I want to add I admire your devotion to Robinson's memory and genius. Do you contemplate writing about him? I knew him for twenty-five years, and between 1909 and 1924 intimately. When no one else in America thought of a collected edition of his works, I did, and urged him, much against his inclination and belief in the practicability of one, to make the suggestion to his publisher to bring one out. His universal recognition began with the publication of the first issue of the *Collected Poems.* In a letter he wrote me after his publisher had consented to bring out the *Collected Poems,* he said: "The idea was yours and I think you ought to be the first to know a collected edition of my poems is to be published." I am quoting from memory. Alas, the letter went with some sixty others at a time of great emergency. How I wish I could repurchase them and all the other rich material of this greatest of our poets which I once owned.

Cordially yours,

Richard A. Carroll, who was to become chairman of the English Department at Spelman College, had begun his teaching career at Johnson C. Smith University when he wrote to ask Braith-waite about the merit of undertaking an exhaustive study of the works of Charles W. Chesnutt.

Atlanta University
Box 333
Atlanta, Georgia.

November 25th 1939

My dear Mr. Carroll: —
I trust you will not charge me with any lack of interest for your letter and the idea therein suggested for a critical study of Chesnutt, because of this tardy response to it. Many distractions these past few weeks, both personal and in relation to my academic associations, have affected deeply the readiness which I should have given to my corre-spondence.

Chesnutt calls painfully aloud for such a study as you propose; really the foremost of our imaginative prosemen has been terribly neglected. As I hinted in the paper in the Locke volume, he stands in a curious relationship to Ameri-can literature, because of his solitariness in a period when a group of white American novelists and story-tellers were discovering the Negro as fiction material under the freedom that had so recently come to him, and were trying to 'fix' him, as Henry James would say, in a pattern that would serve the national social and economic scene. Chesnutt's imaginative study of the 'color line' did something more than create a new milieu in the fiction of the day; it propagated the roots of a truer and more vital relationship between the races in a democracy. Attempting this through an imaginative representation of life and truth, the aim was of course, an equality of opportunity and privilege based upon spiritual values which would in time determine the social and economic status of the Negro both as individual and Race. His solitariness in the age of Page and Cable, and even Dunbar, was that the Negro character in fiction was not fixed, but of a plastic nature, to be shaped and toned by all the idealisms that made the other Americans.

Let me urge you to pursue the study, for it would certainly add to the distinction of American literary scholarship, and what would be of equal, if not greater importance, it would mark the real *beginning* of a sound and critical and, as you say, exhaustive, study of the Negro in American literature.

If I can be of assistance to you in any way in the preparation of the study please do not hesitate to command me. With sincere good wishes for your success, believe me,

Yours very truly,
William Stanley Braithwaite

Olive Lindsay Wakefield gave public readings from the works of her brother, poet Vachel Lindsay. *Black Boy*, Richard Wright's fictionalized autobiography, appeared in 1945.

409 Edgecombe Avenue
Apt. 13-A,
New York, 32,
New York.

June 18th. 1945

My dear Mrs. Wakefield: —
Please pardon my delay in replying to your letter of May
13th, which has been due to some pressing work upon
which the time was limited.

I have read with a great deal of interest the enclosures
accompanying your letter, and I think the object for which
you are working to honor Vachel's memory is both a glorious and desirable one. He dedicated his splendid art to an
ideal that America as a nation and man as the inheritor of
the Divine will and spirit (as Emerson and others so insis-
tently preached) cannot afford to neglect. A true realization
of man's necessary obedience to this ideal will solve so
many of the most perplexing problems of creed and race
that have kept shadowed and disturbing our social and economic relations. Men have, as Micah tells us, but 'to do
justly, and to love kindness, and to walk humbly,' to establish peace and happiness among them, and rid the world of
intolerance and oppression.

I met Vachel first in 1913, here in New York, and when
he came to Boston on his first visit had the honor and pleasure of taking him about and showing the city. From time
to time thereafter for a number of years I would spend time
with him on his visits to Boston.

Are you contemplating a biography? The one by Edgar
L. Masters was not, in my opinion, satisfactory. I don't think
Masters' cynical temper had either the sympathy or understanding to interpret or portray Vachel's art or spirit. Too
little has been done about Vachel's drawings. Have you
communicated with Ridgely Torrence? He has some very
interesting reminiscences of Vachel when he called at the of-

fice of the old *Critic* when Ridgely was on the editorial staff, with manuscripts and drawings.

I am afraid there is an over-emphasis, much as I admire the book, on the kind of philosophy intensified in "Black Boy." The truth is that Jews, Italians, Poles, and the Irish themselves, as my Boston nativity is aware of, have all suffered indignities and injustice in *democratic* America. . . . Nature has kept the secret for all the solutions in her keeping — and always in the end is she triumphant.

Cordially yours,
William Stanley Braithwaite

———————

This letter testifies to the range of Braithwaite's associations and suggests the kind of editorial and promotional service he sometimes provided by arrangement. Braithwaite's "Walter de la Mare and His Poetry" was in the Boston *Transcript*, November 25, 1916. Swallow Press published Pauline Hanson's *Forever Young* in 1948.

409 Edgecombe Avenue
New York 32
N. Y.

July 12th 1948

Sir Walter de la Mare
Athenaeum Club
London, England.

Dear Sir Walter: —

I am not sure that you remember me, but on your first visit to America some years ago, I had the pleasure of meeting you on Staten Island, and riding across the harbor to New York preceding the interview which I did in honor of your visit and which was published in the Boston *Transcript*. You came on that occasion to accept in behalf of Rupert Brooke, the posthumous award of the Loines Prize at Yale. It was also my pleasure to review practically all of your books from "Peacock Pie" on, in the columns of the *Transcript,* and especially those two masterpieces of modern English fiction, "Memoirs of a Midget" and "The Return."

You may be aware of my labors in behalf of contemporary English and American poetry over a long period in the *Transcript,* and the annual series of the Anthologies. After a long period of University teaching, I am once again reviving an interest in the younger poets.

My purpose in writing you at this time is to persuade you to join myself and others over here — Archibald MacLeish, Genevieve Taggard, Mark Van Doren, among them — to give a helping hand to one of the most promising of the younger American poets who is about to publish her first book. This in the form of a brief statement. The poet's work is very delicate, but of a quality that manifests a deep and enchanting sensibility.

You are, of course, to decide whether the verse is worthy of your comment. If you are willing to look it over for this purpose, and will reply to that effect, I'll be happy to send you copies of Miss Hanson's poems. They do not make a bulky content, and can be examined in a very brief time.

I would be deeply grateful for your word of recommendation, if you feel you can give it. And I am sure your countless admirers in America . . . will be grateful too, for your generosity to young talent.

May I offer my congratulations for the Birthday Honor which came to you as a high recognition of the rare and important contribution you have made to English letters?

With deep appreciation and thanks, believe me,

Very respectfully and sincerely yours,
William Stanley Braithwaite

The daughter of George W. Cable mentioned in this letter was Margaret Cable Brewster, with whom Braithwaite was in correspondence as early as 1917. *Scribner's Magazine* published one of her poems in May, 1920.

409 Edgecombe Avenue
New York 32
N. Y.

January 18th 1950

Mr. Philip Butcher
1723 North Broadway
Baltimore 13
Maryland.

Dear Mr. Butcher: —

In replying to your letter of the 12th inst., requesting information about George W. Cable with "various Negroes and with race relations," I wish I could be of more service than is possible.

I did meet Mr. Cable once when he came to Boston from Northampton, where he lived his latter years as you know, to address a gathering of colored citizens. What he said on that occasion, that is in detail, I have now no recollection; the tenor of his remarks was in general sympathy for the plight and treatment of the Race, with references to the courageous attitude he had taken in his native New Orleans, which so aroused public opinion against him that he was obliged to leave and make his home in Massachusetts. This is the general impression I have retained of that meeting.

Some time in the 1920s, I had a brief correspondence with his daughter whose verses I discovered in *Scribner's Magazine*, and had commented on favorably in my *Tran-*

script columns. I do not know what became of the letters, but I do recall vaguely that she referred to her father's interest and sacrifice in behalf of racial justice.

Chesnutt never mentioned Cable to me as far as I can remember.

There was a man of that period who must have had, if I am not mistaken, rich associations with Cable, as he had with many other writers sympathetic with the Negro's cause. His name was Charles Alexander, and though he has been dead these many years, if any of his descendents can be traced, it might yield some interesting material. He was a printer, owned and edited several publications, and carried on an extensive correspondence with interesting people. He came to Boston to live from, I think, some part of Ohio.

Mrs. Charles Williams, of Washington, daughter of Chesnutt, whose husband was librarian at Howard University many years ago — if she is still living, could be helpful in regards to Chesnutt's correspondence. Her sister, whose home was in Cleveland, had, she told me, all of their father's material. But I may be telling you something you already know.

Have you written to Du Bois? If not, and since he lives across the hall from me here, I'd be glad to ask him about Cable. His letters, etc., are being edited and arranged for publication; only last week he told me how, in spite of their great quantity, they have been preserved and filed. With appreciation for your kind personal sentiments, believe me,

Sincerely yours,
William S. Braithwaite

————

Braithwaite paid a later tribute to Marianne Moore, who contributed an essay to his anthology for 1926, than the following letter of congratulation. He wrote this poem in November, 1958:

To Marianne Moore
For Her Birthday

May you reign
In the domain
Of the Muse —
Be profuse
With birthdays
Wreathed with praise —
A goodly sum
Yet to come —
O Queen of syllables
Where magic dwells!

January 15th 1952

Dear Miss Moore: —
May I offer you my congratulations for the award of the Bollingen Prize? It could well have been the Nobel award for the full measure of the deserving recognition that is your due for the contribution you have made to American poetry both as an original poet and as a critical and editorial monitor of poets.

How much, I wonder, does the present generation realize the part you played in introducing Eliot's "The Waste Land" to the public, an act that had a profound bearing upon the tendencies and development of the imagination and technique of a whole generation of poets. It seems fitting that Mr. Auden, a disciple of the prophetic Eliot, should have confirmed the distinction of this award.

With best wishes for an abundant New Year in health and satisfaction, believe me

Cordially yours,
W.S.B.

Letters

Braithwaite's letter to Viking Press editor B. W. Huebsch, once on the Boston *Transcript* staff, is one of several he wrote in 1952 in hope of finding a publisher for a favorite project. His prospectus listed the contributors (some of whom, at least, knew nothing of the plan) as Hugh Gloster, Langston Hughes, Sterling Brown, Alain Locke, Jessie Fauset, Ulysses Lee, Blyden Jackson, Philip Butcher, Arna Bontemps, Arthur P. Davis, and Era Bell Thompson. The introductory essay was to be by Braithwaite, and the contributors were to supply chapters on Richard Wright, William Attaway, Frank Yerby, Willard Motley, Ann Petry, Saunders Redding and Owen Dodson, Ralph Ellison, William Gardner Smith, Chester Himes, William Demby, and Zora Neale Hurston. One result of the idea was the article by Braithwaite on William Wells Brown that appeared in the *Pittsburgh Courier.* Three years later he was in search of a publisher for *A Century of the Negro Novelist,* a book to be composed of passages from selected works together with biographical and critical sketches. This project, too, came to naught.

Dear Huebsch: —
Thanks for the consideration you and your Board gave to my proposal for a symposium on the Contemporary Negro novelist. I was a little surprised, however, that the idea suggested a "review or criticism of literature from the racial point of view," for that was not the intention. The work was intended to be a historical survey of the Negro's practice in fiction, and in this form, of his representation of Negro life and experience in America during the last hundred years. This covers the span of the Negro's existence from slavery to his developing integration into all phases of national life. The work promised, therefore, to be a social history, not only of the Negro, but of his relationships with his fellow-citizens, presented through the terms of an imaginative and creative form of art. It was chiefly a criticism of life by a group of authors conditioned by circumstances, who were

peculiarly equipped by education, tradition, and opportunity, to express this life through the medium of the novel. It is a not unfamiliar pattern in other countries where there has been a conflict of ethnic stocks working towards a solution of understanding and reciprocal responsibility in the national unity.

White novelists have had their say in depicting and relating Negro characters and life, and have had their works appraised critically, from Mrs. Stowe, Joel Chandler Harris, Thomas Nelson Page, Stephen Crane, and William Dean Howells, to Bucklin Moon, William Faulkner, and Sinclair Lewis, among other contemporaries. In this field the Negro has not been appraised, to the extent where his growth and progress have been aesthetically defined . . . through successive generations from slavery to the present participation in our democratic institutions. This wide and dramatic scope of progress may be symbolized by the personality and efforts of the novelist William Wells Brown at one end of the century and Willard Motley or Ralph Ellison at the other end; or by Frederick Douglass, fugitive slave and abolitionist, and the contemporary of Brown, and Ralph Bunche, the diplomat and publicist and Nobel prize winner of today. Within these brackets, spanning a century, it is the Negro novelist who has probed the soul of the Negro as an individual and as a group, and laid bare his anguish and aspirations, his great struggle to achieve a dignified and respected place in the scheme of American democracy.

In this fiction is the eloquence as well as the bitterness of hope and frustration, the humor as well as the tragedy of a people both rejected and encouraged by the destiny that stamped them as American citizens. As beasts of burden they played a major part in laying the foundations of the nation's economic wealth, and in so doing sang their hearts out in folk-songs of religious faith and beauty unequaled in the western world. This spirit saturated the humor of the early fiction until, soured by continued proscription which received no intervention from Heaven, these religious aspirations were turned into instruments of violent protests that permeated the fiction of the middle phase, known as the Negro Renaissance.

Thirty years ago I conceived the idea of summing up the Negro's contributions to American poetry in an anthology. It was a work that needed to be done, but I could not at the time undertake it, and so told James Weldon Johnson about it and urged him to do it. He produced "The Book of American Negro Poetry," which was very successful, and was the first of some half dozen anthologies of the kind successfully published. It seems strange that poetry, which is acknowledged to have none of the commercial appeal of fiction, should have given the Negro author his day in the critical literary court while the novelist has been denied. This lack was what prompted me to propose the work outlined in the draft submitted to you, and I thought it a happy coincidence that the centennial of the first novel by an American Negro should happen to fall in a pattern that had historical significance.

Please forgive this stretched-out expression of my appreciation for the sympathetic attention given the proposal.

Before closing I would like to make a suggestion which I believe has some merit. It is for a Viking Portable from the works of Algernon Blackwood. Works of his, such as "The Education of Uncle Paul," "A Prisoner in Fairyland," "The Extra Day," "Jules Vallon," and the extraordinary group of stories in "Pan's Garden," in so accessible a form, will win the support of old admirers and gain many a new one in this later generation. He had a strange and beautiful power of whimsy that not even J. M. Barrie could out-match; he established in "Pan's Garden," a mystical kinship between the soul of man and the spirit of nature, as exciting as any vision of Blake's. . . .

W.S.B.

———

In addition to his piece on William Wells Brown, "The First Negro Novelist," the *Pittsburgh Courier* published Braithwaite's "Why I Believe in God" (December 22, 1956), but it did not commission the articles he proposed in this letter, written in 1953.

Mr. George F. Brown
Editor, Courier Magazine
Pittsburgh, Pa.

Dear Mr. Brown: —
Thanks very much for the check in payment for my feature article on William Wells Brown, appearing in your issue of May thirtieth last.

May I take the liberty to suggest some articles which will be drawn from my autobiographical material? Appearing in your magazine they would have a twofold significance. First, I think, presented by our leading racial newspaper, they would reveal our literary integration into American literature at a time when a double-standard of criticism was prevalent; and secondly, establish for our younger generation a historical note of importance in the early years of our broadening literary progress.

The idea is to do some sketches of figures with whom I had associations, drawn from my personal experiences. One such would be Col. Thomas Wentworth Higginson, a notable contemporary of the great New England writers, an author himself, a great protagonist of the anti-slavery movement, and colonel of the First South Carolina Volunteers composed of Negro soldiers he commanded in the Civil War, and of whom he gave an account in his book "Army Life in a Black Regiment." This book has been highly regarded as one of the most important documentary records of the conflict. Col. Higginson was also the first to call attention to, and promote interest in, the exalted qualities of the Spirituals. He did this in an article he wrote about them in The Atlantic Monthly, back in the 1870's, which started them on the road to the popularity and appreciation they achieved.

Another figure is Amy Lowell. Since her death a quarter of a century ago, I have been approached many times by writers and editors, to give my reminiscences of her, since it was known how closely I was associated with her during the early years when she was struggling for recognition; I helped her greatly to attain that recognition. But I have refused to give any information to others or to write about her.

There is also Professor Charles T. Copeland — the famous "Copey" — of Harvard, whose influence upon American letters has been exerted through the young men who, taking his courses — Broun, Benchley, Perkins, etc. — went on to achieve distinction. Though stung often by his caustic wit, they made of him an idol. His reputation as an academic teacher is the nearest that we have in America to the famous Dr. Jowett at Oxford. I was responsible for Copeland's famous "The Copeland Reader," and did practically all the work on it. The story of this book is one of the most interesting in American publishing, and has never been told, because I hold the facts and truth of it — which, incidentally, can be confirmed by Lucius Beebe.

I started James Gould Cozzens on his career, having published his first novel when he was a young sophomore at Harvard, and who has been . . . a Pulitzer prize-winner. The same is true of Edward J. O'Brien, author of "The Best Short Stories" and many other books.

These sketches might attract considerable interest from the white world of books and authors, and redound to the literary credit of the Negro. It is to serve this interest that I suggest them.

I shall be deeply appreciative of the consideration that you might give the project.

Yours very sincerely,
WSB

Burton J. Kline, as editor of the magazine section of the *Transcript*, was Braithwaite's principal sponsor during his early years as contributor to the newspaper, and the men became friends. After Kline left the *Transcript*, he became Sunday editor of the New York *Tribune*, which fired him for printing Theodore Dreiser's "Love." A frustrated creative writer, he completed drafts of several novels in his late years.

409 Edgecombe Avenue
New York 32
N. Y.

August 20th 1955

Dear Kline: —
When I was just growing up into youth I swam daily in the foamy seas of English poetry. My discovery of Keats was more startling than the experience Saul had when the Lord exploded a bomb in the soul of the man on the road to Tarsus. There was a line Keats chanted about the 'rosy mantlings of the dawn.' In those days I worked for Ginn & Co., in their plant just across the Longfellow Bridge in Lower Cambridge. Those Marshes that Howells described so poetically lay just north and west of the basin. I rode over there daily from our house up in Sussex Street where the South End tapered into Roxbury. I had to be at work at seven o'clock in the morning, and as I travelled the way in the old-fashioned horse cars, I accompanied the dawn, and luxuriated in those 'rosy mantles' that Keats described. I have seen many a dawn since those far-away days and have never lost the magic of that vision. Later I was to catch a new wonder from the sight when I read Arthur Symons and had him tell me that 'Dawn was the visible delay of Day.' Well, this morning I looked upon the 'mantles' again, as they draped the roof-tops of the Bronx. And the ecstasy drove me to the typewriter and a letter to you. A letter with a touch of anxiety to know that both you and Madeleine

continue to gain in health and tranquility. And I wanted it to testify to my constant thought of you and your work. How better am I to express this than to quote a letter from Erasmus to his friend Servatius Roger? I echo and expose all the feelings and sentiments of Erasmus' words. "You say," wrote the great Humanist, "there is something which you take very hard, which torments you wretchedly, which in short makes life a misery to you. Your looks and your carriage betray this, even if you were silent. Where is your wonted and beloved cheerful countenance gone, your former beauty, your lively glance? Whence come these sorrowful downcast eyes, whence this perpetual silence, so unlike you, whence the look of a sick man in your expression? Assuredly as the poet says, 'the sick body betrays the torments of the lurking soul, likewise its joys: it is to the mind that the face owes its looks, well or ill.'

"It is certain then, my Servatius, that there is something which troubles you, which is destroying your former good health. But what am I to do now? Must I comfort you or scold you? Why do you hide your pain from me as if we did not know each other by this time. You are so deep that you do not know your closest friend, or trust even the most trustworthy; or do you not know that the hidden fire burns stronger? . . . And for the rest, my Servatius, what is it makes you draw in and hide yourself like a snail? I suspect what the matter is: you have not yet convinced yourself that I love you very much. So I entreat you by the thing sweetest to you in life, by our great love, if you have any care for your safety, if you want me to live unharmed, not to be at such great pains to hide your feelings, but whatever it is, entrust it to my safe ears. I will assist you in whatever way I can with help or counsel. But if I cannot provide either, still it will be sweet to rejoice with you, to weep with you, to live and die with you. Farewell, my Servatius, and look after your health."

Thus Erasmus, who in 1487, from Steyn, wrote what in substance is my thought and devotion to you.

In the midst of a busy preparation on the research for the biography of Locke I have given my relaxing moments to a reading of Erasmus. What a mind and what a personality! He shed the spirit of enlightenment in the Northern Renaissance, liberating the spirit of Northern Europe from tradition and the tyranny of the Schoolmen. . . . But like Keats in the garden at Hampstead thrilled by the story of the nightingale, I am halted and pulled back to the matter in hand.

It surprised me to learn a couple of weeks back that I had not lost the urgency to turn out some verses. I was asked to do a poem for the tenth anniversary issue of *Ebony,* a magazine that has developed into an amazing periodical enterprise. It has a circulation of half a million copies. And has mirrored the life and achievements of the Negro during this past decade as no other medium has ever done. Well, when I started on the verse it ran away with me and when I came to the end it ran to two hundred lines. I doubt if they will publish all of it, as the editor thought of it in terms of about one hundred lines. I gave him permission to cut where he would. I wrote it in couplets, so I don't think it will be too difficult to cut — though I couldn't put my own hand to it. . . .

Here we are on the threshold of September! And these winds and rains and floods warning of its approach. They whirled all around you, and I pray gave you not too many anxious moments. In our immediate vicinity we got only the lash of the rain, but roads leading into the city were very hazardous. Yes, before many weeks now, I'll be travelling over to Jersey to see you and that feast of talk for which I hunger. We must make full use of Time to laden the spirit with the old delights that bloomed in the New England years, for how many more Septembers and Aprils there are to be one dare not think. Your novel to get dressed for its birthday party, my biography to get recorded and left as a legacy for those who look back upon our days and wonder how we strove . . . to keep firm hands on courage.

Emma sends her best to you both, and I the safe en-
wrapping of those 'rosy mantles' to multiply and enrich your
day.

Ever
W.S.B.

Sociologist Charles S. Johnson, once editor of *Opportunity*, was
the author of *The Negro in American Civilization* (1930) and
many other works on race relations. Braithwaite's biography of
Locke had to be abandoned for lack of financial support.

409 Edgecombe Avenue
New York 32
N. Y.

February 2nd 1958

Dr. Charles S. Johnson
President, Fisk University
Nashville 8, Tennessee

Dear Dr. Johnson: —
Your beautiful and profound letter, of the second vintage,
endorsing the appeal for a grant to enable the writing of the
projected biography of Alain Locke, has left me breathless
with appreciation and hope. You brought into clear defini-
tion the points that make the need for the biography inevitable. The letter might have come from the pen of Erasmus
whose mind was forever evoking the essentials.

Your letter with the others, complementing the draft
statement, is on its way to the chairman of the Memorial
Committee, Arthur Fauset, and will be submitted immediately to the Carnegie Corporation, which is the first of the
Foundations to whom we will appeal. I will let you know

what progress we make, and should the Carnegie comply at the first asking you will be informed pronto.

In the same post that brought your letter came one from Professor Ralph Barton Perry, who directed Locke's Doctorate at Harvard, and who is now a very old man and ill. These did not deter him from the burden demanded since, as he put it, "I greatly admired his mind and personality and cherish a *very glowing memory of his career and its peculiar meaning.*" The underscoring is mine.

Thanks again, and with warm personal good wishes,
Yours very sincerely,
William Stanley Braithwaite

———

J. Donald Adams, of the *New York Times* Book Review, was preparing a biography of Charles Townsend Copeland when Braithwaite wrote this letter. Adams's *Copey of Harvard* (1960) comments on Copeland's association with Braithwaite.

409 Edgecombe Avenue
New York   32
N. Y.

March 13th 1958

Dear Mr. Adams: —
I am taking the liberty of sending you a copy of the winter issue of the *English Poetry Review*, containing a brief sonnet sequence, *Imminent Harvest*, by Margaret Haley Carpenter which won for her its Greenwood Award. It also won a joint first prize in the Arthur Davison Ficke Award given by the Poetry Society of America last year. Miss Carpenter has completed the authoritative biography of Sara Teasdale to which I rendered some service from my friendship and association with the poet. But perhaps, you have already

seen the *English Poetry Review,* which may well make this calling of it to your attention bothersome.

Quite by accident, the other day, I ran across a Copeland letter which I did not know I had here. I thought all those I had were with the *Braithwaite Papers* in the manuscript division of the Harvard Library. I think this letter might be interesting due to Copeland's expressed concern for the character of advertising and publicity a publisher might use in promoting his book. In any event I am happy to bring it to your attention. I also ran across a copy of the Lucius Beebe's *Transcript* article on Copeland. I daresay you have met with this article among Copeland's papers. But if you want this extra copy for any reason I'd be glad to send it to you. Also enclosed is the invitation to the annual dinner and reading at the Harvard Club for 1925.

May I say how much I enjoyed, and with applauding interest, in recent columns of the Book Review, your discussions of the publishers' commercial attitude toward "bad" second novels by authors who had a great first-novel success, and on the mistaken concepts of method and purpose held by our contemporary novelists? Your criticism was not only penetrating but convincing.

I remember with great pleasure our meeting and talk at the Century Club some weeks ago.

Cordially yours,

With Mrs. Ruby Altizer Roberts, co-editor of *The Lyric,* Braithwaite exchanged several letters. He had poems in the Virginia magazine in 1922, 1956, and 1958, and he was one of several recipients of one hundred dollar Special Citations on the occasion of the journal's fortieth birthday. In 1956 he recorded a tribute to *The Lyric* that closes with his reading of some of his own verse, though he acknowledged that his credentials were not so much those of a poet "as those of a critical student of American poets and poetry through many, many years."

409 Edgecombe Avenue
New York   32
N. Y.

May 14th 1958

My dear Mrs. Roberts: —
Thanks for your kindly and inquiring letter, and the accompanying brochure on the history of "The Lyric." I read "The Lyric Story" with a nostalgic fervor for I was the first to recognize and publicly praise it and its contents at its beginning, in this area. John Richard Moreland came to Boston to see me a year after the magazine's birth in that type-scripted form which was the humble but auspicious herald of a flowering achievement in American poetry. We had several happy days together of dining and talks; and when he left the chilly New England atmosphere was warmer for his presence. Edwin Mims some years ago, in his study of Southern literature, gave me the cherished satisfaction of a service rendered when he wrote that I had through the Anthologies brought the new and contemporary poets of the South to national recognition and appreciation. And Leigh Hanes in a recent letter to a Norfolk friend bemoaned the fact that since the suspension of the Anthology the lyric poets who were away from the New York scene had lost a friend at court. In those days of "The Lyric," Mary Stinton Leitch also came to Boston to see me (I organized and published her first book of poems) as a kind of ambassador from The Norfolk Club, with its five members whose verse I was soon exploiting on the national scene.

You ask me if I am enjoying the "New York poetry circles and the New York poets?" Since taking up residence here in New York I have kept a self-imposed aloofness from them, until very recently. New York is a terribly expensive place in which to live and, unless one has the means from an assured income, a difficult place in which to work. I made terrific sacrifices during all those years I produced the Anthologies and was never able to accumulate any substance to provide for the comforts of these times.

I had not attended any of the meetings of the Poetry Society for many years until last month on the occasion of the Markham tribute. It gave me great pleasure on that occasion when several members whom I had not seen for years came up and told me that I had been the first to recognize and print their work in the Anthologies and the Transcript. It was a strange coincidence that just a couple of days before the meeting I had a letter from the Chairman of the Nominating Board of the Executive Committee, Aaron Kramer, saying that he and the other two members, Frances Winwar and Michel Farano, were extending me the invitation to stand as a candidate for election to the Board for the 1959–1960 term, embracing the Golden Anniversary of the founding of the Society. I was inclined, with the warmest appreciation for the invitation, to refuse; but then I thought as I was one of the two oldest living members of the Society (Witter Bynner being the other) I ought to participate in the direction of events to celebrate the Society's Golden Anniversary. One cannot move about in New York without there being some expense attached to the activities. That is why I have immured myself and declined so many invitations to affairs.

"Are you well and comfortably situated?" you ask. In general health, yes, sound in all the vital organs, that will still let me drive twelve to fifteen hours a day when necessary. I was bothered with an attack of arthritis in the neck some two or three months ago, but with some weekly therapeutic treatments it has disappeared. But my eyes, my eyes! They are my greatest health concern. It is not a wonder when one considers, for long years, the thousands and thousands and thousands of poems and books of poems I read! The right eye is about useless, and in the left is an incipient cataract that I suppose some day must be operated on. They need treatment and special glasses which I have not been able to afford. I am reconciled to the fact that someday I may be blind, but Oh, I shall be grateful for all the Seasons I have known, the multi-colored hue of flowers, the curving lines of the hills, the roll and dash of the sea upon rocks and sands, the still woods under the hood of moonlight, the faces of friends — and even strangers — upon which are written the exultations of love, the pitiful signatures of sorrow and hopelessness. And in the darkness will echo the music of Wordsworth's "still, sad, music of humanity."

Well, it's not a very 'comfortable' situation, is it?

No, I haven't a birthday coming up until December 6th, and which one it will be you can figure from 1878. It is hard to convince anyone who sees me that the years did not begin until twenty years later. And shall I tell you, you being a poet, a secret? That my heart is as fresh in response to the magic of song as it was in those youthful years when life and nature first lifted the curtain upon Beauty. The last four years my consolation has been in making verses, from the long blank verse monologue on Erasmus through lyrics and sonnets and the drafts that are awaiting a polishing and finishing.

Please forgive this long letter in which I have tried to answer your questions, and accept my deepest appreciation for your interest.

Very sincerely yours,
William Stanley Braithwaite

The poetry of Margaret Widdemer, who wrote novels and short stories as well, was Braithwaite's subject in the *Transcript* for December 17, 1921. The letter below concerns the preparation of the *Anthology of Magazine Verse for 1958*, edited by Braithwaite and Margaret Haley Carpenter.

409 Edgecombe Avenue
New York 32
N. Y.

August 20th 1958

Dear Miss Widdemer: —
I didn't mean for this time to go before writing you my thanks for your letter and permission. I must however, tell you, that the other clippings you said were being sent have not reached me. Could they have gone astray? This leaves me with two for inclusion, which I like so much: the "Yea Rooms" and "Spring in the City." Though I have come to the end with the selections that are available, if you will make another piece of your own choosing, and let me have it within the next two or three days — my dateline for the copy is September first — I'll include it.

It has been wonderful the reception and cooperation the poets have given me on my return to the Anthology. From Frost down their replies and consents have been beautiful and touching. He has allowed me to include his long and profound poem "Kitty Hawk" from the Atlantic, and has told his publishers, Holt, to grant me what I wanted for the selections from the previously published seventeen volumes, though they may have been published in his books under copyright. So it seems the years have lightened the weight of their heavy footing.

So let me have the third poem
With best wishes,

Cordially,
William Stanley Braithwaite

It was not unusual for Braithwaite to send notes offering birthday congratulations to fellow poets. This one to Robert Frost may be incomplete.

March 23rd 1959

Dear Frost: —
Well, you have caught up with Landor on the calendar,
though far outstripping him in circling Parnassus. My congratulations, which would be less luminous lacking the
golden gilt of homage.

Old Samuel Smith in his national anthem — which I
still like better than the later officially adopted one — asked
that freedom ring from the country's "rocks and rills." On
this day of our pride, from the rocks and rills, along the
many broad and historic rivers and majestic mountains
there rings from the hearts of your countrymen the love and
homage, the honor and blessing for you as man and poet
who has put her voice and image with the select company
of the world's greatest singers from Homer to Yeats.

––––––––

This appeal to Joseph Auslander is like those Braithwaite sent
to many poets, requesting that they contribute verse to an anthology commemorating the Civil War centennial. When he
asked Langston Hughes for a poem for the book, on September
14, 1959, Braithwaite said he would like to add "another of our
poets" and inquired if the choice should be Arna Bontemps,
Sterling Brown, or Owen Dodson. Many responses to Braithwaite's proposal were favorable, but the project was abandoned.

409 Edgecombe Avenue
New York 32
N. Y.

August 19th 1959

Dear Auslander: —
Dear Friend, I'm waving this letter from the banks of the
Hudson as it is relayed from the banks of the Appomattox.

The meaning of the aforesaid will be cleared up in a moment. Let me preface it with an expression of my deep disappointment that I did not see you in your recent visit to New York. Pesky has told me of your talk with him and of your hope of squeezing a moment from your crowded calendar to have a word with me. Well, I have known how such things are and what of joy and time's recreation can slip from the eager grasp of friendship. But the hope did bring one into the shadows of the Galilean Porch and the tuneful echoes of an evening walk across Copley Square.

Now to the business of Appomattox, when the victor with noble sympathy refused to humiliate the vanquished by accepting his sword.

For a moment let me go back and set the stage for the request I am going to make.

On two notable occasions in the old Transcript days I conceived and carried out a poetic feature that remains, as far as I know, the only achievement of its kind, before or since, in the history of American poetry. I invited a group of poets to write a poem in honor of the centenary of the birth of Robert Browning, and to celebrate the victory of American arms at the conclusion of the First World War. They were astonishingly successful. For the Browning group George Sterling wrote for me an 'Ode' that later won the second award in the Lyric Year contest. The Victory group was published in book form — with an Introduction by Theodore Roosevelt, the last piece of writing that he did — entitled "Victory, Celebrated by Thirty-Eight American Poets."

And now nearly a half century later I am still intoxicated enough with the brew of American poetry of another and later generation to believe in the response of the poets to commemorate the significant event of the Centenary of the Civil War. The historians, military experts, and what not, have let loose their flood of writings in commemoration of the Centenary. Are the poets as a collective chorale, to remain silent: Poetry whose imagination and music expresses the ultimate of Truth and Beauty?

So I am obsessed with the dream that the poets may sing on this occasion. There are countless thematic inspirations to move them. Will you be one of the group of poets I am inviting to write an original poem on this conspicuous Centenary? There will be no limitations set for the effort. If you comply I would like to have the manuscript by February 1st, 1960.

My plan is this: to combine the 1959–1960 Anthologies and include the original poems in commemoration of the Civil War Centenary and set the publication date for October 1960. I think the book will establish a landmark in American literature, from whose tower will shine the inspiring and guiding light of our poets. Of course, we cannot afford to pay what your poem will be worth, but the publisher has agreed to make a token payment. Will you kindly let me know at your earliest that you will comply? Always with warm admiration for the richness of your art and in gratitude for your friendship,

Cordially,

Bibliographer James B. Meriwether had studied the documents at Harvard's Houghton Library pertaining to the publication and promotion of *Confusion* before he sent to Braithwaite the questions mentioned in the following letter.

409 Edgecombe Avenue
New York 32
N. Y.

April 1st 1960

Mr. James B. Meriwether
The University of North Carolina
Chapel Hill, North Carolina.

Dear Mr. Meriwether: —
I am pleased to acknowledge the receipt of your letter with its requests for certain information regarding the publication of James Gould Cozzens' novel, "Confusion," which might be useful to you in the preparation of the Bibliography you are compiling of Mr. Cozzens' works. As you know, being informed by Mrs. Cohn, I believe, I was the founder of the B. J. Brimmer Company and published Jimmy's first novel "Confusion," and rather take pride in being the discoverer of one who has risen since to be perhaps the foremost of contemporary American novelists. To answer the three specific questions about the publication of "Confusion" is not too difficult a task, but they flit through a curtain of nostalgic haze of associated events which I may touch upon as affecting the history of the book and my relationship to its author and the public to its distinction. Let me proceed with the answer to your first question.

> The size of the first printing was 2000 copies, of which 1500 were bound
>
> The book was plated, being manufactured by a firm in Norwood, Mass.
>
> There were no further printings. We sold just 1300 copies.
>
> (This answers No. 2)

No. 3: The balance between the 1300 sold and the edition of 2000 printed were never "Remaindered" by Brimmer.

> The printer retained the Plates, and the balance of the stock that was left, and in the form of "sheets."

I must now revert to the circumstances which overtook the Brimmer Company which had a bearing upon the fortunes of "Confusion" as a Brimmer publication. First let me say that when I accepted and published "Confusion" Jimmy was but nineteen years old and a sophomore at Harvard. So he was a minor when he signed his contract. But he promised me that when he came of legal age, two years hence, he would sign another contract with all the provisions set forth in the first, which had he wished to repudiate his promise would have been invalid. To Jimmy Cozzens' everlasting credit and honor, he kept his word. I say this because he had tempting offers from other publishers, of long standing and with financial resources far beyond that of the Brimmer Company. . . .

Jimmy brought me some chapters of a second novel upon which he was working with the tentative title, "Ignorant Armies," taken from Matthew Arnold's poem "Dover Beach." They did not impress me, and the reason, I have since convinced myself, was because it was so different from the theme and treatment of "Confusion"; but I have also felt, reflecting upon what I remember of it, that it held the seeds of the future novels which have won him fame.

Now this is the story of what happened which lost me the Brimmer Company and . . . any future publishing associations with the now famous novelist James Gould Cozzens. I had obtained from "Copey," the famous Charles T. Copeland of Harvard, a book. Every publisher in the country had been after Copeland for a book, specifically his memoirs. That was what I wanted too, but I soon discovered that it could not be done directly. A brilliant teacher, a marvellous reader, Copeland was not as passionately devoted to "work," and to sit down and write his memoirs was beyond his willingness to attempt. I thought that if one could think of some kind of a book that would bear his name and involved little or no work on his part, which would make him some money, it would lead to a serious consideration of his undertaking the Memoir. This proved right and I got him committed to "The Copeland Reader," on which I did the work.

Well, the larger and well-established publishers in Boston, as well as Scribner's in New York . . . were thrown into a dither, and one of them tried to get Copeland's book by driving the Brimmer Company into voluntary bankruptcy. This certain publisher did not get the book because of a clause Copeland insisted on putting into the contract which tied the book to me wherever I was associated in publishing. But of course, Brimmer was ruined, and Cozzens was lost in the ruins. J. Donald Adams' biography will be out this month, and though I have given him the whole story I wonder how much of it he will record. I wonder if you know how much Jimmy Cozzens turned against that first novel of his? I doubt if Brimmer had gone on if he would have sanctioned its reprinting. . . .

Please forgive this lengthy letter.

Very sincerely yours,
William Stanley Braithwaite

"Mrs. Washburn," included in this volume, was one of the pieces Braithwaite was offering for publication a few months before his death.

The William Stanley Braithwaite Reader

409 Edgecombe Avenue
New York 32, New York

February 24, 1962

The Magazine Editor
The Christian Science Monitor
Boston, Massachusetts

Dear Sir:

I am taking the liberty of submitting for your consideration and publication in The Monitor these two Vignettes on the Civil War. They were suggested by the recollection of my boyhood association with the two women around whom the stories evolve, who gave me a vivid sense of the conflict which raged a hundred years ago.

If you are convinced of the historical significance of these Vignettes at this time of the Civil War Centennial and that they will have an interest for your readers, I have in mind other experiences of a like personal nature which could be added.

With appreciation for your consideration of these sketches, I am,

Sincerely yours,
William Stanley Braithwaite.

Books by William Stanley Braithwaite

1904 — *Lyrics of Life and Love.* Poems. Boston: Herbert B. Turner & Co.

1906 — *The Book of Elizabethan Verse.* Boston: H. B. Turner & Co.

1908 — *The Book of Georgian Verse.* New York: Brentano's.

— *The House of Falling Leaves.* Poems. Boston: John W. Luce and Company.

1909 — *The Book of Restoration Verse.* New York: Brentano's.

1913 — *Anthology of Magazine Verse for 1913.* Cambridge, Mass.: W. S. B.

1914 — *Anthology of Magazine Verse for 1914 and Year Book of American Poetry.* Cambridge, Mass.: W. S. B.

1915 — *Anthology of Magazine Verse for 1915 and Year Book of American Poetry.* New York: Gomme & Marshall.

1916 — *Anthology of Magazine Verse for 1916 and Year Book of American Poetry.* New York: Laurence J. Gomme.

1917 — *The Poetic Year for 1916: A Critical Anthology.* Boston: Small, Maynard & Company.

— *Anthology of Magazine Verse for 1917 and Year Book of American Poetry.* Boston: Small, Maynard & Company.

1918 — *The Golden Treasury of Magazine Verse.* Boston: Small, Maynard and Company.

— *Anthology of Magazine Verse for 1918 and Year Book of American Poetry.* Boston: Small, Maynard & Company.

1919 — *The Book of Modern British Verse.* Boston: Small, Maynard & Company.

— *Anthology of Magazine Verse for 1919 and Year Book of American Poetry.* Boston: Small, Maynard & Company.

— *Victory! Celebrated by Thirty-Eight American Poets.* Boston: Small, Maynard & Company.

— *The Story of the Great War.* New York: Frederick A. Stokes Company.

1920 — *Anthology of Magazine Verse for 1920 and Year Book of American Poetry.* Boston: Small, Maynard & Company.

1921 — *Anthology of Magazine Verse for 1921 and Year Book of American Poetry.* Boston: Small, Maynard & Company.

1922 — *Anthology of Magazine Verse for 1922 and Year Book of American Poetry.* Boston: Small, Maynard & Company.

1923 — *Anthology of Magazine Verse for 1923 and Yearbook of American Poetry.* Boston: B. J. Brimmer Company.

1924 — *Anthology of Magazine Verse for 1924 and Yearbook of American Poetry.* Boston: B. J. Brimmer Company.

1925 — *Anthology of Magazine Verse for 1925 and Yearbook of American Poetry.* Boston: B. J. Brimmer Company.

1926 — *Anthology of Magazine Verse for 1926 and Yearbook of American Poetry.* Boston: B. J. Brimmer Company.

1927 — *Anthology of Magazine Verse for 1927 and Yearbook of American Poetry.* Boston: B. J. Brimmer Company.

1928 — *Anthology of Magazine Verse for 1928 and Yearbook of American Poetry.* New York: Harold Vinal, Ltd.

1929 — *Anthology of Magazine Verse for 1929 and Yearbook of American Poetry.* New York: George Scully and Company, Inc.

1931 — *Our Lady's Choir: A Contemporary Anthology of Verse by Catholic Sisters.* Boston: Bruce Humphries, Inc.

1948 — *Selected Poems.* New York: Coward-McCann, Inc.

1950 — *The Bewitched Parsonage: The Story of the Brontës.* New York: Coward-McCann, Inc.

1959 — *Anthology of Magazine Verse for 1958 (and Anthology of Poems from the Seventeen Previously Published Braithwaite Anthologies,* edited by Margaret Haley Carpenter). New York: Schulte Publishing Company.